india

THE COUNTRY
AND ITS TRADITIONS

JEAN FILLIOZAT

PROFESSOR AT THE COLLÈGE DE FRANCE

india

THE COUNTRY AND ITS TRADITIONS

translated from the French
by MARGARET LEDÉSERT M.A.

PRENTICE-HALL, INC.

ENGLEWOOD CLIFFS, N.J.

FIRST AMERICAN EDITION 1962

© HORIZONS DE FRANCE 1961

ENGLISH TRANSLATION © GEORGE G. HARRAP & CO. LTD 1962

PRINTED IN SWITZERLAND

Contents

FOREWORD

Many books have come out about India in recent years. Some of them deal with what may be considered the bizarre in India; others deal with modern developments and the attempt to industrialize the country. Yet others may contain reproductions of our ancient buildings, especially temple architecture. What these books say or contain is often interesting or attractive. Yet they deal with certain aspects of Indian life which, though important, represent only some aspects of a very complicated and many-sided picture. I often wonder what impression they give of India to their readers.

When I saw Jean Filliozat's book Inde in French and looked through its various pictures and glanced through the table of contents, I felt that this was a different type of book which tried to deal with India more comprehensively in order to give a fuller picture of the country and its background. What effect it produces on the average foreign reader I am unable to say. But it appeared to me to be a worthwhile and commendable attempt, and I am glad that this book is now being issued in an English edition. I hope it will succeed in making its readers realize the long background of India which has conditioned us through the millennia of our history. And yet I wonder if it will not produce a confused picture of the infinite variety of this country. That variety is there, conditioned by geography and our long history and the many experiences that have moulded us in the past. But behind all this fascinating variety there is a certain unity which has left its impress on every part of India. There is an Indianness which distinguishes every part of India, however much the people may apparently differ and however much these various parts may differ from each other. That Indianness is something unique and deeper than the external differences that may strike the casual observer.

India is a curious mixture of an amazing diversity and an abiding unity. It has been fashioned by the initial urge of the Indian people at the dawn of history which has persisted through the ages and which has given them a certain individuality; it has also been moulded by repeated impacts from outside. Throughout this long period of history, people have come to India from abroad and influenced their thinking and the ways of living of the Indian people, thus producing a composite culture which has yet been based on the initial urge that carried our people forward. To-day there is the powerful impact of the industrialized West, and India herself is becoming rapidly an industrial nation absorbing science and technology. There can be no doubt that this new urge for industrialization or the adoption of modern techniques will succeed and change the face of India. How far this will affect what might be called the basic individuality and uniqueness of India is a question which the future alone can answer.

M. Filliozat's book does not deal adequately with this modern phase in India which is introducing a dynamism in a static society. Perhaps it is too much to expect a book of this kind, which concerns itself chiefly with the past, to deal also with the changing present and the emerging future.

But the fascinating question for all of us, not only for Indians but also for others, is what the final outcome will be in this conflict between the past and the changing present. There can be no doubt that India will be industrialized and will take on progressively more and more the appearance of a modern industrialized society. In doing so she will shed many of her superstitions and past practices and develop a new dynamism, as indeed she is doing to-day. But I doubt very much if this change will result in her losing her individuality, which has been her traditional feature throughout her history. Indeed, it would be a pity if she lost her uniqueness and individuality and became merely a copy of the industrialized West.

I believe that India has had something worthwhile in the past, and it would be a tragedy if she lost that uniqueness.

I have been described recently as "A Man of Two Worlds." That description will fit in with many of us in India and indeed with India herself. We live in two worlds, and the problem before us is how to bring about a happy synthesis of the two without discarding either.

India has always seemed to me to have broadly more the feminine qualities than the masculine. Of course, masculine qualities are there and have played an important part in her history. Nevertheless, the feminine qualities seem to me to predominate. Essentially she is gentle and peaceful, even though on occasions she may indulge in brutal and callous behaviour. That is why I think that Indian women, from whatever part of the country one may select them, represent the essence of India, more perhaps than the men. Indian women have excelled in her history in many of the masculine qualities, even in war. But essentially they have remained feminine. We have to-day brilliant women scholars in mathematics and physics. And yet they do not lose their feminineness.

By the coming of modern techniques and industrialization, both rural and, even more so, urban, India is changing fast. I have described the India of to-day as being in the bicycle age. I have done so because the bicycle is now everywhere to be seen in the villages. If I address a public meeting in a rural area, thousands of people come to it on bicycles. It is perhaps a greater change to take to the bicycle from the bullock cart than the automobile from the bicycle. Yet the bullock cart persists just as primitive ploughs persist at the same time as modern ploughs and tractors. The curious thing about India is the persistence of the old and the new at the same time; all the centuries seem to be represented in the India of to-day. There does not seem to be any obvious conflict between them. They coexist, though undoubtedly the past and its methods are giving place to the new.

This concept of coexistence, in the political sphere, is thus basic to Indian thinking. It is not an outcome of some balancing feat of to-day. It fits in with the basic philosophy that has come down to us. We have not been, broadly speaking, a proselytizing people. We accept other religions and faiths tolerantly. We do not think that our view must necessarily prevail over others. There are many aspects of truth, and how can we presume to limit it to one particular aspect which appeals to us?

The political revolution which led to the Independence of India was a major event in our life. And yet it was not quite complete till the French and Portuguese enclaves in India became parts of Independent India. It is only now when these enclaves have become absorbed in India that the political revolution is complete.

Indian nationalism, however, had always a broader basis than the achievement of freedom for India. Even as India had been the classic land for modern imperialism, the freedom of India was looked upon by us as a forerunner of the freedom of all other colonial territories. Also our nationalism had an economic aspect. We have been too powerfully influenced by the poverty and economic backwardness of India to think of political changes only. Inevitably, being an agricultural country, to begin with our agrarian policy absorbed our attention. This resulted in the abolition of landlordism and the creation of peasant proprietors linked together by the co-operative movement. In industry we were inevitably led to State-owned or co-operative industries. Even though we gave freedom to the private sector in industry, our broad outlook was governed by the dominance of the public sector, and the progressive growth of a socialist pattern of society.

To this end we have fashioned our Five-Year Plans. Industrialization has become essential in order to get rid of our poverty and unemployment, and the base of this is the development of heavy industries and the training of our people. Mass education, in addition to specialized and technical education, has grown greatly in recent years, and is likely to cover the entire school-going population soon.

The measure of our general progress can be seen by the marked progress made in the average age of the expectation of life. Previous to Independence this was thirty-two; now it is forty-eight, in spite of the vast growth in our population. This is not only due to better health services and the eradication of some widespread diseases such as malaria, but also to the consumption of more and better food.

Perhaps the most revolutionary feature in India to-day is the spread of what is called Panchayati Raj in the rural areas. This has led to the decentralization of authority and giving of greater power and resources to the village organizations. Also there is a great spread of the co-operative movement. Primarily this is meant to better our agriculture and to encourage various development schemes in the rural areas. But, in the final analysis, it is aimed at the improvement of the individual and making him more self-reliant. Democracy is thus spreading down to the hundreds of millions of our people in the villages, and the old curse of officialdom is lessening.

To us in India this is a fascinating and absorbing spectacle. I believe it is important to the rest of the world too at a time when authoritarian and military rule is playing an important part in many parts of the world, especially in Asia and Africa. It is significant that in India we are proceeding on democratic lines and doing so with a large measure of success. We are not only industrializing the country through democratic processes, but also, at the same time, trying to maintain the unique features in Indian philosophy and way of life and the individuality of India. Thus we believe we shall serve the Indian people best and perhaps the rest of the world also.

JAWAHARLAL NEHRU

NEW DELHI
April 27, 1962

AUTHOR'S PREFACE

No specialist dare venture on the vast and well-nigh impossible task of attempting to describe the peoples and civilizations of India as a whole without initially making known his scruples, in order to guard against any possible misunderstanding of his conclusions, however justifiable he has tried to make them.

But the risks of attempting to describe India must be undertaken, for she has been a major part of world civilization for more than forty centuries, not on account of the ruins of a bygone age which men of to-day can contemplate, but as a living nation, one of the largest in the world. The world as a whole knows little of her, and it therefore stands to reason that the numerous works that describe her give a far from adequate picture. Leaving aside scientific Indian studies inaccessible to the general public, works that treat of the wisdom of India and bear witness to the existence of the outstanding civilization of the country have been preserved since earliest times in European literature, and include the Indian poetry that aroused the enthusiasm of the Romantics of the last century, a whole host of theosophic or spiritualistic writings, and, above all, the ever-increasing number of travel books about India which date back to the sixteenth century, and which are being added to on the one hand by the expansion of the study of history of art, and on the other by tourist literature and the political speculations of journalists.

While making no claim to fill the gaps and to give a true and complete picture of the peoples of India, it nevertheless appears to be a duty to make known their importance, and to try to explain where this importance lies and the reasons for it. This is why this outline description of India is divided into two sections, the first dealing with the current situation and the second with the historical conditions which have led up to it. The latter include not merely historical events but, more significantly, the idealistic outlook that has been present throughout Indian history, which is still valid at the present time, and which appears to a certain extent to be in the process of adaptation to the acquisitions of the modern age rather than being rejected.

The difficulty of writing about India as a whole accounts only for the partial nature of knowledge about her. The lack of understanding of India's place among the nations of the world and the widespread erroneous beliefs about her are due principally to the contents of published works.

But the responsibility does not rest with books alone. Serious students of India, who were more interested in the early days of scientific research in the India of the past than in current affairs, often failed to bring the general picture into focus, and, moreover, many of them had acquired their knowledge of the country only from books. On the other hand the European colonies in India lived apart from the rest of the population, having contact only with their servants and with Indians of European background, and thus had very little opportunity to correct through personal experience their traditional ideas of a suspicious Indian community divided into watertight compartments.

Moreover, during British rule India was not an independent country and therefore of secondary importance, and it was during this period that the most widespread current ideas on the country and its inhabitants were propagated. The British administration certainly compiled a vast and remarkable detailed description of India, but this is not a work within the scope of the general public.

Finally, the general traditional educational system of Europe and America and of the countries in which it was introduced as a sign of modern progress is still very backward in the field of social sciences. Its literary formation is still essentially that of the Western world. History is still taught from the national angle; the civilizations of Biblical and Hellenic antiquity are studied, but those of the living East only in connection with European contacts. Not even in human geography are peoples described in their true background. The man who has not pursued his studies beyond school level has therefore an inadequate picture of India, and it is consequently only natural that he should be ignorant of her true position in the world and accept the legendary conceptions about her. That is why he should have the opportunity of seeing the Indians in their true setting and their rightful importance.

THE INDIAN NATION

1

THE COUNTRY

PHYSICAL ASPECT

The territory covered by the Republic of India consists of the Indian peninsula less two regions, the Indus basin in the west, and Eastern Bengal in the east; these areas were allotted to Pakistan in 1947, when the former British India was divided into two independent states. The political division was carried out in an uncompromising manner, and in the first instance the frontiers were neither geographical nor ethnical nor cultural. A cultural redistribution of population, however, followed close upon the initial separation. Pakistan received peoples of various racial groups, but who were essentially Moslems. India accepted the non-Moslems, though she still retained a certain number of adherents to Islam within her territory. The exchange of population was not carried out without incident. Communities which had lived side by side in harmony separated in an atmosphere of violence, pillage, and reprisal. But no real anarchy resulted, and

the refugees on either side of the frontier settled down to a comparatively peaceful existence, in spite of the disputes which continued between their Governments.

In the long run the separation of Pakistan from India has not resulted in a change in the composition of the peoples of India; it has been a matter only of loss of territory and of transfer of population. The history of India could not be written without taking into consideration those areas that to-day make up the land of Pakistan. Present-day India is no less of an entity than it was formerly, with the same racial background as before the partition, though it has new problems created by political limitations and above all by national independence.

The territory of the Republic of India extends from areas of everlasting snow in the north to lands of perpetual summer in the south, and includes some of the world's highest mountains; the vast plain of the Ganges, which stretches right across it, extending to just south of the Tropic of Cancer; the mountains of Vindhya; and the vast triangular peninsula that extends to 8° north of the equator and the core of which consists of the plateau of the Deccan. In the north the Deccan is dissected by the valleys of a number of east-

Capital decorated with lions (Sanchi)

ward-flowing rivers; it is bordered on the west by the high ridge of the Western Ghats, which follow the Malabar Coast, and on the south by the plateau of Maïsur (Mysore); in the east the land slopes gently down towards the Bay of Bengal; while the Coromandel Coast in the extreme south-east is a land of broad plains and river deltas.

According to ancient geographical tradition, India was the most southern land-mass of the world, bathed by the ocean, and lying at the foot of Mount Meru, the axis of the world and the home of the gods, the peaks of which rose up far away to the north in the polar region. This conception is not so far from reality when one considers the mountain barrier to the north of the country, and the vast expanse of the Indian Ocean, which extends uninterrupted as far as the Antarctic.

The ancient geographers called their country Bharatavarsha, the land of the sons of Bharata, and this is why the official name of the Republic of India to-day is Bharat. Bharata is looked upon as a hero; he was a king renowned for his wisdom, a paragon among those sovereigns of antiquity who, having established order in their kingdoms, handed over the government to their sons, in order to retire from the world and lead a higher contemplative life, thus attaining the ultimate reality of the universe.

When they attempted, with an audacity of which they themselves were unaware, to describe the configuration of their country and determine its dimensions, the geographers of ancient times certainly ventured into the realms of fantasy; but in spite of this they had fundamentally accurate ideas, which are not characteristic of the early geographers of all civilizations. They did not make Bharat the centre of their universe. They recognized the existence of three other countries on the globe, one 90° to the east, one 90° to the west, and the third diametrically opposite Bharat; and they stated that when it was noon in the eastern country it was sunrise in Bharat, sunset in the opposite country and midnight in the western one. In common with other peoples, they considered that the world was bounded by the limits of their own horizon, and were ignorant of the fact that the earth revolves in limitless space. They described peoples who had attained a higher degree of perfection and happiness than their own, but claimed for themselves superiority as far as the possibility of attaining final spiritual perfection was concerned.

This traditional representation of the world has therefore prepared India through the cent-

The Vale of Kashmir with the mountains beyond

Lake in Kashmir

uries to admit the existence of other nations of eminence, and to respect their standing, however proud she may be of her own worth and however jealously she may resist their encroachments.

Climatic conditions in India naturally vary according to latitude, distance from the sea, altitude, configuration of the land, forest cover, and distribution of land and water; but all regions have one feature in common, the regular appearance of the monsoon, and on this depends

the existence of plant life and, consequently, the survival of both man and beast.

The south-western monsoon blows from June until September. It is sometimes preceded by a few thunderstorms in May, but from the beginning of June it brings a heavy cloud cover, with consequent torrential rain, to the Malabar Coast and the Western Ghats. The winds continue towards Northern India, bringing rain to that part of the country, but on account of the mountain barrier of the Western Ghats, the western part of the Deccan receives only moderate rainfall, and its eastern slopes and the southern tip of the peninsula only scattered thunderstorms. The summer monsoon brings sudden fertility to the lands that it waters, and feeds the rivers that have their sources in the western part of the peninsula, thus ensuring irrigation and continuous cultivation in the delta areas of the eastern coast. In the northern plains the monsoon also serves to swell the waters of the tributaries of the Ganges, the volume of which is at the same time increased by the melting of the snows in the high mountains where it has its source.

From October until the end of December the situation is reversed, as the monsoon blows from the north-east; it crosses the Bay of Bengal and hits the Coromandel Coast with full force. But it is a smaller monsoon, less regular, bringing less abundant rainfall, and when it fails it leaves the areas that lie between the deltas completely without resources. It is also occasionally charac-

terized by cyclones which lay waste this coastal region.

Winter and spring are dry everywhere. Grass disappears and herds disperse, except in wooded areas and in the delta regions. The only greenery to be seen is the foliage of the high trees, only a very few of which, in the tropical zone, lose their leaves in spring, and then only to flower with a splendour that contrasts strongly with the general parched appearance of the countryside as a whole.

The north has a continental climate with cool winters, though frost is rare except on high ground, and the lower valley of the Ganges remains warm. In early summer temperatures rise rapidly, and in the period immediately preceding the monsoon exceed 110° F. (45° C.) at Delhi or at Banaras. This is the period of the apparent northward movement of the sun, the *uttarayan*. The heat is nevertheless modified by the rainfall before the overhead sun has reached the Tropic of Cancer, a line that passes slightly to the north

The Dhauli valley in the Garhval massif of the Himalayas. In the foreground a deodar, or Himalayan cedar

Aerial view of the outskirts of Patna (Bihar)

of Calcutta, Jabalpur, Ujjain, and Ahmadabad. After the summer solstice begins the *dakshinayan,* or southward movement of the sun, which continues until the winter solstice.

South of the Tropic of Cancer, throughout the peninsula, temperatures remain high all the year, with seasonal differences becoming less the farther south one goes, to a point where they become almost negligible in the extreme south and in coastal areas. At Pondicherry, temperatures of over 100° F. (40° C.) or less than 70° F. (20° C.) are rare. In this tropical zone there are everywhere two periods when the sun is at its zenith at midday, one on its passage northward towards Cancer, and the other when it is returning southward towards Capricorn.

Throughout India the seasonal incidence of the monsoon and the apparent movement of the sun have combined to spread the popular conception of the regularity of the laws of nature. This is particularly true of the life-giving rain, which is to poet and eagerly waiting peasant alike a symbol of prosperity and of the order of nature.

The mineral resources of the country are extensive,[1] and have enabled industry to be developed. Coal and iron ore are abundant in the east, particularly in Bihar, near the Bengal border; iron ore and bauxite are found in Orissa, in the area lying south-west of Bengal; there is also some iron ore in central India and in the Bangalur (Bangalore) area of Mysore. Man-

[1] See the economic map in the centre of the book.

ganese ore is particularly important in the Nagpur region of central India, at Ballari (Mysore), and in the neighbourhood of the port of Visakhapatnam (Vizagapatam), on the Bay of Bengal. Deposits of mica are to be found scattered through the eastern parts of the peninsula. Some precious and semi-precious stones are also found. Barrages on the larger rivers have made possible the production of hydroelectric power, and further development of this asset is planned.

But India is essentially an agricultural country, though prosperity in this field is due more to the industry of the vast farming population than to the way in which nature has endowed the coun-

Terraced slopes in the Garhval

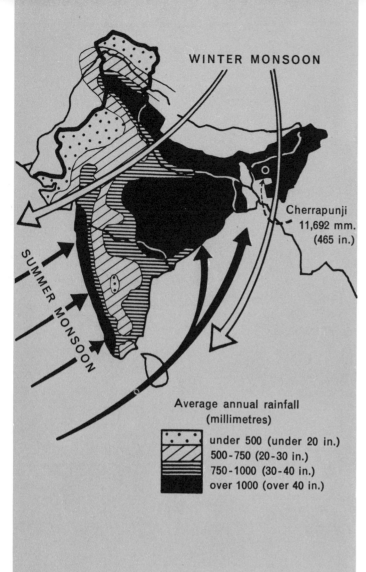

WINTER MONSOON

SUMMER MONSOON

Cherrapunji
11,692 mm.
(465 in.)

Average annual rainfall
(millimetres)

under 500 (under 20 in.)
500-750 (20-30 in.)
750-1000 (30-40 in.)
over 1000 (over 40 in.)

India: Average annual rainfall and direction of monsoons

try; even so, production is not sufficient to feed all the people adequately. The principal food crops consist of rice in the better-watered regions, wheat in the Panjab, and sesame, millets, maize, and peas, which are grown throughout the country. Sugar-cane has an important place in the country's agriculture, and it was from India that the Europe of antiquity first learnt of the existence of sugar; moreover, the Greek word for sugar, *sakkharon*, is derived from the Indian word *sakkhara*. India also taught Europe the use of cotton; she cultivated this crop extensively from the earliest times, especially in Gujarat and Maharashtra. The production of jute is of some significance, though it is more important in the part of Bengal that lies in Pakistan territory. The coconut palm is a valuable resource in the southern coastal areas, particularly the south-west, a region which also produces pepper.

There are considerable numbers of dangerous wild animals, serpents, and venomous insects. Cattle, buffaloes, and sheep are important, but there are few horses. Elephants are diminishing in number.

Though there are relatively few fish in the sea, many Indians earn their living as fishermen. The Gulf of Mannar, between India and Ceylon, is famous for its pearl fisheries.

On the banks of the Brahmaputra

The Brahmaputra valley

TERRITORIAL DIVISIONS

The Indian territory, of some 1,260,000 square miles, is divided into fifteen states,[1] to which must be added seven administrative areas. Northern India, considered from east to west, consists of the states of Assam, the capital of which is Shillong; Western Bengal (capital Calcutta); Bihar (capital Patna); Uttar Pradesh (capital Lakhnau (Lucknow)); and Rajasthan (capital Jaipur); while the state of Panjab (Punjab), the capital of which is Chandigarh, cuts through like a wedge into the two last-named and spreads out across them to the north; in the extreme north of the country lies the state of Jammu and Kashmir (capital Srinagar).

Peninsular India is divided into Orissa (capital Bhuvanesvar) in the north-east, Madhya Pradesh (capital Bhopal) in the centre, and the states of Gujarat (capital Ahmadabad) and Maharashtra (capital Bombay) in the north-west. Farther south lie Andhra Pradesh (capital Haidarabad) in the east and Maïsur (Mysore), the capital of which is Bangalur (Bangalore), in the west. The southern extremity consists of Madras (capital Madras) in the east and Kerala (capital Trivandrum) in the west.

[1] See the map in the centre of the book.

Delhi (New Delhi), the capital of the Republic and the seat of the central Government, is the chief town of one of the seven administrative areas. The others are Manipur and Tripura, which lie respectively along the eastern and western borders of Assam; Himachal Pradesh, which stretches to the northwest of the Panjab; the Andaman and Nicobar Islands, in the Bay of Bengal; the Lakkedive Islands, off the western coast; and Goa, which became an administrative area in 1962.

To a certain extent, though not wholly, these divisions are made on a linguistic basis. From an administrative point of view they may be said to be analogous to what a United States of Europe might be, with a central federal Government, and each state preserving its own individuality and a wide degree of autonomy. India is, however, often considered as a group of ill-assorted states, which have never been unified in former times like the larger countries of Europe. But in fact it is not really comparable to any of these countries. It is not India as a whole, but its separate provinces, and the states which preceded them under former administrations, which may be compared in point of size, diversity of geographical situation, language, and customs with the different European countries; but these differences do not prevent their possessing the

Landscape in
the hinterland of
Bombay, with the
Western Ghats
in the background

Fishing installation
alongside a river

22

fundamental elements of a common cultural background. India, a group of co-ordinated states, represents, indeed, what a federal Europe might become.

Steps were made towards this unification under British rule, but considerable progress has been made since independence. The central Government, which has its seat at New Delhi in the buildings formerly occupied by the British administration, has not limited its activities to making itself a substitute for British rule, effecting the change from Viceroy's palace to Rashtrapati Bhavan, the President's residence. In a few short years it has integrated into the framework of the new union the numerous princely states which formed enclaves in the British possessions, and constituted a dividing feature in the general pattern, even though they were all bound by a common allegiance to the British throne, in a system similar to that of protectorates. The consequences of this recent progress towards unification will be considerable, and in certain regions they have taken rapid effect. The little state of Kach (Kutch), for example, which lies on the western coast to the north of the huge Kathiyavar peninsula, was formed of an island attached to the mainland by a desertic tract of marshland, and thus isolated from the general trade routes, yet not possessing sufficient resources to take the initiative to inaugurate the vast projects necessary to ameliorate the situation. To-day, as an integral part of India as a whole, Kach has been able to draw on the national exchequer for credits for the construction of roads within its own territory and a railway to link it to the mainland. The railway was opened in 1952, bringing an end to its isolation, beneficial not only to Kach itself but to areas in the interior that can now make use of its ports.

Moreover, the fusion of small kingdoms into larger units tends to reduce local differences, to facilitate the movement of individuals and families from one region to another, and to increase the feeling of nationalism at the expense of the caste spirit.

LEGISLATION AND GOVERNMENT

The Constitution of the Republic of India has established the civic equality of all citizens, irrespective of sex, race, caste, or religion, acknow-

Parliament House, New Delhi

Village council in Northern India

ledging the rights of freedom of opinion, speech, and worship. It has legally abolished the ancient caste system.

Legislative power is vested in the parliament, that has its seat in New Delhi and which consists of two assemblies, the lower chamber, or Lok Sabha (House of the People), with 507 members elected by universal suffrage, and an upper chamber, or Rajya Sabha (Council of the States), formed of 250 members, twelve of whom are nominated by the President of the Republic and the remainder elected by the State Assemblies.

The different states promulgate their own laws by means of a Legislative Assembly elected by universal suffrage. The larger states have in addition a Legislative Council.

The executive power of the Republic is in the hands of the President, who is elected by Parliament and the State Assemblies. He is assisted by a Vice-President, who nominates the Prime Ministers and, on his advice, the other Ministers.

A Governor, nominated by the President, is the executive head of each state, and he himself nominates his Council of Ministers.

There is a Supreme Court, the duties of which are to advise the President and to settle any litigation between the states and the Republic or between one state and another, as well as constituting the supreme court of appeal in any judicial matter.

In 1962 the main political parties in India as a whole were, in decreasing order of size: the Congress Party, representing the former consultative body that brought about independence (45.06 per cent. of the total votes); the Communist Party (10 per cent.); the Praja Socialist Party (6.88 per cent.); the Swatantra Party (6.45 per cent.); the *Jan Sangh* (People's Party), the right-wing opposition party (6.38 per cent.). A number of others, none representing as much as 3 per cent. of the total votes, are recognized only in those states where they are particularly active. Some of them are aiming at becoming nation-wide forces, such as the All India Hindu Party *(Akhil Bharat Hindu Mahasabha)*. Others are purely regional, as the *Maha Gujarat Janata* (Great Gujarat People's Party), or resolute partisans of autonomy like the *Dravida KaLagam* (Dravidian Party), a Tamil movement, hostile to Northern India, to Sanskrit, to Hindi, and to the Brahmins.

In general, the Congress Party has a majority in the State Assemblies.

The members of the central Government are thus chosen from among members of the Congress Party. The former President of the Republic, Dr Rajendra Prasad, was secretary of the party in 1922, and president of it in 1934, 1939, and 1947. President now is Dr Sarvepalli Radhakrishnan, a leading authority on both Indian and world philosophy. The Prime Minister, Mr Jawaharlal Nehru, worked in close association with the most famous of all the champions of independence, Mahatma Gandhi.

Outside the Government there are other former associates of Gandhi who are still active, such as Vinoba Bhave, who frequently travelled on foot through the different regions asking landowners for gifts of land *(bhudan),* to be distributed among those who own none.

The motto of the Republic of India is "Satyam eva jayate" ("Truth alone triumphs"), and the official concept of its foreign policy is expressed in five 'rules,' the *Panchsila:* mutual respect for the integrity of national territories; non-aggression; non-interference in internal affairs; equality of rights; pacific coexistence.

Vinoba Bhave marching in quest of gifts of land

Trivandrum

2

THE PEOPLE

Every visitor to India is immediately struck by the diversity of physical types among the inhabitants, a diversity that is emphasized even more by variety of costume and of attitude. This variety is a marked characteristic of the Indian population, but the very differences combine to form a unity distinct from that of any other part of Asia. One Indian may be very different from another, but he will generally recognize a fellow-countryman anywhere, never mistaking for Indian any of the border races: the Iranians of the north-west; the Tibetans of the north; or the Burmese, Thai, Khmers, or Indonesians of the east. But the characteristics which contribute to the measure of unity to be found among the peoples of India are sociological rather than purely physical. It is general bearing rather than details of physique that makes the Indian of Iranian or Mongoloid racial type indubitably an Indian.

Men towing boats on the banks of the Jhelam (Kashmir)

Girl selling cigarettes and betel gum

There are also in scattered areas peoples whose way of life does not conform to the general pattern of Indian civilization; some of them may represent groups which, at a period unrecorded in history, broke away from the general trends; but it is probable that most of them are either groups of natives or of immigrants of the pre-historic period whose mode of life has always been distinctive, and who have continued to exist in isolated areas. The people in question are tribes which differ either in ethnic characteristics or in language from the people who live around them, or, if their racial type and language are similar, the level of their civilization is different.

According to the study at present being made by Professor Georges Olivier, the peoples of India may be divided into three general groups according to the colour of their skins: white in the north and north-west; yellow in the east; and black in the south. To these three main groups must be added another, which consists of the small isolated groups of comparatively primitive tribes scattered throughout the country.

THE INDIDS

If one considers that the white race as a whole can be divided into three groups according to complexion, blond (Nordic), mat, and swarthy,

then the white peoples of India, the Indids, belong to the last-named group. Their skin is very light brown in colour, like that of many of the races of the Mediterranean and Near East, and sometimes even quite dark brown, for the normal pigmentation of the skin can be tanned by exposure to the sun, the degree varying according to the occupation of the person in question. A darker colouring is also sometimes indicative of racial admixture.

The Indids normally have wavy black hair, though it is sometimes chestnut-brown. They have dark or light brown eyes, and very occasionally blue. They are tall or of medium height (5 ft. 5 in.-5 ft. 9 in.), the average height varying according to region. They are either dolichocephalic (long-headed), brachycephalic (short-headed), or mesocephalic—an intermediate type. They have long faces, medium or thick lips, and long, thin noses, either straight or hooked, in the latter case often similar to the type generally described as Semitic. Northern Indians are often very similar in racial type to people one might meet in France or in England, except that they are more swarthy; but there is always that indefinable group characteristic that makes them different from any European, and this has led to the consideration of the Northern Indians as a specific racial sub-group. Even accepting a common origin, all sub-groups have in the course of time grown apart and achieved their own particular

Man smoking a nargileh

Mountain dwellers from Lata (Garhval)

characteristics. The genetic characteristics of the Indids are relatively close to those of the white races of Europe, and their blood groups present percentages similar to those found among the Mediterranean peoples or the Anatolians of Asia Minor.

In physical type the Indids vary considerably, not only from one province to another, but also among people of the same district; an effect of the division into castes. The different castes practise endogamy, or marriage within the group; it therefore follows that the physical characteristics of any one caste are hereditary, and become modified independently from those of any other caste. But the ensuing groups are by no means rigid; new castes grow up, flourish, and then disappear, though the small group which forms the origin of a caste or a sub-caste is characterized by its limited number of chromosomes, different from those of any neighbouring group. Then, finally, the whole of the Indian population can be classified in an infinite number of large and small groups on a basis similar to one of geographical environment, each group being characterized by parallel evolution. This is true not only for the Indids of the north, but also for the Melanids of the south; it is true for Hindus, Moslems, and Christians alike, and it is significant to note that even Christians often practise endogamy within the caste. Considered super-

ficially, these peoples present a general impression of homogeneousness, but studied caste by caste reveal significant differences brought about by endogamy and by living conditions.

The physical type of the Indids also varies according to regions. The ones who may be considered as most typical are those of the north: Kashmir, the Panjab, the region between the Ganges and the Yamuna (Jumna), and part of the Rajput country. They are the Indo-Afghans of Risley's classification, the Proto-Nordics of Guha, the north Indids of von Eickstedt. They have a lighter skin and a more delicately shaped nose than the other Indids. They are tall, long-headed, sturdy in body, and have an abundant growth of hair. A well-known example of this type of Indid is the Sikh. Anthropologists would like to have classified them with the Nordic races, but this would have involved the theory of a separation before a hypothetical evolution had given rise to the typical Nordic fair hair and blue eyes.

To the east and west of the region occupied by this dolichocephalic group are areas inhabited by brachycephalic peoples. The western one consists of the valley of the Indus, Baluchistan, and the Sind—that is, roughly speaking, Western Pakistan. The racial type living there is variously described as Turko-Iranian, Indo-Iranian, or Alpo-Dinaric. They are a round-headed people, often with a flattened occiput, similar in type to the Iranians and the Anatolians of Asia Minor. In the eastern area, Bengal, the inhabitants are also characterized by their round heads, but they have shorter faces and their skin is almost brown, of a shade intermediate between that of the Indids of the north and the Melanids of the south.

There is also a third group to be found in Uttar Pradesh, the Ganges valley, and Orissa that may be considered as a link between the preceding groups. Risley called them Hindustani, and considered them as intermediate between Aryans and Dravidians. Von Eickstedt, on the other hand, considers all these brachycephalic groups as "Gracil-Indids," smaller and darker-skinned than the others, with finer and more handsome features. Georges Olivier appears to classify the Bengalis, the Hindustanis, the inhabitants of Orissa, and the Rajputs as forming a group of Indids with some Melanid admixture, considering the shape of the skull as a secondary characteristic, possibly a comparatively recent development, and not a determining racial factor.

◄ *Basket-seller from Rajasthan*　　　　*River craft in Kerala*

While the yellow races are to be found only on the periphery, in the areas bordering Tibet and in Assam (Naga and Khasi), and in racial admixtures in a few groups, the Melanids form an important element in the population of India as a whole. It was von Eickstedt who gave them the appellation, but they are more often referred to as Dravidians, though the name has no real anthropological significance. 'Dravidian' comes from

belongs racially to the Iranian group and has no link with the peoples of Southern India.

The Melanids are dark-skinned, with a colour ranging from light brown to black, but their features are those of the white races. They are, however, generally lighter-skinned than the Negroes of Africa or the inhabitants of Melanesia. They are below average in height (under 5 ft. 6 in.), and their bodily proportions are intermediate between those of the black and white races. They have elongated heads, broader noses, thicker lips, and more rounded faces than those of the white races;

Tea-picking in the Mannar area (Southern India)

the Sanskrit *dravida,* which means the population of Southern India in general, and more particularly the Tamils. Custom has decreed that the term be applied linguistically to a group of languages spoken principally by the people of Southern India, but also by groups of differing racial types living in scattered areas throughout India, and also outside the Indian territory, as, for example, the Brahui, a tribe of Baluchistan which

is the hair of a white race, though rather more curly.

Each race has its own particular genetic characteristics. A map of the distribution of the blood groups A, B, O divides India in two; though in all regions 15-20 per cent. of the inhabitants have blood of the A group, the proportion of those of the O and B groups varies from north to south, as follows :

	Group O	Group B
South	60—65 per cent.	15—20 per cent.
Centre	50—60 per cent.	20—25 per cent.
North	50—55 per cent.	25—30 per cent.

This table naturally does not include the primitive tribes (Veddids).

In the matter of fingerprints, which are inherited and quite independent of environment, the Melanids have patterns similar to those of the white races, and in no way resemble the Negroes. The same is true for their colour perception and their aptitude to discern the bitter taste of certain products.

The most characteristic Melanids are the Tamils, a major linguistic and cultural group inhabiting the south-east part of the peninsula, the Coromandel Coast and its hinterland. Three main facial types can be distinguished: *(a)* the small, thin face, with straight nose and fine features, frequent among the younger inhabitants and the lower castes of all ages; *(b)* the long, broad, fleshy face, often with a hooked nose, found among older, well-fed people and the higher castes in general; *(c)* a coarser, broad, lozenge-shaped face, less harmonious and more difficult to describe, with a narrow forehead and prominent cheek-bones; it is often broad-nosed, sometimes with slight prognathism, and is frequently associated with particularly curly hair. It occurs only in small isolated groups.

THE SCATTERED TRIBES

The numerous tribes which live outside the general pattern of Indian civilization inhabit mainly mountainous areas to which they appear to have retreated under the pressure of the expansion of that civilization. Some of them may be the descendants of the original inhabitants of the country, but others seem to have lost status within historical times. They have little in common

at the same time they in no way resemble Negroes, and if any comparison with other races can be made it is with either those New Caledonians who are believed to be racially mixed with Oceanians, or the finer-featured inhabitants of Madagascar who are considered to be racially mixed with Indonesians. The proportion of finely featured Melanids is striking, so that one is tempted to disregard the colour of their skin and to classify them as a white race, particularly as they have the same shape of eyes and eyebrows as the whites.

The black races are characterized by prognathism, a forward projection of the lower part of the face. A few Melanids have this characteristic, accompanied by projecting upper teeth; but it is curious to note that the phenomenon occurs almost exclusively among the higher castes, and only very exceptionally among the lower, who have in general darker skins. It cannot, therefore, be considered as a Negroid characteristic.

Another important racial characteristic is the type of hair. The hair of the Melanids is wavy or curly, never woolly like that of the Negroes, nor straight and sleek like that of the yellow races. It

A typical Moslem

anthropologically or linguistically, though none of them has a written language; but they are grouped together because of their way of life.

Physical characteristics vary considerably from one tribe or group of tribes to another. Most of them have dark-brown skins, broad noses, thick lips, and are long-headed with curly (not woolly) hair. They are below average in height. Genetically they are characterized by the low percentage of the gene N, the small numbers of taste discriminators, and the frequent occurrence of sicklemia.[1] A high percentage of them belong to the

[1] A genetic variation in which the red blood cells are more or less crescent-shaped.

A Bengali mendicant pilgrim carrying
the ektar with which he accompanies
singing. The ektar bears an
inscription in Bengali

blood group O, at the expense of group B; but there are great variations, doubtless on account of isolation, and all types of blood are encountered. Normal anthropological development implies a mixing of the genes as a result of marriage with other blood groups; but in a closed society characteristics develop gradually, differentiating the group from others or from the original group from which it has sprung. This explains why not one of the isolated tribes really resembles any of the others.

The whole group of tribes has been given the generic classification of Veddids, and the name, which means "hunters," indicates the general

The poet Rabindranath Tagore, surrounded by a group of
his students, girls from the University of Santiniketan

Transplanting rice. In the background, raising water from
a well with oxen. Coromandel Coast

Tamil girls

A typical Sikh

level of civilization, and is taken from the Veddas of Ceylon. Within the general classification, von Eickstedt has distinguished two sub-groups, the Gondids of Central India and the Malids of the South.

The Gondids, or Kolarians, have as prototypes the Gonds who inhabit parts of Madhya Pradesh, particularly in the Nagpur and Jabalpur areas. Their skin is lighter than that of the other Veddids, their hair is more abundant, and they have longer faces and finer features, though somewhat infantile. Some of these primitive peoples are very near the white races in general appearance.

In addition to the Gonds and tribes related to them, the Gondids include the Munda group (Munda, Santal and Sora); each tribe of this group has its own particular language, belonging to a group classified with a so-called Austro-Asiatic family and including the Mon-Khmer languages of the Indo-Chinese peninsula. The Munda inhabit areas of Eastern India, to the north and east of the Gond territories, Chota Nagpur,

41

Orissa, and even areas as far north as parts of Bihar and Bengal.

The Malids are relatively small and dark-skinned, often with lozenge-shaped faces that appear asymmetrical; they have receding foreheads, eyes that appear to be sunk into their orbits, and broad noses. They sometimes have prominent superciliary arches like the Veddas of Ceylon. They are occasionally characterized by slight prognathism, emphasized by a receding chin. Though their hair is never woolly, this sub-group appears to have some slight Negroid affinities, and certain writers have claimed for them traces of a Negrito relationship.

Fish-seller

3
LANGUAGE

The languages of the peoples of India differ from one state to another as do the languages of the different countries of Europe ; and as the languages of Northern Europe are mainly Germanic and those of Southern Europe Latin, so the languages of India fall into two main groups, those of the north being Indo-Aryan and those of the south Dravidian. The difference between the Indo-Aryan and Dravidian groups is, however, far greater than between the Germanic and Latin languages, which both belong also to the great Indo-European family, while the Dravidian languages form a distinct linguistic group.

In addition to the two main groups there are other groups of languages spoken in India, such as the Munda dialects of small tribal minorities and the Himalayan languages of the northern frontier tribes.

INDO-ARYAN

The modern Indo-Aryan languages are derived from Sanskrit or Old Indian, passing through the stage of the *prakrits* ("natural languages") of the different regions—that is to say, the various modifications to which Sanskrit was submitted throughout the course of time. This intermediary stage may be described as Middle Indian. Sanskrit itself is still preserved as a literary language.

Hindi is the Indo-Aryan language spoken by the greatest number of people, and is the native tongue of the inhabitants of Madhya Pradesh, Uttar Pradesh, and Rajasthan. It is also spoken in the Panjab concurrently with Panjabi. It has numerous dialectical variations, not only in the spoken language of the different regions, but also in its literature, which goes back for several centuries. There is, however, a tendency towards uni-

formity, brought about by education and by the Press and characterized by an effort to follow the example of good modern writers, particularly those who make an effort to write in a style acceptable to all. The language is in the process of rapid development, if not even of creation, for until recently authors, all of whom had received a Sanskrit education, tended to write in a Hindi highly influenced by Sanskrit, often almost unintelligible outside learned circles. The language is derived from Sanskrit, but is no nearer to it than Italian is to Latin. Current vocabulary includes a large number of words of Persian, Arabic, Turkish, and English origin, derived from the Moslem and Mongol invasions of Northern India and from the period of British rule.

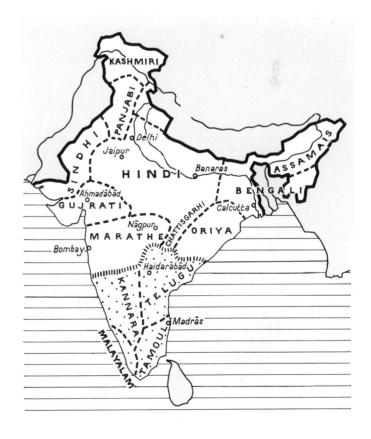

India: simplified linguistic map

43

*One of the inscriptions
of King Asoka
(third century B.C.)*

Urdu is a language very similar in grammatical structure to Hindi, but its vocabulary, especially on the intellectual side, is derived from Persian and not from Sanskrit. It may be considered as the Hindi of the Moslems, and was at the time of the Moslem domination the language common to the whole of Hindustan; it is because of this that the word Hindustani came to denote a language, sometimes referring to both Hindi and Urdu, and sometimes to Urdu alone. Urdu is spoken in the same regions as Hindi, and also in parts of Bengal and the Deccan plateau.

As Hindi is the most widely spoken of the Indian languages it has been chosen as the official language of the republic, and may gradually replace English, with which it is now used concurrently as the language of the Government. But although Hindi is the most widely spoken language it is not used by the majority of the population; even the combination of Hindi-, Urdu-, and Panjabi-speaking peoples accounts for a total of only 150 to 180 million. Hindi is not even understood in a great number of states, whereas English, though not a native tongue, is understood throughout the country by many people, particularly civil servants. This problem features prominently in the Press. Some Indians affirm that national unity must go hand in hand with a national language, and that a foreign tongue like English could not conceivably serve that purpose; therefore Hindi should replace English. Others retort that the various languages of the different states of India are all in themselves national, and that to many Indians Hindi is a language more foreign than English, which has already been established throughout the country as the one means of communication between the different parts of the nation. There is therefore a movement in favour of the retention of English as an official language. Very few refer to the example of Switzerland, where there are three or even four official languages; but it is true that the Indian problem is on a much vaster scale.

Problems of this nature are never solved by State Assemblies or by Governments but follow the natural course of events. Any language can become an effective means of communication, provided that it is taught throughout the country and in standard form. Before the advent of English, which was a language adopted naturally through relations with British officials and spread by means of the schools, rather than one imposed upon the Indians, the common language of the various Indian states was Persian, propagated at the time of the Mogul domination. Before Persian, Sanskrit performed the same function, not only for purposes connected with religion, as it is sometimes thought, but also in purely secular matters, because Sanskrit formed the basis of the teaching of the educated classes, to whatever region they belonged.

In India to-day teaching in the primary schools is normally carried out in the native language, as children cannot be expected at that stage to absorb any other except as a foreign-language study. Secondary education is sometimes given in the native language and sometimes in English. Higher education is mainly in English. In order to become a nation-wide language Hindi would have first to be adopted throughout the country at the secondary-school stage. Even then English would probably remain as a subsidiary common language, because of its international importance and the position which it has already acquired.

After Hindi the most important Indo-Aryan languages are the Bengali spoken in Bengal, the Gujarati of the state of Gujarat, and the Marathi of the state of Maharashtra. Each of these languages has a literature of considerable significance. Bengali was the language of Rabindra-

nath Tagore, the poet of world-wide reputation. It is also the principal language of Eastern Bengal (Eastern Pakistan). Assamese is the main language of Assam, though some Tibetan and Burmese dialects have intruded. To the south-west of Bengal, in Orissa, Oriya is the language spoken, while Kashmiri and Dogri are used in Jammu and Kashmir.

DRAVIDIAN

The Dravidian languages are those of the southern states, Andhra Pradesh, Mysore, Madras, and Kerala. The most widely spoken is the Telugu of Andhra Pradesh, while the one with

A treatise of modern anatomy in Sanskrit

Adults learning Urdu and Hindi in a village school in Uttar Pradesh

the longest and most important literary history is the Tamil of the state of Madras. Apart from Sanskrit, which is taught throughout the country, but which is not really a living language, Tamil is the only Indian language that through the course of centuries has provided a complete traditional education. Treatises on all aspects of the arts and sciences were written from a very early date in Tamil, while elsewhere a classical education was available only in Sanskrit, whatever the native language of the region was.

Kannada (Kannara, Kanarese) is the language of Mysore, while Malayalam is spoken in Kerala. Malayalam, unlike Kanarese or Telugu, is very similar to Tamil, and up to the Middle Ages was no more than a dialect of it. In Telugu and more particularly in Kanarese there is a traditional literature and a classical educational system, less old-

established than the Tamil and more dependent on Sanskrit culture.

There are other Dravidian languages which, though interesting from a linguistic point of view, are the native tongue only of scattered minorities and have no written literature. One of these languages, Brahui, belongs to an area outside India; it is spoken by a group of mountain dwellers of Baluchistan, who racially belong to the Iranian group and not to the Southern Indians.

'ಸದಾಶಿವ'ನ ಐದು ಸೃಷ್ಟಿಗಳು

ಶ್ರೀ. ಬುದ್ಧಯ್ಯನವರು, ಪೂರಾಣಿಕ

ಪುರಾಣಗಳಲ್ಲಿಯ ಸದಾಶಿವನು ತನ್ನ ವಿನೋದಕ್ಕೆಂದು ಚರಾಚರ ಸೃಷ್ಟಿಯನ್ನು ನಿರ್ಮಿಸಿದರೆ ಹ್ಞಾನಗಳ ಸದಾಶಿವ ಯೋಗಿಯು ಲೋಕದ ಜನರು ಸುಖಿಗಳಾಗಲೆಂದು ಹೊಸಯುಗವನ್ನೆ ನಿರ್ಮಿಸಿದನು. ಆ ಸದಾಶಿವನದು ಸ್ವಾರ್ಥ ಸೃಷ್ಟಿ. ಈ ಸದಾಶಿವಯತಿಯದು ಪರಾರ್ಥ ಸೃಷ್ಟಿ. ಈ ಯತಿವರನ ಜೀವನವೇ ಒಂದು ಸರಾರ್ಥ ಲೀಲೆಯಾಗಿ ಪರಿಣಮಿಸಿತು.

ಸದಾಶಿವಯತಿಯು ಅನಿಮಿತ್ತ ಬಂಧು ಶಂಭುಲಿಂಗನ ಸನ್ನಿಧಿಯಲ್ಲಿ ತಪವ ಮಾಡಿ ಲೋಕದ ಕಷ್ಟವನ್ನು ನಿರೀಕ್ಷಿಸಿದನು. ಆ ನಿರೀಕ್ಷಣೆ ಕಾರುಣಿಕ ಇಚ್ಚೆಗೆ ಪ್ರೇರಣೆಯನ್ನು ನೀಡಿತು. ಆ ಇಚ್ಚೆಯ ಹೊಸ ಸೃಷ್ಟಿಗೆ ಚೈತನ್ಯಕೊಟ್ಟಿತು. ಹ್ಞಾನಗಳ ಶ್ರೀ ಸದಾಶಿವಯೋಗಿಗಳ ಪವಿತ್ರ ಇಚ್ಚಾಶಕ್ತಿಯೆ ಶಿವಯೋಗಮಂದಿರ-ಮಹಾ ಸಭೆಗಳ ರೂಪದಲ್ಲಿ ಮೈದಾಳಿ ಬಂದಿತು. ದಿವ್ಯ ದೃಷ್ಟಿಯಿಂದ ದಿವ್ಯ ಸೃಷ್ಟಿಯಾಯಿತು.

ಮಾನವ ಜೀವನ ದೃಷ್ಟಿ ಲೌಕಿಕ ಪಾರಮಾರ್ಥವೆಂದು ಎರಡು ವಿಧ. ಆವೆರಡನ್ನು ಶ್ರೀಗಳವರು ಎರಡು ಸಂಸ್ಥೆಗಳಿಂದ ಸಾಧಿಸಿದರು. ಶ್ರೀಗಳ ಅಂತಃಶಕ್ತಿಯ ಐದು ದೃಷ್ಟಿಗಳಲ್ಲಿ ಒಡಮೂಡಿತು. ಶಿಕ್ಷಣ, ಮುದ್ರಣ, ರಕ್ಷಣ, ಉದ್ಯಮ, ವಾಣಿಜ್ಯ- ಇವು ಶ್ರೀಗಳವರ ಐದು ದೃಷ್ಟಿಗಳು. ಅವುಗಳಿಂದ ಐದು ಸೃಷ್ಟಿಗಳಾದವು.

೧. ಶಿಕ್ಷಣ ಸೃಷ್ಟಿ

ಲೌಕಿಕ ಪಾರಮಾರ್ಥವೆಂದು ಶ್ರೀಗಳವರ ಶಿಕ್ಷಣ ಎರಡು ಆವೆರಡು ಶಿಕ್ಷಣಗಳ ಸಮನ್ವಯ ಸುಂದರವಾಗಿತ್ತು. ಮಾನವನ ಪ್ರವೃತ್ತಿ ನಡೆಯಬೇಕು. ಸಮಾಜದ ಮಕ್ಕಳು ಮೊದಲು ಮಾತೃ ಭಾಷೆಯಾದ ಕನ್ನ ಶಾಲೆಗಳನ್ನು ಶ್ರೀಗಳವರು ಸ್ಥಾಪಿಸಿದರು.

ಧರ್ಮ-ಸಂಸ್ಕೃತಿಗಳ ಪರಿಜ್ಞಾನ ಪಡೆಯಲು ಸಂಸ್ಕೃತ ಭಾಷೆಯ ಪಾರಮಾರ್ಥಿಕಗಳ ನಾಡಿನಲ್ಲಿ ಮೊದಲು ಸ್ಥಾಪಿಸಿದವರು ಶ್ರೀಗಳವರು; ಕಾಶಿ ಸಹಾಯ ನೀಡಿ ಪಂಡಿತ ಮತ್ತು ಶಾಸ್ತ್ರ ವರ್ಗವನ್ನು ಮುಂದೆ ತಂದರು. ಇಲ್ಲುದಿಟ್ಟಿ ಪರಿಯ ಪ್ರಕರಣದಲ್ಲಿ ಸಮಾಜಕ್ಕೆ ವಿಜಯ ಸಿಕ್ಕುವಂತೆ ಸಾಧ್ಯ ಶ್ರೀಗಳವರು ಕೊಟ್ಟ ಪ್ರೋತ್ಸಾಹ ಅಪರಿಮಿತವಾದುದು. ಶ್ರೀಗಳವರ ಸ್ಥಾಪಿಸಿದ ವಿಚಾರ ಮಾಡಿದರು; ಶಿವಯೋಗಮಂದಿರದಲ್ಲಿ ಸಂಸ್ಕೃತ ಸಾ ಶಿಕ್ಷಣ ನಿರಂತರವಾಗಿ ಸಾಧಕರಿಗೆ ಸಿಗುವ ನವಶಕ್ತಿಯನ್ನು ಮಾಡಿದರು.

ಧರ್ಮಪ್ರಸಾರವನ್ನು ಜನಮನರಂಜನೀಯವಾಗುವಂತೆ ನಟಸಭೆ ಜನಕೊಟ್ಟರು. ಅವರ ಸ್ಥಳೀಯದಲ್ಲಿ ಇಂದು ನಾಡಿನಲ್ಲಿ ಸಂಗೀತ ಕಲೆ ಗಮಾಯುಗವರ ಶಿಕ್ಷಕೋಟಿ ಕೆಟ್ಟು ಜನತೆಯಲ್ಲಿ ಸಂಗೀತಕಲೆಯು ಕಡಿಮೆ

रामचरितमानस ।   १२८

बीच बीच बरबास बनाए । सुर-पुर-सरिस संपदा छाए ।
श्रसन सयन बर बसन सुहाए । पार्वहिं सब निज निज मन भाए ।
नित नूतन सुख लखि अनुकूले । सकल बरातिन्ह मंदिर भूले ।
दो०—श्राधत जानि बरात बर सुनि गहगहे निसान ।
... राज रध रहसर नगर लेन चले श्रगवान ॥३३६॥

भाजन ललित श्रनेक प्रकारा ।
...ति भाँति नहिं जाहिं बखाने ।
...वि भेंट हित भूप पठाई ।
...ग मृग हय गय बहु बिधि जाना ।
...हुत भाँति महिपाल पठाए ।
...रि भरि काबँरि चले कहारा ।
... श्रानंदु पुलक भर गाता ।
...दित बरातिन्ह हने निसाना ।
...ल्लुक चले बगमेल ।
...त बिहार सुबेल ॥ ३३७ ॥
...उदित देव दुदुंभी बजावहिं ।
...नय कीन्ह तिन्ह श्रति श्रनुरागें ।
...ड्ढ बकसीस जाचकन्हि दीन्हा ।

ஓவியக் கலை   59

"யாவையும் எனக்குப் போய்யெனத் தோன்றி
மேவரு நீயே மெய்யெனத் தோன்றிணை
ஒவியப் புலவன் சாயல்பெற எழுதிய
சிற்ப விகற்பம் எல்லாம் ஒன்றில்
தவிராது தடவினார் தமக்குக்
சுவராய்த் தோன்றும் துணிவு போன்றனவே"*

சுவர் சித்திரங்கள் பெரிதும் பயிலப் பட்டிருந்த
படியிஞல்தான், "சுவரை வைத்தல்லவேலா சித்திரம்
எழுத வேண்டும்" என்னும் பழமொழி வழங்குவ
தாயிற்று.

"படம்"

காவிரிப்பூம் பட்டினத்தில் இருந்த உவவனம் என்னும்
பூங்கோட்டம். ஒவியக் கலைஞர் திரைச் சீலையில் அழுகுபட
...ாட்டம் போல இருந்தது என்று சித்...
...யிருஞர்.

...இயற்றிய விளங்கிய கைவிணைச்
...செய்கைப் படாம் போர்த் தததுவே
...தோன்றிய உவவனம்...."†

...லத்தில் திரைச்சீலையில் சித்திரம் எழு
...ந்தது என்பதை யறியலாம். இதை
...று சிலப்பதிகாரம் கூறுகிறது.‡

সন্দীপের আত্মকথা

যেটুকু আমার ভাগে এসে পড়েছে সেইটুকুই আমার, এ কথা অক্ষমেরা বলে আর দুর্বলেরা শোনে। যা আমি কেড়ে নিতে পারি সেইটেই যথার্থ আমার, এই হল সমস্ত জগতের শিক্ষা।

দেশে আপনা-আপনি জন্মেছি বলেই দেশ আমার নয়— দেশকে যে দিন লুট করে নিয়ে জোর করে আমার করতে পারব সেই দিনেই দেশ আমার হবে।

লাভ করবার স্বাভাবিক অধিকার আছে বলেই লোভ করা স্বাভাবিক। কোনো কারণেই কিছু থেকে বঞ্চিত হব প্রকৃতির মধ্যে এমন বাণী নেই। মনের দিক থেকে যেটা চাচ্ছে বাইরের দিক থেকে সেটা পেতেই হবে, প্রকৃতিতে ভিতরে বাইরে এই রফাটাই সত্য। এই সত্যকে যে শিক্ষা মানতে দেয় না তাকেই আমরা বলি নীতি, এই জন্যেই নীতিকে আজ পর্যন্ত কিছুতেই মানুষ মেনে উঠতে পারছে না।

যারা কাড়তে জানে না, ধরতে পারে না, একটুতেই যাদের মুঠো আলগা হয়ে যায়, পৃথিবীতে সেই আধমরা এক-দল লোক আছে, নীতি সেই বেচারাদের সান্ত্বনা দিক। কিন্তু যারা সমস্ত মন দিয়ে চাইতে পারে, সমস্ত প্রাণ দিয়ে ভোগ করতে জানে, যাদের দ্বিধা নেই, সংকোচ নেই, তারাই প্রকৃতির বরপুত্র। তাদের জন্যেই প্রকৃতি যা-কিছু সুন্দর, যা-কিছু দামি সাজিয়ে রেখেছে। তারাই নদী সাঁতরে আদবে, পাঁচিল ডিঙিয়ে

DIFFERENT SCRIPTS

I. **KANARESE** (Kannara)

2. **HINDI** (from the *Ramayana* of Tulsidas)

3. **TAMIL** (from a history of Indian art)

4. **BENGALI** (from original version of *The Home and the World*, by Rabindranath Tagore)

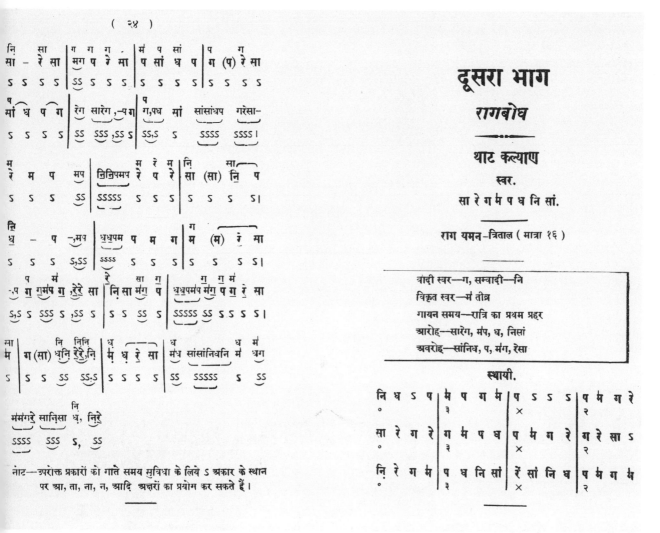

Nagari musical notation

SANSKRIT

Sanskrit remains a very important language in present-day India, even though it is spoken as an everyday tongue only in a very few exceptional families. It is for India and the countries of Indian influence and civilization what Latin was to mediaeval Europe, and occupies a far more important position in modern India than Latin does in the Western world of to-day.

Sanskrit is not only the language of Indian classical literature, but modern literary works are still composed and even some modern scientific manuals published in Sanskrit. Moreover, many educated people are sufficiently familiar with the language to write letters in it and also to speak it. They use it in preference to English for discussing subjects relative to Indian civilization and culture; and though a detailed study of the complex grammar of the language is necessary in order to understand the literature, which has been in existence since over a thousand years before Christ, there is also a modern, simplified version, suitable for practical needs to-day. It should also be noted that all the Indian languages contain vocabulary of Sanskrit origin; this is even true of the Dravidian group, the grammar of which has no connection with Sanskrit. As every Indian has thus a basic Sanskrit vocabulary in his own tongue, there is a case for the establishment of Sanskrit as a pan-Indian language, and there is

48

obviously some truth in the assertion that the general use of it could help to achieve unity in modern India. Some scholars have even proposed that Sanskrit should be used for the creation of new technical terms to replace the international scientific vocabulary which a few of them believe to be specifically English. They argue that the new terms thus created would be more readily comprehensible to the Indian, who has no knowledge of Greek roots, and for whom words of Greek origin constitute a mere assembly of foreign sounds, difficult to master. But the fact that the student understands the etymology of a word will not dispense with the necessity for his learning its exact scientific definition; and a Sanskrit substitute for a modern technical term is likely to be as conventional as the international one, while it would have the definite disadvantage of having no international significance and would necessitate a much greater recourse to dictionaries for Indians reading scientific works in a foreign language.

INDIAN SCRIPTS AND BOOK PRODUCTION

Most of the Indian languages have their own particular form of writing, and until the last century Sanskrit generally followed the local form of script. There is now, however, a growing tendency to write and print in the *Nagari* script, used for both Hindi and Marathi. In the Tamil country, Sanskrit has its own script, which is known as *Grantha,* but this is now giving way to *Nagari.*

Although the various Indian scripts present considerable diversity, some angular, some rounded, some simple, some complicated or 'flowery', they nevertheless have unity of structure and a common origin in a script of simple, geometrical lines which goes back to the inscriptions of the reign of King Asoka in the third century B.C.

Modern books have adopted a standard European form, with the exception of some religious

A bookstall at the entrance to a temple in Kanchipuram

and classical works which are more often printed lengthways on rectangular sheets; these are not bound, but are preserved between two boards and wrapped in material. This is the traditional Indian form of book, and many ancient ones have been preserved in public and private libraries. The traditional Indian book was written or engraved on either palm-leaves or long, thin sheets of paper which were threaded together through one or two holes punched in the middle of the top of each. In the North it was customary to write in ink on fairly broad palm-leaves. In the South narrower palm-leaves were used and the text engraved; the leaves were then covered with black powder, which was dusted off, leaving the incised characters black. In Kashmir the writing was often done in ink on sheets of birch bark. Fine calligraphy is held in high esteem, particularly in the North and West, but it does not aim at attaining the studied and elaborate character of Persian calligraphy, except in some Urdu manuscripts which are written in Persian script. Illuminated manuscripts are comparatively rare. In Nepal, Bengal, and Gujarat there are some ancient illuminations on palm-leaves; while throughout Northern India there exist manuscripts of relatively recent date written on paper and ilustrated with paintings that show the influence of Persian art.

An autographed poem by Rabindranath Tagore

SOCIAL BACKGROUND
AND TOWN LIFE

THE CASTES

Indian society is traditionally divided into castes, now officially abolished by the present Constitution, which has suppressed all distinctions of religion, race, caste, sex, and place of birth. As in Europe the nobility has survived the abolition of its privileges, keeping no specific rights, so in India caste still counts, though to a lesser degree, in matters of personal relationship, and this gives Indian society its characteristic structure.

Bombay : Marine Drive

Bombay: public washing establishment

groups and with a way of life that does not correspond with the general trends of Indian society.

The Constitution has also legally abolished the incapacities arising from the idea of 'untouchability'—that is, discrimination against certain categories of men and women considered as unclean.

Society, according to the classical tradition, was considered as consisting of four ideal divisions, the *varnas* (classes), each fulfilling a different function. They were the *Brahmanas* (Brahmins), who engaged in religious and intellectual occupations, the *Kshatriyas,* or warriors, the *Vaisyas,* or businessmen and landowners, and the *Sudras,* whose duty it was to serve the others as artisans, workmen and peasants. To-day these four classes, except to some extent the Brahmins, have no real social significance, and it is the other divisions, the castes and sub-castes, reputedly over three thousand in number, that really count.

The term 'caste' is a translation of the word *jati,* used in Sanskrit and most of the modern languages, and denoting 'birth' or 'race'. The castes are closed groups, in theory practising endogamy and not eating with members of another caste. It is in vain that one looks for any precise definition of group. In modern India belonging to a caste implies no more than an acceptance that one is a member of it; intermarriage and fellowship in eating are no longer even fast rules, and belonging to a caste need not even imply recognition by other similar groups. In both country and town, especially in the latter, members of different castes eat in the same restaurants, and mixed marriages are more and more frequent, while many castes or sub-castes do not recognize the claims of others to be considered as such. But though they are not charac-

The Indian Constitution has also been obliged to take special measures in respect of part of the population not integrated into the general social scheme, in order to enable them gradually to exercise the rights legally granted to all citizens. The peoples in question are the Scheduled Castes and the Scheduled Tribes living in scattered

Bombay: juxtaposition of Anglo-Indian and modern buildings

Street in the centre of Srinagar (Kashmir)

Street barber in Poona (Maharashtra)

terized by any clearly laid-down objectives, and may be constituted in a variety of ways, the castes have a very real existence for those who recognize them, and sometimes their importance is even over-estimated by the people who are trying to abolish them.

In theory the castes represent hereditary occupations, thus constituting groups similar to guilds, but in practice this distinction is maintained in only a restricted number of them. It is common to-day, and there is written evidence to show that this has always been so, for sons to adopt different occupations from that of their father. Only lack of general education, limiting the possibilities of apprenticeship, and the opposition of groups wishing to retain their monopoly of certain trades, have restricted the choice of an occupation, and have frequently compelled sons to take up their father's calling. A caste defending its means of livelihood becomes a closed corporation. Members of professional groups, even if of differing social origin, working for the common interest of the group, have in the past and until recently constituted castes or sub-castes. On the other hand, members of a caste may follow different occupations. Some of these have as basis religion or sect. Even religions such as Mohammedanism and Christianity, in which discrimination of social origin is a matter for condemnation, cannot, by reason of the strong caste feelings of the majority of Indians, prevent their adherents from being considered as members of a caste. It is, moreover, true that in these religious castes there is a strong tendency to maintain social standing, and Moslems and Christians alike form from among themselves groups of people of similar social background, in order to maintain their position and to prevent unsuitable marriages. Among the Moslems there are *Sayyid,* who claim to be descendants of Fatima, daughter of the Prophet, and the *Sheikhs,* who are reputedly of pure Arabic origin; these two groups form sub-castes which practise strict endogamy. Without this they would long ago have lost their identity, but they are proud of their descent and wish to preserve their inheritance, even though they are members of a community which claims to consider all men as equal.

Most of the castes, naturally, are of Hindu religion, and many of them are differentiated according to the sect or the priestly functions of their members. The latter therefore constitute groups which have both religious and occupational basis. Some of the Brahmanical castes have the privilege of recruiting priests for the service of certain temples from among their members.

But caste is no more frequently a question of religion than it is of occupation, though it is always a matter of prestige and solidarity of milieu, whatever reason its members had in the first place for considering themselves a group of associates. Questions of birth play an important rôle in the formation of this feeling of solidarity, but they are by no means always the essential factor; the tradition which binds them may have its root in the belief in some legend, possibly invented after the formation of the group, to explain a

unity arising from circumstances rather than from common social background.

The Brahmanical class, the only one of the four great classes of Indian society that still has any stability, is composed of a large number of castes, allegedly divided on a basis of ancestry, region, beliefs, and particular functions, but all of them have in common a code of ritual and customs and a reputation for purity of descent which they guard jealously. Brahmanical autonomy, strictly observed in traditional circles, has served as a model to all the other social groups found in India. It offers an example of rigorous maintenance of an acquired position and of a standard at which other groups might aim, though knowing that they can never achieve it. The superiority of rank of the Brahmins has long been recognized and envied, and it has spread among other Indians feelings of rivalry and of desire to improve their position. Many of the castes still imitate Brahmin customs, in order that they may achieve a status nearer to that of the Brahmins, and if that appears impossible they

Modern houses in Bombay close to slums

strive to place themselves above other castes. The humblest, who cannot rise, take a pride in being faithful to their own position and have a sense of propriety about the place they occupy in society, however lowly it may be in comparison with others.

It is under these conditions that social inequality, condemned to-day, has existed for so long, and it may well continue to exist, seeing that it is purely theoretical, an inequality of standing in no way based on fortune. The high position of the Brahmins has never automatically implied wealth or power, and members of lower castes are often richer than the Brahmins. A Brahmin may

be a high official or a great landowner, but he can also be a servant in the household of another Brahmin. The rule of life followed by a Brahmin, which ensures the ritual purity of his every activity, implies that the wealthy Brahmin must be served by a poor one.

It is by reason of historical circumstance, and not of their privileged place in Indian society, that the Brahmins have, at various periods, attained distinction of position, honour, and power; and their supremacy has often been of short duration, in a purely regional setting. Rank and wealth are by no means more inseparable in India than in any other country. Indeed, pride

Delhi: drug-seller and snake-charmer ▶

Mathura (Uttar Pradesh): vegetable-seller sitting near a pillar-box

Photographer in the market at Delhi

The Red Fort, Delhi: view on to the gardens

of rank can prevent a Brahmin or a member of one of the higher castes from seeking his fortune in a trade which he would consider unworthy of his position; this attitude, of course, is not exclusively Indian. Members of the higher castes would not demean themselves by working as launderers, as this occupation is considered unclean, because of the dirty linen which has to be handled. Moreover, the launderers would resent an intrusion into the trade that provides them with their means of livelihood.

At the present time caste distinction and the following of the ancient caste traditions are becoming less and less marked in large cities and industrial centres, though this is less evident in small townships and rural areas. In the industrial centres questions of birth are no longer of importance, and members of all castes work together and take their meals together, though in theory members of different castes should follow different diets and eat separately. An association through work carried out together has superseded the idea of caste. And though most marriages are concluded within the framework of the caste, marriages between members of different castes are becoming more and more frequent.

The position of the former Untouchables has changed more than anything else, as it has been attacked by the liberal movement as the element which causes the most flagrant obstacle to the principle of equality.

The word 'untouchable' does not represent the translation of a traditional Indian appellation. In the various Indian languages, a wide range of names is used to refer to the Untouchables, some of which are frankly pejorative and others euphemistic. The most frequently used are *candala* ("boor," "uncultured person") and *antyaja* ("the lowest by birth"). It is therefore clear that these people are not generally considered as literally untouchable, and the cases where contact with them would necessitate ritual bathing are far from numerous. Where great crowds are gathered together for some festival, fortuitous contact with them would not call for purification of any sort. But if access to the areas inhabited by the higher castes, and to the temples frequented by them, was frequently forbidden to the Untouchables, it was chiefly due to the exclusive policy of certain communities. The extreme case of a Brahmin leaving his meal because the shadow of an Untouchable has passed over it has unfortunately been described as a rule in superficial books depicting life in India. In actual fact the segregation of the Untouchables, even when it was a general rule, was far less strict than the segregation of the Negroes in certain areas governed by white populations. Many villages or parts of villages, known as *cheri (ceri)* in Southern India, were set apart for the Untouchables. Nevertheless houses occupied by Brahmins were often built in close vicinity. The Brahmins, however, generally live near the principal temples, in groups of mansions *(agrahara)* often allocated to them by some pious foundation.

The term *pariah* is one used mainly by Europeans, though the word is Tamil in origin *(paraiyan*=a man with a drum). As with other derogatory appellations, or appellations which have acquired a derogatory meaning, it is now generally replaced in India to-day by some more euphemistic term, such as the *Harijan* ("people

New Delhi: India Gate, a memorial to the Indian soldiers killed in World War I

and his unmarried daughters, all in the same home. It is now comparatively rare for three generations to form such a unit. Living conditions in the large cities make it difficult; and even in the smaller towns and rural areas such family units are found only in the high-caste traditionalist milieux, among important landowners. It is now more frequent for sons to leave the family home after a few years of married life, if not from the very day of marriage. On the other hand, a son-in-law rarely goes to live in his father-in-law's home, unless he himself has no parents, as the family structure is fundamentally patrilinear.

of God") popularized by Gandhi, or *adivasi* ("primitive inhabitants"), a term brought into use through confusion between the humbler classes and the aborigines.

The structure of Indian society is not only one of division into hierarchical groups; it also rests upon a complex idea of family and kinship, often the real basis of the groups termed castes. This conception naturally varies considerably, especially according to religion, being less differentiated in some sects than in others. The adoption of Christianity does not necessarily imply a change in the conception of family relationships; Christians are singled out from the other members of the social group from which they are recruited by their adoption of a common faith and religious practices, but they often maintain their original views with respect to kinship and marriage. The adherents of Islam are, on the other hand, more closely bound by the traditions and rules of their religion in matters of family relationship and social contacts. Hinduism presents a great variety of social conceptions, owing to the vast number of social classes and sects, though there is a growing tendency to disregard the previously accepted structures, which were long maintained in face of foreign domination, first of the Moslems and later of the Europeans. With the advent of independence, egalitarian legislation, and the wider contacts of modern life, there is now much less reason to preserve them. It is a matter of urgency for sociologists to study these structures in the field while they still exist, for certain fundamental conceptions are beginning to collapse. This is certainly true of the traditional idea of the family unit, where the father as head of the family lived with his sons, grandsons, their wives and children,

Amber (Rajasthan): the Temple of Jagacchiromani

THE STRUCTURE OF SOCIAL
AND ECONOMIC LIFE

The life of the Indian community as a whole is characterized by the teeming masses of its population and in detail by its subdivision, on a social or economic basis, into many compartments.

The total population according to the census of 1951 was about 360 million; by 1961 it had reached 438 million. The total area, partly on account of the deceptive appearance of wealth of the tropical lands, is by no means sufficient to ensure enough food for all the inhabitants. The problem of over-population is therefore a serious

New Delhi: the Central Secretariat

one, and measures being taken to encourage a diminution in the birth-rate will obviously be insufficient. A more even distribution of consumer goods throughout the country is clearly necessary, together with imports from abroad and an increase in the area and yield of arable land. While Indian artisans can supply a certain number of export products, it is evident that a modern

Delhi: The Red Fort ▶

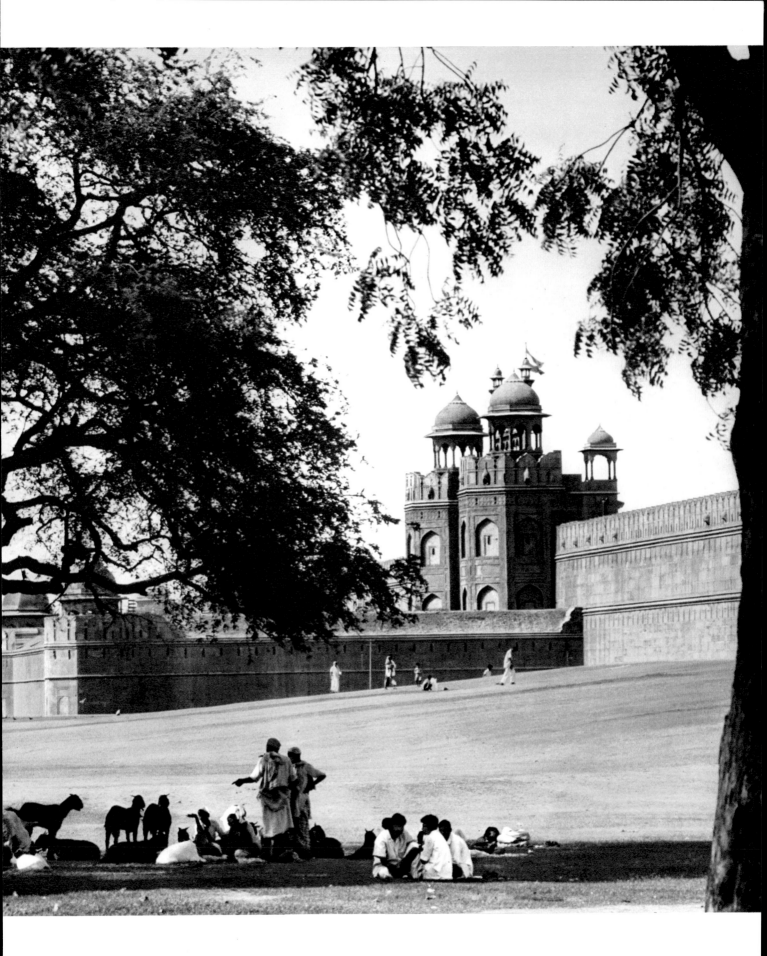

industrial system is necessary in order to exploit fully the mineral resources of the country, to give employment to the surplus labour force, and to supply the home market, so that luxury imports may be restricted in favour of necessities, and the currency and goods required for foreign trade provided. Therefore, by means of a series of five-year plans, the Government is orientating an increasing proportion of the activity formerly directed to agriculture, trade, and the production of the craftsmen towards modern industry. These State plans for expansion have brought about the creation of an extensive new class of civil servants, technicians and specialists in the central and local Governments, transport and public services, education, scientific research, and the armed forces. But, as industrialization has been developed partly by private enterprise and in certain spheres by foreign aid, and as education is in part the responsibility of private individuals or religious communities, there has grown up also in these sectors of the modernization of the nation a whole new category of office employees and workers.

Thus a general division of Indian society into agricultural and industrial workers, artisans, civil servants, and office workers has taken the place of the traditional classes, and no occupation is any longer, in theory or in fact, the prerogative of any category. The Brahmins, the only group ever to have had any real unity, and to have maintained its individuality, and to whom certain religious functions were assigned, have now no claim to any special calling; and if a certain *esprit de corps* may at times operate in their favour, they are in general at a disadvantage where employment or promotion is concerned, because of the reaction of the non-Brahmins against their former privileges, real or imaginary.

The effects of the division of Indian society into exclusive groups are noticeable on a local rather than on a national scale, in the details of the everyday occupations of the individual. In small townships or rural districts the carpenter, blacksmith, potter, and policeman keep their distinct and necessary functions and the means of livelihood of their particular group because they are trained for no other, resent any outside competition, and have created for themselves a pride in their occupation. In privately owned commercial organizations with country-wide relation-

Udaipur: the lake and the palaces

Anglo-Indian architecture: a Jain temple in Calcutta

ships there have grown up links of a less localized nature, consisting of exclusive groups with only their background and calling in common; one such group is the *Marvari*, who originally came from Marvar (Rajputana), but who are now to be found throughout India; they are generally members of the Jain sect, and carry on in a very exclusive manner their business of commercial transactions and money-lending. In such groups the idea of caste is perpetuated by the refusal to marry outside the group or even to take meals with members of other groups; they have also certain conventions of lesser significance, and sometimes have a type of mutual-benefit system restricted to members of the group.

The groups which have as their basis both a common geographical background and their occupation may have purely local significance or a much wider field. As people travel frequently in India, members of any one occupational group may have closer and more frequent contact with members of similar groups in different parts of the country than with their neighbours belonging to other groups, with whom they have in common only normal commercial relationships. Thus the social differences are more important than the geographical, and this has led to the grossly exaggerated statement that for the Indian patriotism means caste. The sentiment of nationalism has greatly increased since independence has given it a more concrete aspect, and a feeling of affection for his birthplace is an important factor in the outlook of an Indian, giving rise to strong provincial patriotism, which in extreme cases is expressed by demands for regional autonomy. Patriotism means to the Indian the love of the area in which he was born and the language he spoke as a child, together with the way of life of the community in which he lives. Thus the different social groups have this affection for their background in common, even if they are not formally associated. They will work for this

common cause, as has been evident in numerous debates on the division of the states. Marathas, Tamils, Andhras, or Bengalis form distinct nations, the unity of which resides in their common local allegiance and language, even though they are subdivided into separate communities which may not be confined to the local state.

There is no question of enmity between the different groups. Their relationships are restricted to the interchange essential to daily life, but, apart from occasional rivalry and dispute, they consider each other as necessary and complementary, an accepted part of an order of things that may be far from satisfactory, but which they take for granted, up to the point of regarding with suspicion any fundamental change. They may assert their rights or engage in disputes over matters of immediate interest, but they live in an atmosphere of mutual toleration, not one of perpetual latent strife. The groupings place no limitations on wealth and standard of living, and,

though they restrict some members of the community to lower social categories, they at least protect them from the encroachment of others. All are guaranteed security of position in their own sphere. The division into castes does not exclude a general participation in the life of the community as a whole, in which each of the separate groups plays its distinctive part. Moreover, the links between similar social groups in different parts of the country form an element that contributes in no negligible manner towards the unity of India as a whole.

There are thus two conflicting tendencies in the social background of India, the nation-wide movement towards broader social contacts and the tendency to retain characteristic local differences. The former is the more significant, for the legal abolition of the caste system has made the social groups much less exclusive; and if local custom discourages them from mixing freely, it does not prevent them from playing their part as

Banaras: one of the ghats leading down to the Ganges ▶

64

members of the community as a whole. The castes formerly had their own system of jurisdiction, with a council headed by a chief who could condemn and fine members of the caste who infringed its customs or violated its code of honour. For serious crimes one of the punishments consisted in leading the criminal in procession round the village streets, mounted on a donkey, with his face painted in a grotesque manner. This was often carried out without recourse to any legal jurisdiction. The offender was subsequently expelled from the caste, a disgrace comparable to that of excommunication in Europe in the Middle Ages. As one could not transfer from one caste to another, the victim found himself outside the pale of Hindu society. He could either leave the country, become a Moslem, and enter a tribe where Hindu custom was not observed, or he could join other outcasts and with them form a new, low caste. To-day, if the caste acknowledges a leader, his rôle is merely that of an arbiter of custom. The group can no longer openly exert any jurisdiction over its members, nor impose fines and punishments. Its only resource is to

exclude members of whom it disapproves from any festivity. But disapproval of the group may be disastrous to any member who depends upon it for his livelihood.

Women are often deemed to hold a very subordinate and dependent position in Indian society, acting very much as domestic servants to their husbands and even to their children. But in fact, though it is considered a woman's duty to attend to the wellbeing of the household, her task is considered a noble one, and her position is by no means despised. A mother is deeply respected, and she herself considers her tasks an honour. She wields, moreover, considerable authority. In wealthier families the wife's task is limited to the supervision of the household; but poorer women fulfil tasks outside the home, such as fetching water from the well, pool, or river, helping in the fields, transplanting the rice (though not ploughing), and even acting as labourers, carrying gravel or earth for the maintenance of the roads, or transporting lime, mortar, and bricks for the masons.

Hindu marriage is traditionally arranged by the parents, though child marriage is no longer practised. The parents consult marriage-makers who are familiar with the family background and position. Once a marriage is planned, an astrologer is consulted about the compatibility of temperament and the future of the young couple as revealed by their horoscopes. The marriage ceremony is a very solemn one, its main rite consisting of a procession round a fire, and a large number of relations and members of the caste are invited. A procession, which may include musicians, dancers, jugglers, lamp-bearers, and fireworks, is organized to present the newly wed couple to the village or district in which they live. This public entertainment, together with the reception in the house, the banquet, and the presents, represents a considerable expense and may entail ruinous debts, but it is considered essential as a matter of family prestige. Among poorer people there is obviously less ceremonial, and for the humblest the wedding-day is possibly the only day in their lives when they do not really feel the pinch of poverty. Great sacrifices are often entailed in order to make the most elaborate display possible.

Apart from a few sects which admit divorce and remarriage, a Hindu marriage is considered indissoluble. It was a tradition that no widow

Street in the centre of Calcutta

should remarry, and it could happen that a girl married in early childhood might lose her husband without ever having known him. She was nevertheless considered as a widow, condemned to remain at home all her life, dressed in white without any ornaments or jewellery, and forbidden to take any direct part in public festivities. The strict attitude towards widows has been fiercely contested, and has disappeared in certain milieux. But the sacred and binding character of marriage has resulted in the fact that wives in general are completely faithful to their husbands, and it has made many widows unwilling to consider a second marriage. In former times this attitude of devotion to the husband led in its degenerate form to the sacrifice of the *sati*, the burning of a wife alive on the funeral pyre of her husband.

In addition to the classes of Indian society engaged in active occupations, but depending on them for their livelihood, one important marginal group, the beggars, has been estimated as totalling five millions. Beggars are to be found in large numbers at the entrances to the temples, in the stations and markets, in places where public festivities are in progress, and around places frequented by tourists and hotels patronized by foreigners. This explains why the foreign traveller often thinks that they are even greater in number than they really are. The total number of beggars, moreover, is not due, as in other countries, only to poverty, unemployment, social degradation, laziness, or despair. There exists a whole category of men who consider themselves impelled by religious motives to live solely by receiving alms. They are the *sannyasi*, Hindus who have renounced the world in order to concentrate on their own salvation, with the feeling that they are also contributing to the general good, for there is a belief in India that it is beneficial to society as a whole to support a large number of religious men and to acquire personal merit by giving them alms. They are therefore called *sadhu* (good men). These religious 'beggars' have only to present themselves at the doors of the houses where they normally receive alms, or to station themselves at the entrances to temples or among the crowds at times of pilgrimages or religious festivals. They are easily recognizable; many of them are practically naked, and cover their bodies with white ashes; others are draped in ochre-coloured cloth; they have long hair, generally gathered up into a knot on the top of the head, but occasionally floating loosely; like other mem-

Street scene in Old Delhi

bers of their sect they bear a distinctive mark on the forehead, and they carry religious symbols such as strings of beads, pikes or tridents, and the shells in which they collect their alms. Many of them in theory, in accordance with vows which they have taken to mortify the flesh, practise terrifying acts of self-torture such as exposing themselves to the full sun, lying on beds of cacti or spikes, paralysing one of their arms or legs by keeping it for an indefinite space of time in an uncomfortable position, or piercing their tongue or cheeks with knives or spikes. They are well known throughout the world from descriptions given by travellers, who refer to them as *fakirs*; the name is not correctly used in this context, as it comes from the Arabic *faqir* (poor man), and is properly applied to all beggars, and in particular to Moslems, not Hindus. Some of these beggars predict the future or consult horoscopes, though these occupations are generally carried on by professionals rather than by beggars.

The numbers of the authentic *sadhu* are inevitably augmented by a host of unscrupulous imitators, who profit from public charity, and who may even be criminals seeking refuge from the police. There is therefore a campaign in progress to take a census of all beggars and to issue the genuine *sadhu* with identity cards.

Many Hindus who have renounced the world do not live as beggars, but establish themselves for at least part of their lives in a *math* (monastery) or an *ashram* (retreat). These are communities organized under the supervision of a master and maintained by pious foundations, gifts, and the work of those of their members who have not wholly renounced the active life.

The non-religious beggars are either cripples or destitute in appearance. They demand alms of the passer-by with outstretched hand, addressing him in terms of flattery. It is they, rather than the *sadhu*, who importune the foreigner or any other person whom they have seen giving alms. Many of them are children, and not always those who look most hungry. Some of them have other occupations and resort only from time to time to begging, as an additional source of income, or even to provide necessities when their jobs do not offer them an adequate means of livelihood.

In the large cities beggars are often grouped in small communities living in the same district, especially when they come from the same region, speak the same language, and have similar customs. Many of the beggars in Delhi come from distant areas, hoping to find good opportunities for receiving alms in the rapidly developing capital city; there is a large colony there of beggars from the Madras region. Many of the beggars speak several languages. Throughout the country there are to be seen groups of those lepers who are not confined to colonies, but who live by begging.

According to a survey made in Delhi in 1955 and 1956, it was estimated that the *sadhu* re-

Madras: street sanctuary

View of Pondicherry from the old pier ▶

Calcutta: the waiting-room
of a station

ceived on an average 15 annas a day, the crippled beggars 13, the apparently healthy beggars 12; and that the amount of alms given in a year throughout the country totalled 900,000 rupees.

LIFE IN THE TOWNS

An Indian city presents a most varied picture, with the contrasts between the different districts, the vivid animation, the teeming population, and the brilliant colours of the many kinds of dress. To the stranger nothing could be more disconcerting than the roadways of the populous districts, which are by no means restricted to the vehicular traffic of all kinds, pedestrians and animals which stream along them. Whole crowds of people are to be found there, sitting or lying on the ground, sometimes on an old piece of cloth or matting, offering their small quantities of humble wares to the customers; they sell seeds, fruit, second-hand books, monkey nuts, or modest household goods. Some of them carry on a trade; there are shoe-menders, barbers, and bicycle-repairers. The shoe-mender often sits upright, with his knees as far apart as possible and the soles of his feet touching, so that he can hold a sandal between them as in a vice, leaving his hands free to sew; he may even hold the shoe between two of his toes. The barber squats opposite his customer, and shaves him amid the throng of passers-by. The bicycle-repairer prefers to take up his position at the crossroads, with one or two spanners, a piece of inner tubing, a little glue, an old tin full of water, and a pump. Fortune-tellers

71

Shops in Pondicherry

await their clients beside a roughly drawn hand, with the lines painted crudely on it. Astrologers show their calling by displaying an open book illustrated with horoscope designs. Some of the traders have a little cart like that of a barrow boy, piled up with seeds, fritters, or sweetmeats, often enclosed in a glass-topped box; some of them have presses for extracting sugar from the cane, or a grater for making delicately coloured water ices.

Some people sit idle, watching the scene of animation around them. Others sleep in the shade of the walls or in doorways, in the midst of all the noise and movement. Here and there one sees a placid bull, ruminating with dignified indifference. And the whole street, a strange mixture of bustle and immobility, is lined with rows of shops — or, rather, of stalls, which jut out into it in front of the shop buildings. They are narrow and piled high with goods, and raised up one or two steps above the general level of the street; some of them are covered with a cloth. There are small passages in the middle of each and a place for the shopkeeper, who sits beside the casket which serves him as a till. These stalls are in no way attractive, and display nothing but es-

sentials. They are protected by awnings of canvas or palm-leaves, or by a tiled roof supported on posts. Some of the shop signs are in English and some in the local language or languages, or in a phonetic transcription into the local script of English words, such as 'ice cream' or 'modern radio'.

Among these stalls are vegetarian restaurants to which all sections of the public are admitted. They are generally run by Brahmins, with Brahmin cooks and waiters, for, though the Brahmins may receive food and water only from members of their own group, there is nothing to prevent their serving others. These restaurants are far from luxurious; their walls are often in poor repair, covered with ancient though brightly coloured religious pictures. The price of the various dishes is posted up, and the furniture consists of marble- or zinc-topped tables, rustic benches and stools. At the back there is a display of cakes and sweetmeats, from which the client may make his choice, though he is not allowed to touch them. Along one wall is a wash-basin with running water, or large water-jars with taps. Near the door is the desk where the customer pays, as he leaves, the bill made out to him by the waiter.

The larger restaurants include a room reserved for customers who prefer to eat sitting on the ground or on a low board with their backs against the wall, and who have their meals served on the ground in front of them. The food is generally served on metal dishes and plates, except in the South, where people prefer 'plates' made out of banana-leaves for the main meals and small, round 'plates' made of leaves sewn together for snacks. The food consists of pancakes, chapati, fritters, heavily spiced stews, curry (the Tamil word is *kari*), and vegetables, served in little heaps on the dishes or leaves, and mixed by the customer with split peas or rice, which may be served with *ghi* (melted butter). After washing his hands and rinsing his mouth, the client sits down and eats, using his right hand only, mixing the soft foods and breaking the pancakes. Water is the usual drink, and no alcoholic drinks may be served in these restaurants, where smoking is also forbidden. In the South it is customary to serve coffee with sugar and milk, which is made to foam by being poured from a height into a broad-topped shallow cup.

One of the humbler shopping streets in Calcutta, with advertisements for films, medicines, and hair-oil

Mutton or chicken curries and various other non-vegetarian dishes are served in the Moslem restaurants and in those labelled in English "Military Hotel."

In the evening the shops are lit by electricity, except the poorer ones, which have storm-lanterns or oil-lamps. They do not close until late. The goods are then taken inside and the doors fastened with large padlocks. Then the people settle down to sleep, if they have not already done so, wrapping themselves up in covers and lying down on the ground, on the steps, in the doorways, or even on the window-sills. Some of them have beds, consisting of a wooden frame on legs, with a net on which to lie, which they drag out from the shops or houses, and they may even have a mosquito-net to cover them. Not all of these people are homeless, but their rooms are so small and so airless that they prefer to sleep in the street. In the morning they all go to wash in the nearest river, pool, or fountain, for these people who sleep on the none too clean earth like to bathe as often as possible. It is, indeed, a characteristic feature of Indian life that even the most wretched bathe and wash their clothes frequently. It is only the lack of water and the difficulty of finding a clean and dry place in which to establish themselves, and not indifference to personal cleanliness, that make the poorer town dwellers sometimes remain dirty.

Indian towns do not always present the aspect depicted above, as the crowded streets described, which are so striking to the foreigner, are the poorer shopping districts, which either replace the market or bazaar or are to be found in the area near the bazaar. The bazaars in large towns are extensive covered market-places, or elsewhere a district in which all the shops are grouped together. The stalls are arranged according to the type of merchandise for sale: vegetables, fruit, flowers, fish, meat, spices, seeds, ironmongery, materials, or books. Brightly coloured displays are characteristic of the piles of fruit, garlands of flowers, and glass or plastic bracelets encircling in their hundreds the rolls of cardboard on which they are mounted. No traffic is allowed in the streets of the bazaar, but the passers-by have to mingle with the women seated on the ground selling their meagre wares, or arranging flowers in garlands or hair ornaments, and mounting them on sticks to form regular compact bouquets.

In the districts near the bazaar are the streets where the artisans and certain specialized shop-keepers have their establishments. Whole streets may be given over to a particular type of trade, such as the sale of materials, seeds, oil, or copper-ware, or the workshops of the tailors, the gold-smiths and silversmiths, or the potters. The houses are low and fronted by a veranda, on to which opens the stall or workshop. One can see whole streets where men — not women — sit working on the veranda all day long at sewing-machines. Others present a vast display of gold and jewellery, while in the streets consecrated to the potters the wares often spill over from the veranda into

Banaras: northern bathing-place

Delhi: villagers at the Red Fort ▶

Canal in Kerala

the street. The same is true of the gaily coloured displays of silk and cotton goods, piled high on the stalls and spilling down from them or hanging in the entrances to the shops.

These shopping streets are generally in the old districts where the temples stand, surrounded by the houses of the Brahmins or the wealthier people who do not earn their living by trade. The most prosperous of these houses have double wooden doors with a carved framework opening on to a veranda. One of their typical features is an interior courtyard surrounded by a gallery supported by large columns, on to which the rooms open. The two-storeyed houses sometimes have a double gallery. The roofs are generally flat, and the courtyard may be covered with an awning of palm-leaves supported on poles, thus protecting it from the sun and rain and at the same time letting the air penetrate.

The districts where the public buildings are to be found are characterized by the British colonial influence of their architecture. In the largest cities, such as Calcutta, Bombay, and Madras, they are to be found in the vicinity of the Fort. These districts have wide streets and large squares filled with statues and lined with trees. An example of a particularly striking square is the Maidan at Calcutta, which contains the Victoria Memorial, a huge white building. The houses in these Westernized areas are several storeys high and often have arcades which protect the pavements from the sun and rain, and on to which open shops which are European in aspect. The official buildings, stations, large hotels, and university buildings are vast and heavy in style, overdecorated, with bow-windows, towers or little turrets, and columns. They contain elements of the architecture of many periods; some of the older ones have details imitated from the Greek;

the more recent ones are a mixture of Victorian Gothic and Mogul architecture; while, particularly since independence, some of them are characterized by features of Hindu art. The huge Taj Mahal Hotel in Bombay is rather reminiscent of certain hotels in Russell Square, in London. The churches are relatively small, and many of them have spires in the English style. And in the midst of all this modern buildings of an international style are being constructed.

In the towns of Northern India such as Delhi, Jaipur, Agra and Lucknow, the Anglo-Indian buildings are dwarfed by the architecture of earlier periods ; there are the Mogul forts at Delhi and Agra ; the mausolea, such as the tomb of Humayun at Delhi and the famous Taj Mahal at Agra; and there are also important mosques and Hindu palaces.

New Delhi, the capital, is particularly distinctive. It is built outside the Mogul walls of Old Delhi, and it is characterized by its vast, imposing buildings in red or ochre-coloured sandstone. It contains many elegant, single-storeyed houses, built in extensive grounds and lying back from the broad avenues lined with trees that radiate from a series of squares, remarkable for the green of their lawns. Commercial activities are largely confined to the Connaught Circus area, which lies between Old Delhi and the administrative centre of the city, dominated by Rashtrapati Bhavan, the residence of the President of the Republic. Apart from this, only a few small groups of humbler shops or stalls are to be found amid the avenues and parks.

On the opposite side of Old Delhi lies an older residential district, where the houses are built in large grounds in a similar way to those of New Delhi, but where the avenues follow a less regular pattern.

The residential districts of the other cities are similar in type, characterized by bungalows [1] built in extensive gardens. These areas have been considerably extended in recent years, and the new houses, though more modern in style, and usually with terraces, follow the same general pattern as the older ones.

An extensive residential district of a different character has been erected on the sea-front at Bombay, along a broad avenue. It consists of tall blocks of flats without gardens, built in the square, modern style with large windows and painted in different light shades.

---

[1] From Hindustani *bangala* = house.

In the midst of these varied districts of solid construction, or on their outskirts, there are still areas of village-like straw huts, or even temporary encampments. Along the sea-front at Madras, between Fort St George and the old town of Mayilappur, lie the extensive buildings of the university, a number of administrative buildings, and the new construction of the All India Radio; between them and the sea stretches a long avenue of ornamental trees; and below them, on the beach, a row of rickety fishermen's huts; behind the official buildings there is a group of precarious-looking tenements.

This haphazard mixture of poor and wealthy districts, overpopulated and deserted areas, separated by parks and stretches of waste land, gives to many of the towns in India an appearance of disorder. It is in a way typical of the country itself, where many different elements exist side by side without really mingling, where men live in a spirit of toleration combined with ignorance of their neighbours and their way of life.

Throughout the country vast constructional enterprises are being carried on under private and public initiative, and every year new buildings are being erected among the old ones, filling up unbuilt spaces and overflowing into the suburbs and countryside, and replacing straggling groups of huts with rows of small white houses. Thus numerous modern blocks *(nagar)* are coming into existence, and if shanty towns are to be seen alongside them they are merely the temporary dwellings of the building workers and the small traders who sell them the goods they need.

Besides increasing the size of the towns, this building activity has added to their general bustle. According to the census of 1951, there were 76 cities of over 100,000 inhabitants, and their total population represented 7 per cent of the total population of India. The three largest cities were Calcutta (4.6 million inhabitants), Bombay (2.8 million), and Madras (1.1 million). Old Delhi had 915,000 inhabitants, but it is New Delhi that is increasing, as not only is it the capital, but it also has land available for expansion. Its total population is now 2.5 million.

The building programme gives direct employment to large numbers of workers, while others benefit from it indirectly. It has made a considerable amount of work on the roads necessary, and has also made greater demands upon transport, not only for the supply of building materials, but also for the consumer needs of the growing population of the cities and the increased trade

Calcutta: street scene with rickshaw ▶

occasioned by their expansion. Means of transport are frequently insufficient, and the more modern equipment is supplemented by a whole host of small-scale carriers and porters.

It is on account of lack of transport that in both towns and villages a large percentage of the population travels on foot, even for long distances. Loads are carried on the head or, particularly in the north-east, on either end of a pole slung across the shoulder. Porters are frequently employed to carry goods, as are men who push or pull handcarts; the latter are even employed for some of the work in large ports like Madras, where generally three men are needed to push or pull the heavy carts. The rickshaw, which was introduced into India from Japan in the nineteenth century, and the name of which is believed to be of Japanese origin, is widely used both for passengers and for the transport of goods. The continued use of the rickshaw has shocked one part of Indian public opinion, but a recent attempt to abolish it in Calcutta was abandoned

because of the impossibility of finding alternative employment for the rickshaw men. Rickshaws pulled by a tricycle (motorized or otherwise) are gradually tending to replace the hand-drawn vehicle. The pedal cycle is widely used, and sometimes serves for transporting small loads. The various litters and sedan chairs described in many books about travel in India have now ceased to exist.

Pack animals and draught animals are very widely used. Donkeys are employed throughout the country to carry the laundrymen's bundles of washing to the rivers and pools; there the linen is dipped in the water, then put to steam over fires lit in mud-built ovens, and finally washed and wrung out by being banged against stones. In Northern India loads of considerable size are carried on the backs of large buffaloes. In the North-West dromedaries are used for this purpose; these animals are also often harnessed to four-wheeled drays. But most of the carts are drawn by buffaloes, oxen, cows or horses. The

horses, few in number, are small in size, and are used mainly for passenger vehicles; they are usually harnessed to two-wheeled carriages with a semi-cylindrical canvas covering, and the passenger squats on the floor. These vehicles are known as *tanga*. The buffaloes pull the heavier carts, while oxen and cows are most frequently used for light ones. In the South dwarf oxen or small, wiry cows, led by a rope passed through the nose, trot along like ponies, and are swifter than the horses. Larger oxen or cows harnessed in pairs draw the heavy carts, and, as they have prominent withers, their yoke, instead of joining the base of their horns, consists of a cylindrical piece of wood placed across their necks. Elephants are luxury animals and are not used for commercial transport. They are to be seen in the temples and are used in processions at festivals.

Though it is still far from adequate for the needs of the population, mechanized transport is increasing rapidly. There have long been trains to link cities with their suburbs. Trams are now disappearing, as in European cities, and are being replaced by buses, sometimes of the double-decker type, as in Bombay. The numbers of lorries and private cars are increasing, but not rapidly enough to take the place of men and beasts as means of transport.

This state of affairs not only means that in the towns of India a large proportion of the population appears to be engaged in small-scale transport and that many animals are led through the streets; it also partly accounts for the presence of birds of prey and stray animals, a thing that seems strange to foreigners. There are municipal services to clean the streets and collect the rubbish, but anything dropped by the teeming crowds attracts crows and other birds of prey, and is rapidly seized by them.

Moreover, the presence of cows in the streets is not due to a veneration for the animal, as many travellers have stated. Religious scruples certainly lie behind the respect for the cow and the attitude that it would be an act of desecration to kill it. It is nevertheless treated as a beast of burden and beaten if the need arises; but it is well cared for because it is valuable, not only as a beast of burden but also as a source of milk, an important element in vegetarian diet. Lack of transport often means that milk from the country cannot easily be supplied to the towns, so cattle are kept within

Chandigarh: women students from the Panjab

Banaras: one of the ghats

ing, and has extended far beyond the limited circle of those who have adopted the type of building, furniture, clothing, and equipment typical of Western civilization. On the other hand, as also happens in the Western countries, certain Indians, obsessed with a desire to be modern, have only a very superficial cultural background, and are content to follow European custom by using Westernized equipment, even though it may be ill-adapted to the climate in which they live.

A happy medium is often achieved by those who are able to reconcile the possibilities of their own country and the recent progress made in the technical field, and to adopt only those things that are useful to them and which they can afford. Cars, scooters, bicycles, the cinema, and the radio are among the modern inventions most widely adopted in India. They are the first to have been produced in the country itself, and have done much to animate the life of the towns. Above all, the cinema, which ranks among the foremost in the world, attracts a large percentage of the population, in spite of the limited means of the middle classes and the poverty resulting from lack of stability in employment.

The incomes of civil servants, doctors, lawyers, and office workers of all categories are, indeed, very limited, and those of artisans and workmen extremely small. A salary of a few hundred rupees a month (1 rupee = 1s. 6d.) is well considered, and wages as low as 30 rupees a month are quite common. It must be borne in mind also that figures quoted by various authors are apt to differ considerably according to whether they wish to emphasize the poverty or the relative prosperity of life in India. The same wage can be presented under a different aspect according to whether the writer takes into account the wages in kind that the worker often receives in addition to the basic monetary payment. In considering how some of the workers in the large cities can live at all, however precariously, on the slender means at their disposal, one should take into account the simplicity of their way of life, with very little household equipment, and also the high purchasing power of the rupee in the matter of basic necessities. Though a small car of Indian manufacture costs 13,600 rupees, a substantial Indian-style meal in a modest restaurant costs from half to three-quarters of a rupee (9d.-1s. 1½d.) and only 2.5 rupees in one of the better vegetarian restaurants. These are, moreover, inclusive figures, as tips are not custom-

the city limits. Cows that have outlived their usefulness are often abandoned, and wander about the streets until some charitable individual or institution takes pity on them. Cattle have now been banished from large cities such as Bombay, and dairies have been set up on the outskirts to supply the population with milk, the problems of keeping it fresh and transporting it having been solved.

Members of all the social groups are naturally to be found in the cities, where administrative centres, commercial and industrial establishments, and educational institutions are all represented. Some of the great landowners, whose income is derived from the country, also live in the towns.

Some of the wealthier people live in European style, and it is only they who can do so, in view of the expense entailed by this mode of life. But the spread of European culture is not limited to those who follow European customs. The knowledge of Western learning and ideas is develop-

Chandigarh: University students ▶

ary, except in European establishments; and there has even been a recent campaign to suppress these. These examples nevertheless show that the greater part of the Indian population lives at subsistence level, at the mercy of any misfortune or increase in prices, and without any possibility of saving to achieve an increase in their standard of living.

In the towns progress is being made in the development of the medical services offered by the doctors and in the hospitals and dispensaries, but, as the former services were grossly inadequate, the present resources are not yet equal to the needs of the population. The existing medical services, however, are efficiently run, as are the public health services in the towns, with a result that the death-rate is decreasing in the country as a whole.

Some cities, like the well-known Banaras (Varanasi), have a huge shifting population of pilgrims who come to visit the sanctuaries, perform ritual ablutions, and carry out rites in memory of the dead, and who are received by the numerous priests as soon as they arrive in the city, along the roads or at the stations. The ablutions are carried out at the foot of flights of steps that lead down to the river or pool in question; in Banaras it is the Ganges, and there the priests are established at the top of the staircases or ghats. The Hindu custom of burning all the dead except young children and *yogi* has given rise to the establishment of places of cremation in the towns; they are particularly numerous in the holy cities, where old or sick people retire to die, so that their ashes may be scattered over a sacred river.

In all towns the temples and churches are built in the areas where the people who are members of the particular religious sect live. The Hindu temples are larger and more numerous in the South; there are sometimes very large mosques in the North, but they are also numerous in certain southern areas; Jain temples are to be found in the West and particularly the North; there are also Catholic and Protestant churches and, throughout the country, along the roadside, at a crossroads, or under a tree, little popular wayside sanctuaries; they consist of some roughly carved image that is placed in a rustic shelter, often no more than a few stones piled up at the foot of a tree, without any roof to cover them.

Banaras: cremation site

5

WORKING CONDITIONS

RURAL LIFE

According to the 1951 census, nearly 70 per cent. of the population of India is dependent on agriculture for its livelihood, and if one adds to this the number of people living in the country and engaged in occupations other than farming, it means that 83 per cent. of the total population lives outside the large urban agglomerations. The important landowners, their farmers and families, account for less than 12 per cent. The small-scale landowners and their families, numbering 47 per cent. of the total population, form the lar-

gest group. But it should be borne in mind that the working population, which is less than half of the total population, has to supply the needs of the remainder, and that this is true of all groups, irrespective of social position.

Many detailed descriptions have been written of Indian villages in various regions. These show that there are basic features common to all, but that the aspects of life in the countryside or in the coastal areas naturally vary according to the different climates and economic resources of the region.

In spite of the fact that the land is divided up into a large number of small independent farms, the villages appear to live on a broad communal

Flower market in Southern India

Buffaloes grazing on an irrigated plain (Coromandel Coast)

basis. Not only do small-scale farmers help each other in turn in tasks such as ploughing, sowing, irrigation, and harvesting, and have their flocks and herds tended all together; each village also obviously has its group of traders and professional men who serve the whole community: potters, blacksmiths, coppersmiths, goldsmiths and silver-smiths, cartwrights, barbers (whose wives are traditionally the village midwives), healers, priests, writers, astrologers, and shopkeepers. The real communal aspect of this organization is that the services of these traders and professional men are paid for, in proportion to the contribution which they make, not in money but in kind, either from the produce of some part of the village land allotted to them or by contributions made by different families in the form of part of their harvest.

The Government has encouraged the re-establishment or the continued activity of the *pan-*

chayat or village council, under the leadership of the *patel* (" chief ") ; and this organization is now to be found in most villages. Neither the chief nor the members of the council have the authority of civil servants, but they represent the interests of the village in dealings with Governmental authorities, and are responsible for village matters that do not come within the scope of the central or state Government or the legal authorities. A joint *panchayat* is sometimes constituted to deal with problems involving a group of villages.

There also exist bodies which are committees of the leading members of the different castes of one or more villages, but these are tending to disappear in some regions, as, distinction of caste being legally abolished, they have no official standing, and cannot compel members of the caste to follow their verdict in matters of accepted custom. In practice, however, when the caste is really a professional association, a purely

Ghogargaon: country scene ▶

private action carried out by its members acting as a group can have considerable significance. Such an action could, for example, prevent the engagement of a worker outside the group for a type of employment considered as being the privilege of the group. Thus in small communities and even in towns a domestic servant who is not a launderer will refuse to wash linen as part of his regular duties, not, as is sometimes believed, because of scruples about the purity or dignity of his own caste, but because he fears the action that would be taken against him by the *dhobi* (launderers), even though they have no legal right to intervene.

Thus the closed-shop principle has done much, particularly in rural areas, to maintain Indian society in self-sufficient groups, the members of which marry within the group and have no social relations with those outside it; they have built up for themselves a feeling of pride in their group, are almost obstinately attached to customs or prerogatives that may seem futile to others, but which to them mark the justification of their autonomy. In order to justify their exclusive attitude the more cultured of the groups cling to the idea of the legendary order of society, quoting national religious tradition and the reasons for the original formation of their group, the functions of which are ennobled by their utility, however humble they may be. The more coherent the group is, the more it feels it necessary to carry out its functions to the best of its ability, partly to com-

A picottah *(machine for raising water from a well for irrigation)*

Market scene in Pondicherry ▶

bat the possible risk of being deprived of them, and partly because the feeling of tasks conscientiously carried out raises its own self-esteem, whatever position in society it may hold.

In the regions where water is not in short supply at any season of the year, and where the land is not waterlogged, the villages always look clean, even though poor. Most of the houses are low and built of mud, roofed with palm-leaves or thatch, and set fairly close to each other. Cooking is done either in the open air on a fire built between three stones or in an earth-built oven under a lightly constructed shelter. The people spend most of their time out of doors; this explains why their tiny dwellings are really sufficiently large.

In the larger settlements there are varying numbers of brick-and-tile houses. These are often fronted by a veranda consisting of a raised platform and supported by posts. They are sometimes isolated and sometimes form streets, particularly when they are to be found in the vicinity of a temple, and then they are the homes of the Brahmins serving there and of the wealthier landowners. The shops are to be found in a different part of the settlement, either forming a bazaar or consisting of stalls bordering a street.

The water-supply is derived from rivers, pools, or wells, and the women go to fetch their water in vessels of burnished copper, dull metal, or earthenware. They carry them either on their hips or on their head. Alongside the rivers and pools are places reserved for bathing and for

Furnace for extracting lime from sea-shells

Srirangam: millstone for crushing stone or shells to obtain lime. Note the symbol of Vishnu on the temple wall behind

Banyan-tree on the banks of the Hooghly, between Chandernagore and Calcutta

washing linen, which when wet is beaten on stones and then stretched out on the ground to dry. Custom ordains that the despised classes shall not have access to the same bathing-places and wells as the more highly considered groups; as the drinking-vessels of the former are reputedly unclean, they must not plunge them into the water used by the others. This custom is not observed where the water flows in a channel; hence the widespread saying, " A well has a caste, but a tap has none."

In villages much frequented by travellers, drinking-water is distributed to people of all categories, who are not allowed to draw it from the well themselves. For this purpose jars are placed under a tree, in the care of a member of a so-called pure caste, who pours out the water for the passers-by. This service is usually provided either by a charitable institution or by a private benefactor. Similar feelings of consideration for others have led to the tradition of establishing roadside shelters open to any traveller, and also stone constructions of the same height as a man, where the traveller can rest the load he is carrying on his head without bending. These facilities are available to members of all castes, as it is considered that the sun and the wind exert a purifying action.

The central Government is at present making an attempt to improve living conditions in the country by constructing rows of small houses, sometimes with a courtyard, to replace the poor huts. In particular, settlements are being built for the accommodation of the former Untouchables, the least-favoured class of society. They are provided with wells, or, in districts where water is abundant and electricity available, with public fountains. The new houses are small and airless, retaining the heat in their bricks, with the result that they are accused of being hotter than the huts, which were equally small but not so enclosed. Their tenants therefore sometimes cover them with palm-leaves and build on to them a type of hut where they live, using the original house merely for storage.

The cleanliness of the villages, more noticeable in the South, is due to the absence of heaps of manure, as the cows are rarely kept in byres and the dung is regularly cleared and dried, to be used either as fuel or as fertilizer. Any rubbish that can be burnt is used as fuel, on account of the scarcity and high price of wood and coal. Any organic rubbish is quickly disposed of by the countless carrion crows, other birds of prey, or the rats.

The clothing of the villagers varies according to region and occupation. Men who are not engaged in manual work wear the *dhoti,* a piece of cloth wrapped round the loins. In the South this cloth is allowed to hang down to the feet; in the North it is caught up between the legs. In the North trousers are also sometimes worn. The upper part of the body is covered by either a long collarless tunic or a type of loose shirt or a large shawl. When the temperature warrants it a sleeveless waistcoat or a woollen garment is worn above these. Those who are not bareheaded wear a turban or, if they belong to certain castes, a cylindrical skullcap; many Moslems wear a cap in the shape of a truncated cone, which is often made

Rice-harvesting, Kanchipuram (Southern India)

*Village temple at Viliyanu
(Southern India)*

of velvet or sheepskin, even in the hottest regions. While working the men either hitch up their *dhoti* to leave their legs free or else are completely naked, apart from a piece of material worn between the thighs and hanging from a rope tied round the waist. In the hotter regions young children are completely naked, though some of them wear round their waists a string from which hangs, in the front, a little silver plaque in the form of a heart.

In the North-west the women wear trousers and a long, loose tunic open at the sides. Elsewhere they wear a *sari,* a long piece of brightly coloured material that is wound round the body and may end in a type of scarf draped round the head. When working in the fields they fasten up the skirts of this garment in very much the same way as the men do their *dhoti.* Moslem women favour materials with large floral designs, though when out of doors they cover themselves in voluminous black or white cloaks, which they draw across their faces; they may even cover their

heads completely, leaving only a slit in the material, level with their eyes.

Many women work in the fields, particularly for transplanting the rice, and also as labourers, principally on the roads and in the building industry, carrying materials on their heads in little spherical baskets or metal bowls. In the South especially the bright colours of their costumes make a striking contrast with the green of the rice-fields or the dust of the roadways.

The carts used are nearly all drawn by oxen, cows, or buffaloes, except in the North, where horses are more numerous. But a large proportion of the country is provided with bus services, which run between the main centres of population and the larger villages. The fares are not high, and extensive use is made of this means of transport.

In regions where electricity is available in sufficient quantity there is lighting in the houses and public buildings, and radio and cinemas are widespread. Village cinemas are large closed-in buildings, constructed of light mater-

Woman pounding condiments on a grindstone ▶

ials, timber, bamboo, palm-leaves, and thatch.

In the rice-fields electrically driven pumps are gradually replacing the old means of irrigation; they are installed either by the Government irrigation services or by the co-operatives, the establishment of which is greatly encouraged by the central Government. There are still very many of the ancient forms of raising water in use, the two main types of which are operated by animals, generally oxen, or by men. In the first type the earth is banked up on one side of the well, forming a sloping surface; at the top of the well is fixed a pulley or a rotating horizontal axle. Through this central point passes a cord, to which is attached a skin water-container which is filled, and pulled up by the oxen as they walk down the slope. The water is poured into the irrigation channel and the oxen walk backwards up the

slope again, the container dropping back into the well to be filled with water once more. The second type of apparatus consists of a long rod mounted on an upright pole. The rod plunges the container into the well or pool and lifts it out again as a man operates the rod with a lever movement, to the rhythm of a song. One or more assistants seize the container as it rises and pour the contents into a runnel.

Farm implements are simple and rudimentary, but of good design and well adapted to their tasks. Indian farmers are generally efficient and characteristically hard-working, even in areas difficult to cultivate and subject, in spite of the regularity of the seasons, to periods of extreme drought or flooding, which may be disastrous.

The traditional plough is a simple wooden instrument, generally with a pointed tip of iron,

Winnowing

River craft at Quilon (Kerala) ▶

Women pounding rice in a mortar

which does no more than skim the surface of the soil. But it offers three important advantages — its low price, its lightness, which enables the farmer to carry it across his shoulder, and its superficial action, for the layer of fertile soil is often extremely thin, and a plough that struck too deeply would bring sterile soil to the surface. For rice cultivation the muddy earth in which the seed is sown requires only light treatment, consisting of the passage of this small plough to dig in the stubble and the trampling action of men and beasts to break up the clods and loosen the soil. Once the rice begins to grow it has to be pulled up and transplanted in a field that is maintained under water until the ears of rice arrive at maturity. The work of replanting is generally undertaken by women, who stand in rows in their brightly coloured *saris* to receive the clumps of plants that the men pull out and throw to them.

Rice-harvesting is done with a sickle. The grain is extracted not by threshing but by trampling the ears on the rice-field itself or, better still, on a flat threshing-floor. The sheaves are scattered over the ground, and oxen, led round on them in pairs, trample them and the grains of rice emerge.

The chief fertilizer is cow dung, and as this is inadequate, since much of it is used as fuel, it is supplemented by branches of certain trees — for example, the *Thespesia populnea,* or portia-tree — which rot quickly in the water of the paddy-field. The Government authorities also encourage sowing leguminous plants near by, so that they can be used as a green fertilizer.

Crops grown on the dry lands are certain species of rice, wheat, maize, millet, groundnuts, and many varieties of lesser cereals of high food value such as *Eleusine coracana (ragi)*. After ploughing the seed is sown at the beginning of the rainy season. These crops require or can withstand deeper ploughing, and mechanical ploughs are advantageous where the areas under the crop are extensive.

New farming methods advocated, such as the Japanese system of cultivating rice, are reasonably well accepted by the Indian peasant if he can observe successful results on trial-grounds on his own land.

The monotony of village life is broken by frequent journeys. Whole families will undertake pilgrimages, and individual journeys from one village to another are often made. Festivals, marriages, and cremations, to which considerable numbers of people are often invited for several days, can at times be ruinous in an economy characterized by extreme poverty. Families often incur debts which they have no hope of redeeming, on account of the high rate of interest and the common clause which excludes partial repayment. No profits are made on a scale that can envisage the repayment in one lump sum of both the loan and the current interest. But although it seems absurd from an economic point of view, this vast expense for a wedding can be justified from a psychological angle. In an existence characterized by never-ending poverty, increased privations are of little account, but the relative splendour which breaks on one occasion

the monotony of this situation of permanent nonentity produces a feeling of liberation from hopeless inferiority, and in the eyes of his neighbours raises the individual and his group fully, if only momentarily, above the level of wretchedness and oblivion.

It would be incorrect to think that the Indian peasant has no thoughts beyond his handful of rice, which is so frequently unavailable that he is forced to learn to do without it. It is his position in society that is dear to his heart; it is one of the few things which really belong to him, something that he must defend and, if possible, improve.

Fisherman on a raft made of tree-trunks lashed together

THE INDUSTRIAL CENTRES

Work in the modern industrial centres and the important public services is organized in much the same way as in the rest of the world, as the requirements of output and productivity are similar. One important exception, however, lies in the fact that though the equipment and organization of work often follow the pattern of the most recent technical developments, the workers have not the same industrial background as those of other countries. In India the graduate engineer has had a training similar to that given in other parts of the world, and his general way of life is not vastly different; but the unskilled worker is still normally recruited from among the farm-labouring community. While workers' settlements are rapidly being built in the permanent industrial centres, they have not yet replaced the temporary camps that are generally to be found in proximity to the new factories, and where overcrowding and promiscuity make the life of the majority of the inhabitants more wretched than in the country.

The movement into the industrial centres of workers of all classes of society from all regions is bringing about a fundamental transformation in the Indian way of life. The small specialized hierarchical groups of the villages, organized for the protection of their local monopolies, are giving way to new trade groups formed in a new setting of mass production and technical organization. The wage-earner, transplanted from his original caste, finds himself a member of a group of workers who are developing new allegiances and who are facing a different type of competition. The exclusive attitude of the castes is disappearing in communities where living quarters are no longer separated and where all work together irrespective of social background and eat together in a communal canteen. At the same time the caste tradition is still maintained in family life, and many marriages, arranged by the parents, still take place in the native village or town of the worker, rather than in the area in which he is employed. Some of the wives brought to the industrial centres, and living among strangers, have a tendency to adopt some of the stricter conventions of higher castes. They feel that they can raise their social status in a way

Tobacco factory (Andhra Pradesh)

The Howrah Bridge, Calcutta

that would have been impossible in their original homes, where they would have been subjected to the protests or the scorn of their neighbours. While conditions of employment are tending to break down the barriers of caste, and there appears to be a general trend towards abolishing them, they are at the same time upheld to a certain extent by feelings of rivalry and questions of status.

Life in India in the material and the intellectual fields is influenced by tradition as well as by equipment and education. The young worker's choice of a career depends not only on the openings offered in the present state of industrial development, and his own level of instruction, but also on the outlook of his own family group.

Third-class compartment in a train

TRANSPORT

Transport was the first sector of the economy to be developed on modern lines, and still represents the field of activity in which the Government is making the greatest effort. While the density of the road and rail networks is low compared with the large extent of territory, all the regions are served, if not wholly adequately.

To the existing road and rail communications has been added the efficient air network of the Indian Airlines Corporation. The large cities of Bombay, Delhi, Calcutta, and Madras are international airports served by world airlines, or have direct links with all the continents through the Indian company Air-India International. The four cities are further linked by regular day and night air services, and each of them is the focal point of a network of secondary airlines.

As far as land routes are concerned, the railway is the most reliable for long-distance transport, as there are viaducts and bridges over the major rivers and land liable to flooding, while this is not always true of the roads. Nevertheless the section of the Public Works Department responsible for road maintenance is very active, and its efforts have been increased as a consequence of the series of five-year plans. The duty of this department is to keep the main roads and many

of the secondary ones (especially in Southern India) in good repair, to construct new roads, and to increase the number of bridges. Work so far undertaken has made possible a considerable amount of road transport, by means of lorries and extensive bus services.

Some sections of the rail network are electrified or in the process of electrification, but steam traction is the general rule. Work is in progress on the modernization and renewal of rolling-stock, and now third-class trains with air-conditioned compartments and numbered seats help to ease the problem of the ordinary, overcrowded trains. German industry has recently acquired the patent for an improved transmission system for diesel engines invented by the Indian engineer Suri.

Bus and rail fares are not expensive — for example, the bus fare from Madras to Bangalore, a distance of more than 300 kilometres (over 185 miles), in a new, well-equipped vehicle is 10 rupees (15s.).

While the conditions of inland transport are favourable to trade, there are few ports; with the exception of Visakhapatnam, which has a naval shipyard, and Madras, which is an artificial port, the east coast ports consist only of open roadsteads, which are dangerous when the north-east monsoon is blowing and threatens to sweep craft on to the coast.

POWER AND INDUSTRY

The extensive potentialities for the development of hydroelectric power on the one hand, and the deposits of both coal and iron ore in certain regions, such as the Bihar and Western Bengal area, make possible the development of irrigation, electrification, and the steel industry. The five-year plans and international co-operation have contributed towards the construction of dams and steel-works, and an atomic power station has been established at Trombay, near Bombay.

Many industrial enterprises have been set up, or are in the process of development, either by private enterprise or with Government aid. These include textile mills, locomotive works, and plants for the manufacture of motor vehicles, bicycles, sewing-machines, and many other commodities. In order to co-ordinate production it has sometimes been necessary to build factories that would appear to be of very limited utility; for example, a considerable area of uncultivated land in the south-west is suitable for the development of rubber plantations (*hevea*), but the immediate needs for tyres for the motor-vehicle industry are such that it has been found essential to set up synthetic-rubber plants to meet interim needs.

But while large-scale industry is in process of development, it is still the craftsmen who supply the mass of the population with consumer goods.

Dam across a river

Construction of the dam for the Nugu reservoir (Mysore) ▶

THE CRAFTSMEN

The craftsmen form a very large percentage of the Indian industrial population. Their degree of skill is extremely varied, but in certain fields, particularly in weaving, they produce goods of an exceptionally high quality. These products are quite different, naturally, from mass-produced factory materials, and are typically Indian in design.

In 1952 the Government established the All India Handicrafts Board in order to help the craftsmen. Its object is to preserve the traditional arts that are of value in themselves and which help labour problems by the employment they offer. It also aims at maintaining the regional or national characteristics of the finished product, discouraging the output of the over-stereotyped or commonplace. But it is not merely an institution for encouraging the production of luxury articles of high artistic value.

The family spinning and weaving industry is helped by a system for the supply of raw materials and small-scale equipment and the collection of the finished product. Indeed, one of the most important organizations to help the prosperity of the craftsmen is that of the production and sale of *khaddar,* or *khadi,* a material woven in the homes, not even an output of specialized craftsmen; it is a development of the earlier campaigns led or inspired by Gandhi, whose aim was to provide India with cotton goods produced from the local raw material without the intermediary of the English mills.

Carpenters

Woman weaving woollen cloth at Mana

108

The *khadi* system exists for the silk industry, but the major product is cotton. The materials are simple in design and strong, though some are much finer than others, and they are marketed at relatively low prices. They are sold either by the yard or metre or in strips finished with borders ready to make into *dhotis* or *saris*. There is a small production of ready-made goods, such as towels, handkerchiefs, and scarves.

Though part of the production of the craftsmen benefits from Government aid, or even represents industries created by the Government, most of it comes under the scope of large or small scale private enterprise. Certain industries are to be found in all centres of population, whether large or small, though others are typical of certain regions or districts. Potters, ironmongers, and shoemakers are to be found almost everywhere, and manufacture standard articles for current consumption, but there is also an output of certain specialized products of these industries, confined to particular regions and villages. As transport is becoming more easy each village tends to have fewer different industries and to obtain its supplies through middlemen who collect or receive the products of the specialized groups of craftsmen. Any particularly specialized product of these groups is also marketed throughout India, through a special Government department. Thus, although often produced in small local centres, the same types of mats, basketwork, materials, jewellery, carpets, ivories, carved wooden objects, and metal goods are sold throughout the country and sometimes even exported.

A characteristic of the work of the Indian craftsman is the skill and ingenuity used to transform very rudimentary materials into the finished article. The craftsman traditionally learnt his trade from his family or caste, and still often does so; this tends to make him over-specialized, but gives him a degree of skill in his trade which astonishes the outsider.

Man selling baskets

The development of the output of *khadi* by craftsmen has led to progressive industrialization, passing through the stages of specialization by craftsmen and technical improvements. The production group, originally an individual family, has become organized into a sort of guild, which supplies the Government sales service with the finished goods. Commercial centres for this trade have been established in the towns and large villages, and they supply the craftsmen with the raw materials and collect, check and sell the finished product.

Implements for fanning the fire

Potter at his wheel

A less commendable characteristic is the too frequent lack of finish and presentation of the article, which the Westerner or Japanese finds displeasing. This is due to the fact that the Indian craftsman has to produce his goods at as low a price as possible because of the very limited means of his customers, and it is therefore accepted that everything should be sacrificed to the essential. Some of the imperfections in the finished goods also arise from the fact that in addition to the skilled craftsmen there are large numbers of untrained workers. It is true that in all fields Indian labour is very uneven in standard, because of the vast numbers of uneducated or untrained workers who have to find employment where they can. As soon as more extensive training facilities are available it will be possible to orientate workers towards the trade for which they show an aptitude; but in the meantime there is a vast labour force which, without adopting an apathetic attitude towards the improvement of its status, can manage to live or survive in conditions of poverty which the workers of many other countries would be incapable of accepting. This is one aspect of the essential strength of India, a country that is not the slave of a complex system of material equipment without which living would be considered impossible. While the Indian can enjoy material comforts, he can also do without them. He is accustomed to poverty, but even when wealthy his tastes are simple; and this fact, together with the climatic conditions of the greater part of the country, makes the minimum living wage lower than in most industrialized communities. India therefore has a large cheap labour force, but as many of the workers are undernourished and untrained the individual productivity is low.

Production costs are therefore often high, in spite of low wages, because of the large numbers of workers who have to be employed. On the

Woman spinning
(Southern India)

Painting on matting (Calcutta)

other hand, industrialization and the further development of the activities of the craftsmen should do much to increase the general standard of living; and, in any case, the present organization of the craftsmen and the use of craftsmen's methods in different branches of activity are offering a considerable amount of employment and are making possible a production programme which would otherwise have had to wait a long time before costly machinery could be imported.

EDUCATION AND
SCIENTIFIC RESEARCH

India is considered to have one of the highest percentages of illiteracy among the major countries of the world. Nevertheless teaching is available throughout the country, and people who cannot read are by no means always without some cultural background. The traditional teach-

ing in India has always been principally if not wholly oral. Innumerable stories, legends, songs, proverbs, and sayings are familiar through repetition to all classes of the population. Grandmothers, wandering story-tellers, and men who recite the legendary epics are teachers without realizing it; and the popularity of films on legendary and mythological subjects shows that they are well known among a wide section of the public, literate or otherwise. These films do not teach the masses, who are familiar with the subjects and criticize the production, having preconceived ideas on how the themes should be presented.

Formal education is available at all stages under both the Indian and the English systems. The Indian education is less comprehensive, being confined mainly to Sanskrit language and literature and, to a lesser degree, to modern languages. In the South, however, Tamil studies are available as well as Sanskrit, and do do not depend upon it, as the Tamil literature covers all aspects of Indian culture except the specialized branch of Vedic studies. In the North,

Woman at a loom (Calcutta) ▶

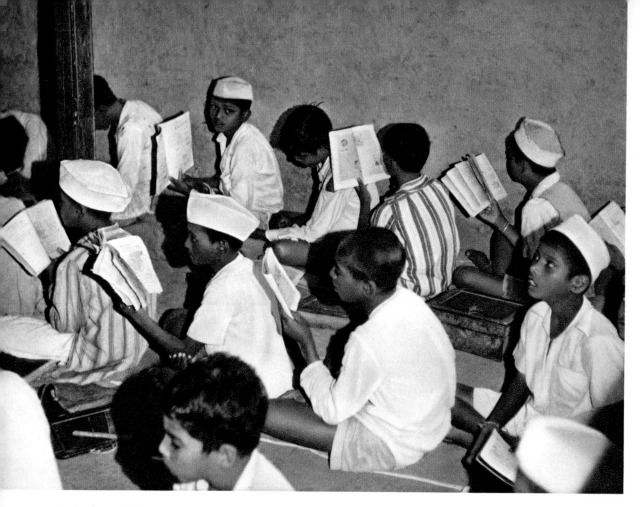

Village school at Ghogargaon (Aurangabad region)

as the languages spoken derive from Sanskrit, and most of the learned texts are written in Sanskrit, the study of modern languages depends on Sanskrit even more than the study of European languages depends on Latin, Sanskrit being far more important in modern India than Latin is in Europe to-day.

There are schools that specialize in the Indian traditional medical studies, *Ayurveda* (the science of longevity), which have been improved by certain elements taken from the universal study of medicine. Some schools are very inadequate, and many of the healers do not even study at them. Some of the partisans of the traditional methods, which are not without their value, recommend an official reorganization of the schools, in the belief that the danger of the old methods consists largely in the incompetence of the practitioners. Modern doctors, however, oppose any official recognition of the *Ayurveda,* which would serve only to perpetuate it. It remains true, however, that modern medicine is insufficiently widespread and too costly; a considerable part of the population is therefore still

at the mercy of ignorance and charlatanism, and could benefit from the traditional methods of treatment if they were adequately administered. But as it would be scarcely more difficult to train a large number of modern doctors than to train the same number of competent practitioners of the *Ayurveda,* the solution lies in the extension of facilities for the teaching of modern medical science, at the same time not neglecting any useful knowledge acquired through the *Ayurveda.*

Primary education on English lines is generally carried out in the local Indian language spoken by the majority of the pupils. Secondary and higher education are largely if not wholly in English. Attempts in the universities to teach modern subjects in the language of the state in which they are situated have so far given rise to difficulties. The absence of books in the languages concerned is only a temporary problem; the production of educational books on a large scale in languages spoken by millions of people is a wholly legitimate conception. Nor is the absence of technical terms in these languages really an obstacle: the transliteration of the existing international terms, generally with Greek roots, is a comparatively simple problem, and Sanskrit is as well adapted as Greek for the formation of new ones. The real difficulty arises from the fact that once the student is qualified he may have the opportunity of a post in a state where a different language from his own is spoken; if his higher education has been in his state language, then he is fitted only to work in his own state ; if he has been taught in English, then he can mix in any official circles or with any other educated Indians. The universities can abandon teaching in English only if some other language such as Hindi is substituted throughout the country.

Teaching according to the English system, with its early specialization and manuals which the Indian students learn by heart, does not always provide the Indian with a good general education, while in England family background can often supplement the deficiencies of the curriculum. Indian students, moreover, have very few books at their disposal apart from the textbooks required for passing their examinations. Under these conditions it is very difficult to train adequate professorial staffs for the universities.

There has, however, been considerable progress in India in the development of basic scientific research through the installation of laboratories, and thanks to the international reputation of Indian scientists, particularly in the realms of physics and mathematics, where important results can be achieved without costly installations.

Government establishments carry out research in the applied sciences, particularly in the fields

Madras, University buildings

Jamnagar : the new college of electricity and naval technology (1955)

117

Embroidery work (Kashmir)

of geography, botany, forestry, agriculture, geology, and statistics. Special mention should also be made of the institutes of physics and medicine in New Delhi and the institute of electronic studies in Bangalore.

Technical and professional training are relatively undeveloped. The primary need is for trained workers and for increased opportunities for employment in technical posts; but it is, moreover, essential that technical training should develop at the same pace as the demand for skilled personnel created by the expansion of industry.

Machine tools in an instruction shop at Ambarnath (near Bombay)

6

ASPECTS OF CULTURAL LIFE

India's cultural heritage includes Hindu, Islamic, and European — or, more particularly, British — traditions, which are coexistent rather than intermingled; and though there are many Indians who are influenced by all three, they form but a small minority of the country's vast population. Even smaller in number are the Parsee intellectuals, who still keep the traditions of pre-Islamic Persia, whence they sprang; their education includes the mastery of several European languages, and they have a particularly broad outlook on mankind as a whole. A much larger group enjoys the advantages of Western civilization and Indian culture, both classical and modern, through Hindu religious and philosophical teaching. Even more numerous are the Indians

Man in meditation near a sacrificial fire

who have but a single cultural heritage. Some have not really been enriched by British culture, as they have acquired it at the expense of their own native traditions. This was true initially of some eminent Indians of recent times, such as Gandhi and Aurobindo, who, after exclusively English studies, discovered much later in life the wealth of Indian outlook and achievements. Such men at least finally acquired the traditions of the two civilizations, but they are few. The vast majority remain bound by the limits of their early educational formation, and disdain anything beyond it. There are some who have a superficial acquaintance with both Western and Indian tradition, who like to compare them in a way that does not really penetrate below the surface, and either take a naïve pride in finding in their past history the discoveries of the modern world or, obstinate in their insistence on things modern, make a point of disowning their background.

Knowledge of India's past varies considerably. Outside truly scholastic circles there are many who believe that the whole scope and chronology of India's past is contained in the *Puranas* ("old traditions") which, though varied in the many accounts written at different times, nevertheless present a relatively coherent whole. According to this tradition the world revolves in an everlasting cyclical and periodic movement around the axis of the North Pole, the home of the gods of nature. At the end of each major period everything is dissolved in chaos, then is reorganized into a new era, at first a kind of Paradise, where *Dharma* ("Right Order") reigns, only to decline gradually in power until the fourth and worst age, the *Kaliyuga,* is reached; it is this fourth age in which we are living at present.

This tradition, unlike that of some other nations, does not put India in the centre of the universe. It admits the existence of other continents and other peoples, some of whom are happier and better than the Indians themselves. But

▲

Mamallapuram : Somaskanda cave. Vishnu recumbent (seventh century). Siva, Uma, and Skanda are inside the central shrine on the right

Mamallapuram : Somaskanda cave. The goddess Durga fighting a buffalo-headed demon, Mahisha (seventh century) ▶

An ascetic saint, Karaikkalammaiyar, sitting at the feet of Siva dancing, and listening to the final echo of the cymbals

Temple of Madurai (sixteenth century). The pool of the Golden Lotus and two towers (gopuram)

the way in which foreign countries are described has little in common with geographical and ethnological fact.

The literature consists of mythological stories and lists of the royal dynasties. They place a Supreme Being, Reality, above everything; all the different transient forms of Nature participate in this Reality, which alone is unique and eternal. Reality, which is shared by all, by individual man as well as by the universe, and which is the "self" *(atman)* of each and every individual, is the one true God, the Supreme Self *(Paramatman)*, or Brahman. Reality also appears in manifestations of power, in the forms of the different divinities, in the incarnations *(avatar)* and in human forms.

Pattadakal : Lambani women dancing ►

Lambani woman (Mysore)

HINDUISM

In Hinduism there are two main religious currents, for there are two major parallel cycles of the representation of the Supreme Being, those of Siva and Vishnu. They are the two main currents of Hinduism, Saivism and Vaishnavism—the religion of the Hindus, as opposed to the beliefs of other Indians, whether Moslems, Christians, Parsees, or those who follow any other faith.

Saivism is the larger group and possesses the greater number of temples. The Supreme Being is Siva, the Propitious, Sadasiva, the Ever-Propitious, or Rudra or Bhairava, the Terrible, one Being with two opposing aspects, commanding the universe. The force *(sakti)* that moves him and that inclines him to manifest himself in one or other of his two aspects, or in the eight forms of the elements that constitute Nature and Ritual, is evoked by his two corresponding female manifestations, Uma or Parvati ("daughter of the Mountain"), a goddess of sublime beauty and sweetness, and the terrible goddess known as Durga ("the Inaccessible"), or Kali ("the Goddess of Time" or "the Black Goddess"), or sim-

Mamallapuram: group of monolithic sanctuaries sculpted in the rock (seventh-eighth centuries)

ply as Devi ("the Goddess"). Siva and his consort have many other names corresponding to their greatness or to the countless forms in which they manifest themselves in Nature or in tradi-

Unfinished sanctuary of Durga, carved in a rock, north of Mamallapuram (eighth century)

125

tional legend. The sentiment of this greatness exalts believers and transports them towards the deity in a wave of thankfulness and love, even through the contemplation of the terrible forms, for they see beyond them, behind the fantastic and shifting manifestations, the perpetual serenity of the Eternal Being towards whom they are led by knowledge and faith. The image of Natesa ("The Dancing Lord"), who appears in a circle of flames above a trampled human body, represents the triumph over the blindness by which man in his passage through the world forgets that he is part of the Eternal Being.

The doctrine of Saivism, following the teaching of the ninth-century philosopher Sankara, preaches the non-duality *(Advaita)* of the Supreme Being. The only element common to everything for which we find an image is the mere fact of existence. The changing aspects under which both objects and individuals appear are created by Illusion *(Maya)*, which can be pierced only by knowledge *(jnana)*. Man is like an ignorant beast held in the grip of Illusion, but the Supreme Being liberates him and receives him by revealing himself to him. Man has also a psychical indiv-

iduality, composed of the sum of the impressions made upon his mind by the previous psychical activities which have accompanied his actions *(karma)*. This individuality does not die with the body, but is reincarnated in another form according to its leading tendencies. It is thus drawn into the phenomena of the illusory world, passes through a successive series of existences, is carried along in the stream of transmigration *(samsara)*. It is finally absorbed in knowledge, which, when the illusory images that have brought pleasure or suffering have faded, reduces everything to the pure fact of existence in the infinite plenitude of the potentialities of Reality.

It must not be concluded from this that every Saivite is a philosopher who considers life as a dream. His ideal is a goal to attain, not a situation which has been achieved. Man is a traveller on the path of Illusion, and he should guard his steps so that he progresses towards Deliverance *(mukti* or *moksha)*. He can do this by resorting to a psycho-physiological discipline, *Yoga,* which is a mastery of both body and mind, teaching man to control all the elements of his individual existence. He can do this also by acts

Terra-cotta statues of warriors of the god Aiyanar on the road between Villapuram and Selam

Baranas : a temple visited by monkeys ▶

of worship, which consist of making offerings, reciting sentences of adoration or hymns of praise and devotion, and reading or listening to holy stories or contemplating images which evoke them. Finally there is ardent personal devotion, for love of the deity, even in his terrifying form, which is the witness of his power and an instrument to destroy ignorance, is a deep-rooted feeling in Saivistic circles.

The typical symbol of Siva, and of all the Kumara, is often added. Siva's mount is a bull known as Nandi, and a statue of it is traditionally placed in front of the shrine.

The most important part of the temple is the sanctuary, above which is built a tower *(vimana)* of varying height; it is preceded by an antechamber, and generally stands in the middle of a courtyard surrounded by high walls, the gates of which are surmounted by towers *(gopura)*. The act of worship consists of anointing the divine

Temple musicians at Bahur

"Lords" who are other forms of this Supreme Being, is the *linga,* a simple cylinder mounted on an oval, horizontal base, the *yoni,* and this dual image initially symbolized procreation. It is to be found in the centre of all the sanctuaries of Siva. Representations of Siva in various human forms, with three eyes and four arms, with or without Parvati, are equally numerous. The image of a young child, their son, Skanda, or image, presenting offerings of food from the vegetable kingdom, of coloured pastes, incense, leaves of *vilva (Aegle marmelos)*, garlands of flowers, and lights. The worshippers then consume the offerings of food. They mark their foreheads and often their shoulders and chests with ashes, making three white horizontal lines; this is the exterior symbol of their religion.

The religion is not an exclusive one; it recog-

*Procession bearing the statue of the goddess Draupadi
(heroine of the* Mahabharata*)*

nizes the existence of other deities, and particularly of Brahman, from whom the world emanates, and of Vishnu, who pervades and preserves it, though these deities are considered to exist, as do all other beings and objects, only through Siva. There is thus a threefold representation of the divinity, the *Trimurti*. Devout worshippers of Siva, well known through their works and the legendary stories of their lives, are venerated in the temples side by side with the divine forms. In the south of India they are known as the sixty-three *Nayanmar*.

There are also two very popular cults connected with Saivism, the worship of Skanda, or Kumara, a son of Siva and Parvati, a young warrior hero with six heads, represented mounted on a peacock, and their other son Ganesa, the god with the head of an elephant, who is portrayed mounted on a rat, the leader of the hosts of the genii; he is called Pillaiyar in Tamil, and upon invocation will clear away the difficulties from any enterprise. Not only does everyone invoke Ganesa, at least as a secondary invocation, but this cult, like that of Kumara, is sometimes considered as an autonomous religion.

This doctrine is propagated by the *jagadguru* ("preceptors of the world"), who represent the tradition of the philosopher Sankaracharya. The main places where this teaching is carried out are Sringeri in Mysore and Kumbakonam and Kanchipuram to the south and west of Madras respectively. These *jagadguru* are the heads of the *matha* (monasteries) and are, like their founder, Sannyasin, men who have renounced the world and religious rites.

Other important Saiva movements are the Saivasiddhanta, the "perfect achievement of Saivism," found mainly in the Tamil-speaking area; and the Virasaiva or Lingayats, who are widespread in the Kanarese territories. Both place more importance on attainment of Knowledge than on rites, and admit the possibility that people of any social class may attain Knowledge.

The principal temples of the main cult are served by Brahmin priests, but those of secondary cults may be served by members of lower castes who have specifically embraced these cults; this is true for the worship of Sitaladevi, or Mariyammai, the goddess who offers protection against smallpox, to whom sacrifices of cocks are made. This cult is linked to Saivism only by identification with one of the forms of the great goddess Devi, to whom, in the form of Kali, sacrifices of kids are offered, especially in the well-known modern temple of the Kalighat at Calcutta.

A cult of confidence and love is also dedicated to Kali. She is considered as the mother who gave birth to the world, and one has only to yield oneself wholly to her to be saved, to become part of the Supreme Being, for she is in essence this unique Being. The love of Kali the mother of all, together with the philosophic belief in unity of the Supreme Being, characterizes the beliefs of the Ramakrishna Mission, a movement powerful in India and spread outside the country by missionaries. This mission was founded in the name of the Bengali saint Ramakrishna (1834-1886) by his disciple Vivekananda and his followers.

Vaishavism contains ideas very similar in general principles to those of Saivism, but it is Vishnu and not Siva who is considered as the embodiment of the omnipresent Reality that penetrates all creation. For most of the followers of Vishnu the world is considered as real and not an illusion. It is real in the sense that Vishnu is present everywhere, dwelling within man himself as his supporter, supporting even nothingness itself, for without participating in Reality nothingness would not exist. Knowing this, the faithful worshipper sees God in everything and within himself, but more clearly in the outstanding

Modern statue of the god Aiyanar, guardian of the fields

Har ki padi (Hara's staircase), a place of pilgrimage at Haridvar

manifestations of the deity and in his direct incarnations which are made famous in legends and epics such as the *Mahabharata,* the *Ramayana,* in the traditions of the *Purana,* and in the hymns of adoration of the devout.

The incarnations *(Avatar)* are of animal form. They include the fish, who saved humanity from the deluge; the boar, who extracted the earth from the waters of the ocean ; some are hybrid, like the man-lion, who tore to pieces an unbelieving Titan despot. There are also the purely human incarnations of Rama and Krishna.

The real miracle is above all the grace by which this Absolute Being descends, marvellous and human, within reach of man, and offers himself to the transports of man's worship and to his gratitude for his deliverance and his union with the Absolute. Man's devotion in its most ardent form can never hope to achieve this deliverance and this union, so exalting is the quest, and

abasing oneself before the glory of God is already so much supreme happiness.

Vishnu is worshipped in human aspect, not in a symbolic form, in the temples which are similar in plan to those dedicated to Siva. Sometimes he is represented by a standing figure, generally with four arms, bearing among other attributes a conch-shell and a discus, and is often accompanied by his usual vehicle, the bird Garuda. Sometimes he is depicted lying asleep on the coils of a mythical serpent, which itself is floating on the Ocean of Chaos. He is also represented under the human incarnations of Rama or Krishna, and the faithful like to invoke him using these names, though at the same time they think of him as the Supreme Being appearing simultaneously in all his many forms. He is equally often depicted as the Man-lion, tearing to pieces with his claws Hiranyakasipu, the king of the Asura or Titans, who had defied him,

Entrance to the temple of Jagannath at Puri (Orissa)

raging at the devotion which his wise son Prahrada had sworn to him.

Rama is the hero of Valmiki's great Sanskrit poem the *Ramayana,* and of other similar epics in all the various modern languages spoken in India; he also figures in other poems, legendary tales, and choreographer's themes that stretch beyond the bounds of India into Siam (Thailand), Laos, Cambodia, and Indonesia.

Rama is an example of faithfulness to *Dharma* ("Right Order"), which it is man's supreme duty to respect and defend. He was exiled by the king his father because of a rash promise made to his stepmother to expel him so that her son might reign; so he left the northern land of Ayodhya, and journeyed towards the southern forests in the company of his faithful wife Sita and his younger brother, Lakshmana. He fought the monsters and savage tribes that opposed the establishment of the Brahmanic Order. But

Offerings presented to Krishna ▶

132

the lovely Sita was seized by terrible Ravana, the king of the monsters *(rakshasa)* who lived in Lanka (Ceylon). With the help of the monkeys and the bears Rama attacked Lanka, killed Ravana, and delivered Sita, whose subsequent trial by ordeal proved her fidelity to the whole world. Rama is often represented armed with a great bow and arrow and accompanied by Sita and Lakshmana; the huge ape Hanuman, who could leap prodigious distances, and whose devotion knew no limits, is associated with him. Hanuman is the object of a separate cult, yet one which is not wholly independent; for Hanuman is worshipped because of his supreme devotion to Rama, in much the same way as the famous saints of Vaishnavism, the *Alvars* of the Tamil country. Indeed, extreme humility is one of the characteristics of certain devotions of the Vaishnavites, who invoke the saints who have devoted themselves to the divinity, while not daring to address the deity himself. The most usual distinguishing mark of the members of the sect is a white V on the forehead, in the middle of which is a vertical red line, symbolizing the footprints of Vishnu on the head of his humble worshipper.

The struggle between Rama and Ravana is by no means only a traditional theme brought down to modern times through learned literature; it remains a powerful source of emotion and wonder in all classes of modern Hindu society. The *Ramayana* composed in Hindi in the fifteenth century by Tulsidas, and now published with translations into modern Hindi, is one of the most popular books in Northern India. Readers or wandering reciters of the Bengali *Ramayana* by Krittibas can easily gather around their candles in the evening, on the quaysides of Calcutta, a group of humble folk who are eager to listen to the old story.

In the south passionate politicians have made the story of Rama a matter for conflict. To the autonomists of the region Rama figures as the invader who established and consolidated the usurping class of the Brahmins in the country, and for them the real hero is Ravana, unfortunate but sublime, a national hero. There have been in the recent past serious fights at Tanjavur (Tanjore), between the partisans of North and South on the occasion of a play based on the *Ramayana.*

The worship of Krishna is equally important. Krishna is the prodigal, mischievous child, in the presence of whom women overflow with feelings of maternal tenderness; the young, charming,

Chariot decorated for a religious procession

humorous hero, at the sight of whom maidens are filled with the transports of love. The tale of his greatness is told in the *Mahabharata,* a philosophic epic of a hundred thousand stanzas, linked by the theme of the fratricidal war between two factions of the descendants of Bharata, the Pandavas and the Kauravas. A part of this vast work is the famous *Bhagavadgita*; Krishna had become the coachman of the Pandava hero Arjuna, who, at the moment of battle, hesitated, because his adversaries the Kauravas were also members of his family. At this point Krishna preached the importance of acting in accordance with the duty of the condition in which one finds oneself, regardless of personal feelings, a duty that must be carried out in the knowledge and the love of the Supreme Being, the essence of whose glory he

made to celebrate the games of Krishna and the *gopi,* the girl cowherds whom he charmed with his flute and who experienced with him, as do all mystical souls who love the deity, the loneliness of abandonment, outbursts of jealousy, and the transports of union with the Supreme Being.

Thus devotion *(bhakti)* dominates the Hindu religion, and, though it is shown more by outward manifestations in the worship of Vishnu than in the worship of Siva, it is for both a fundamental force. *Bhakti* is linked by faith to the unique Supreme Being, the universal Self, the essence to which human individuality belongs, man's self on his path through life, the *jivatman,* confined within the limits of earthly life as a portion of space is enclosed in a vessel. This *jivatman* is forced to carry out his part in life as an actor plays his role, leading each successive life as though playing a series of parts on the stage. But even during this life it is possible for him to recover his true nature, through knowledge directed towards the deity; and, when the body is dissolved in death, it can become reintegrated with the infinite, as the space within a vessel when the artificial walls that have enclosed it

revealed in himself. But this literature is a common heritage of Indian cultural tradition as a whole, and the worship of Krishna has as more specific sources other works, the main one of which is the *Bhagavata Purana.* King Kamsa, Krishna's maternal uncle, disturbed by a prophecy, wanted to have him killed at birth, so he was hidden on the banks of the river Yamuna in a community of herdsmen; he grew up and played, killed monsters amidst his games, and radiated a feeling of love, so that the infinite greatness of cosmic reality could be seen in him.

Krishna figures in great works of art and literature throughout India, but not outside the country, as Rama does.

The love of Krishna and Radha, a symbol of the union of the soul with the deity, is celebrated in many ways, particularly in Bengal, in the holy places associated with the legend on the banks of the Yamuna, at Mathura and at Vrindavan. Poems, hymns, litanies, cantilenas, and ballets have been composed and statues and paintings

Modern steatite statuette of Subrahmanya

Jain monks at Delhi

crumble, and return once more to the dust.

In this outlook, which can be described as "gnostic," where *jnana* (knowledge) and *bhakti* ("inclination" or "devotion") hold supreme place and offer to man the possibility of transcending his earthly condition, ritual counts in principle merely as a means of approach to the deity, and service of the various forms in which God has manifested himself to man becomes the only true form of worship. This service is that of the court of a prince, and includes awakening and putting to sleep, offering homage, ablutions, clothing, adorning with jewels, giving banquets, and amusing the image of the deity; and, at festivals, processions with the image enthroned in a litter or a chariot. In principle also, following the logical conclusions of such a concept, the faithful worshipper can attain knowledge and salvation, no matter to what social class he may belong. But in practice it is commonly admitted that certain advantages of birth give some men advantages in matters of knowledge and devotion, by reason of tendencies that they have acquired in former lives. This is a reintroduction of the legitimacy of the distinctions of the hierarchical castes, as it is considered that the caste into which a man is born is determined by

the actions of his former lives. This accounts for a certain resignation to their present position on the part of the lukewarm, who carry forward their hopes of advancement towards a future existence, which they must prepare for long in advance by exact observances of the moral code, acts of worship, and charity.

This has brought about fairly wide-scale introduction of ritual observances disdained by those who have reached the heights of doctrine and faith, but to which many remain attached, all the more so because they are largely ignorant of the reasons for their existence, and are unaware of what retributions they may bring upon themselves by disregarding them.

These observances consist in maintaining a strict standard of conduct in all matters, in individual worship and in attending the temples for morning and evening worship and participating in festivals and pilgrimages to holy places. One of the essential rites performed when making a pilgrimage is carrying out ablutions at the *tirtha,* the ford where ablutions are believed to wash away all sin, and where the object of adoration is the *linga* of Siva, a footprint of Vishnu, an image, a tree, or any other object which local tradition has associated with miraculous virtues or the

Bronze statuette of Virabhadra

power of salvation. Ablutions in the *tirtha,* which may be a river like the Ganges at Banaras or the Phalgu at Gaya, or sometimes an artificial lake, are believed to be more efficacious than the great legendary sacrifices of the Vedic period, which are no longer practised. In places of pilgrimage there are groups of priests who await the pilgrims, to guide them and officiate for them in their acts of worship.

The festivals in the temples and holy places attract vast crowds, who often come from great distances and sometimes consist of whole families bringing the greater part of their household goods with them. The place where the festival is to be held and all the neighbouring district is transformed into a huge camp, where traders set up stalls for the sale of seeds, fruit, cakes, implements of various kinds, books, jewellery, and toys, and where the crowds can find amusement in the travelling zoos or entertainers, while professional beggars ask for alms. These beggars consist of cripples or men who pretend to be infirm, and of the *sadhu,* sometimes incorrectly called *fakirs,* who are bound by vows to acts of self-torture, such as lying on a bed of nails or thorns. At some festivals the devout practise certain forms of mortification of the flesh, either individually or collectively; for example, a group of people may walk over a bed of burning embers. These devout people, however, do not ever beg.

Followers of Hinduism form a varied and complex group that is nevertheless quite distinctive. They are divided not only into Saivites and Vishnavites, but also into a host of different communities with definite traditions who are distinguished by the ritual they observe, their religious attitude and philosophical tendencies.

There are some particularly important movements. Those already referred to include the Saivasiddhanta, the origin of which dates back further than the tenth century; the Virasaiva, who became organized in the twelfth century; and the Ramakrishna Mission, which dates from the nineteenth century. There is also the group that professes a mystic love for Krishna, which, founded in Bengal in the sixteenth century, rapidly spread throughout most of India. Under the influence of Chaitanya and his disciples, the *gosvami,* this group revived, even in its region of origin, the cult of Krishna, which had been eclipsed for a time by Islam.

The Sikh sect is an even more closely knit and discernible community; its members are the disciples of the "spiritual master," the *guru*

Nanak (1469-1538), and of his successors as leaders of the movement. This community holds in veneration a sacred text, the *Adigranth* ("Original Book"), which consists of a collection of the works of numerous religious writers of the mediaeval period, who were not sectarians but ardent worshippers of the divinity and enemies of formalism; some of them are acclaimed by the Moslems as well as by the Hindus, as is the case of Kabir. The Sikhs are distinguished by their egalitarian ideas, repudiating all distinctions of caste, by their liberalism, and by certain exterior characteristics. The principal feature by which the foreigner can recognize them is their turban, which is wound round a pile of hair that has never been cut, their beards, which are never trimmed and are sometimes worn in a fine net, and their abstinence from the use of tobacco. But their essential characteristics are the cohesion and the dignity of their community.

On the confines of Hinduism, yet Hindu in that it was founded in India in an ancient period before the Islamic conquest, is the Jain sect, which flourishes in Gujarat and Mysore. There are also Jains in all the large cities, such as Bombay, Delhi, Calcutta, and Madras. The Jain community consists of monks and lay members of differing degrees of wealth, who are mainly engaged in commerce and banking. Generally speaking, the members belong to the wealthier, educated, and liberal classes. The origin of the movement goes back to at least the sixth century B.C., and it developed parallel with Buddhism. The latter, after a long period of evolution in India, spread through three-quarters of Asia, only to disappear subsequently from India in the Middle Ages. But though the Jain faith has never been propagated outside Indian territory, it has been maintained within its boundaries. Its doctrine is one of doubt as far as the world and metaphysical problems are concerned, but one of certitude that man must attempt to rid his psychic individuality of the bonds of the world. This can be achieved by following the rules of conduct taught by the twenty-four *Tirthakara* ("ford-makers"), who help man to cross the river of worldly allurements. The adoration and the hymns of the worshippers are addressed to

A pilgrim camp

these sages, the *Jina* or conquerors of transmigration, and not to a supreme deity. The general attitude of the members of the sect is dominated by a high ideal of virtue, mastery of self, and charity towards one's neighbour. The law of doing no injury to others *(ahimsa)*, so general in Indian life, is nowhere more scrupulously observed than among the Jain community. Among their members are not only those who are strict vegetarians, but also those who make it their duty never to harm any living creature, not even the insects that they sweep aside before sitting down, or the gnats that might be killed in their mouths or nostrils if they did not cover them with a piece of linen. The conscious destruction of animal life is believed to stain man's psychic individuality, which he endeavours to keep pure; even the involuntary killing of a creature would leave its mark on the spirit. The monks are divided into two groups, the *Svetambara,* those robed in white, and the *Digambara* ("clothed in space," i.e. naked); they carry out a psycho-physiological discipline similar to Yoga with rigorous asceticism. One of their acts of physical mortification is to practise tonsure by pulling out their hairs one by one. Among the most ascetic of the Jains it is highly considered to commit suicide by letting oneself die of inanition.

The Jain sect is distinguished by its large, immaculately kept temples, by the publishing, distribution and preservation of religious works, and by its societies and charitable institutions. The last-named include a number of well-known homes for aged and sick animals, but they are of little importance compared with the institutions for social welfare and education. These institutions maintain their position, in spite of the popular belief in Hindu society that the condition in which a man finds himself is due to himself alone, being the automatic consequence of the acts committed in his former lives; the fortunate man is therefore worthy of merit, and the unfortunate a sinner whose sin is revealed by his wretched condition; therefore, though one should abstain from killing or ill-treating an animal in order to avoid burdening oneself with the crime of an act of violence, one can pitilessly abandon an unfortunate man to his own wretched state.

Delhi : Moslems at prayer

Mosque at Delhi at the time of a religious festival

THE MOSLEMS

Side by side with the Hindus live groups of Moslems and Christians, but, though their outlook on life is profoundly different, there is no open conflict between them.

After the division of the subcontinent into the states of India and Pakistan in 1947, there was a tendency for Pakistan, the essentially Moslem country, to encourage the immigration of Moslems and to expel Hindus; at the same time considerable numbers of Moslems remained in India, where there was no State religion. The movement of population from India to Pakistan was largely confined to the areas near the frontiers with Eastern or Western Pakistan. In the south there was little emigration, and the original coexistence of members of different religious communities continued. Throughout the country mosques are still in use as Islamic places of worship. The Indian Moslems belong to the two major opposing sects, the Sunnites and the Shiites. The Shiites, who flourish particularly in Persia, are numerically strongest in India in Lucknow and the surrounding areas. They have a particular veneration for the descendants of Ali, the son-in-law of Mahomet, whose rights to the succession of the Prophet they claim to have been usurped by Abu Bakr, Omar, and Osman, held by the Sunnites to be the legitimate heirs. The Ismailian sub-sect of the Shiites is found principally in Western India. There are also other sects and reform movements, though these divisions do not give rise to any serious dissensions. Moslems of all beliefs and even Hindus will often indiscriminately participate in commemorations which are in principle strictly Shiite, such as the period of mourning, which takes place at the beginning of the month of Muharram,[1] for Husain, son of Ali, and members of his family killed in the battle of Karbela. It should also be noted that Moslem practice in India is frequently not strictly orthodox.

Numerous tombs of Moslem saints or *pir* are venerated locally in different regions, and many of the practices recall those of the Hindus. While

---

[1] The first month in the Mohammedan year. As the Mohammdan calendar is based on a year of 354 days (355 in a leap year), there is no equivalence of the months with the Christian calendar.

Moslem society in theory repudiates caste discrimination, different groups, based on birth, region of origin, or occupation, have nevertheless formed in the midst of the Hindu social groups. The Sayyids or descendants of Husain, grandson of the Prophet, and the Sheikhs, who are reputedly of pure Arab stock, traditionally practise endogamy. The Pathans are Afghan in origin. The Malliks are reputed to be descendants of Mallik Muhammad Ibrahim, one of the generals of the Sultan Muhammad Ibn Tughlak (fourteenth century). The Mumins, who are the most numerous, are traditionally weavers.

The Moslems in India have mainly kept the custom of dressing differently from the Hindus, chiefly in the south, where they wear caps in the shape of a truncated cone, and swathe their hips in a multi-coloured check garment known as the *kaïli;* but there is a tendency for the young men to wear a *dhoti* like the Hindus and to go bareheaded, or to wear European-style shirts and trousers.

In the north and west Moslem women are completely veiled in black, with a piece of net in the veil level with the eyes. In the south they are not so strictly veiled, but, to go out, wear voluminous white robes over their floral garments.

THE CHRISTIANS

There is a total of only a few million Christians in India, some of whom are Catholic and some Protestant. Among the Protestants there are many different denominations, including Anglicans, Baptists, and Seventh Day Adventists. The Catholic communities are strongest in the states of Kerala and Madras; some of them are descendants of the members of the Nestorian and Syro-Malabar churches, established before the time of the earlier Portuguese settlements; a few communities owe their origin to the Portuguese clergy, but most of them came into being through

Saiva monk receiving massage. Deccan, eighteenth century

Catholic church in Kerala

the activities of the missionaries of the Society of Jesus and later the Foreign Missions. There is a tendency for these Churches no longer to consider themselves as Christian communities founded by foreign missionaries and therefore incurring the reproach of being of foreign origin, but rather as national Indian Church recognized by the secular central Government, the constitution of which guarantees complete freedom of worship. But they find themselves in opposition to the Hindus, who form a majority in the country as a whole, and who in particular dispute the Christian influence over the isolated tribes that have yet to be integrated into the Indian nation.

Caste distinctions still persist in Christian communities, especially in matters of social relations and marriage. Christians of different castes often worship in different churches, but this can be explained by the location of the churches in districts inhabited by different caste groups. The Christians have formed castes distinct from those

of either the Hindus or the Moslems, as differences of religion have to be considered in addition to differences of social standing.

Though most of the Christians have been drawn from the lower ranks of Hindu society, this is not the invariable rule in all regions or in the towns, where many Christian families belong to the higher castes.

Indian Christians have a number of holy places. There are those in the region of Madras, associated with St Thomas the Apostle, whose martyrdom is said to have taken place at St Thomas Mount and whose tomb is to be found at Mayilappur. There is also the tomb of St Francis Xavier at Goa. There are in addition modern places of pilgrimage, such as Our Lady of Fatima at Velangani, on the Coromandel Coast, south of Nagappattinam.

The important Christian feasts, pilgrimages, and processions attract great crowds, where Hindus commonly mingle, as they do in the Moslem festivals. Christian asceticism is easily

Kraunca, white bird of the marshes. Mogul miniature, eighteenth century

accepted in this country where the discipline of the body is normally linked with the discipline of the mind and with religious practice in general. In all regions are to be found Christian schools, charitable institutions, orphanages, hospitals, dispensaries, and leper hospitals.

PHILOSOPHY

There are many schools of philosophy in India, just as there are many religions. Some follow the ancient schools of thought, some Western philosophy, and there are new trends where the two traditions intermingle.

The most important theories of philosophy today following the purely Indian tradition are those of the *Vedanta*. They are generally linked with Hinduism, though not necessarily, for they have been retained as metaphysical concepts on the nature of man and the universe by men who have repudiated or who neglect the Hindu mythological tradition and rites. *Vedanta* is the ultimate achievement *(anta)* of knowledge *(veda)*. It consists of the representation of the ontological substratum of the phenomenal world, which is considered as an object of practical knowledge. It may be divided into three main schools, the *Advaita*, the *Visishtadvaita*, and the *Dvaita*. The *Advaita* of Sankara has already been referred to in connection with Saivism. The *Visishtadvaita* of the philosopher Ramanuja (twelfth century) is generally associated with Vaishnavism; it is a belief in the "oneness" *(advaita)* of the Supreme Being with every particularized phenomenon *(visishta)* which can be perceived with the senses and the mind. The *Dvaita* of the philosopher Madhva (twelfth to thirteenth centuries) establishes duality between the Being of God and the Being of the world. The Madhvists are also Vaishnavists, and are organized in a community which has its principal centre at Udipi (Mysore), but which also includes some divergent schools.

Sri Saccidananda Sivabhinava Nrsimha Bharati, philosopher of the school of Sankara, jagadguru *1879-1912*

145

Vedantic philosophy, with its interest in the Being and in appearances in general, has eclipsed other ancient speculations like the *Purvamimamsa* ("primary investigation"), which concentrated on the nature and efficacy of speech, a creative principle in its power of injunction and an instrument for the conveying of knowledge. It has also eclipsed the *Samkhya,* an analytical enumeration of the realities *(tattva)* that constitute the universe, and the *Vaiseshika,* an atomistic theory of the universe. It has, on the other hand, links with *Nyaya,* the theory of reasoning, the logic that studies the criteria of validity *(pramana)* of judgements, which may be made by direct constatation, comparison, inference, or by means of reliable witness; it is an enumeration of the different types of reasoning and the different forms of error. Finally, Vedantic philosophy is completed by Yoga, a psycho-physiological theory and even to a larger extent a practical discipline for the mastery of the body and the mind, destined to remove from the psychic being all external sensations, and to adapt it to that state of sheer existence which *Vedanta* sees in all finite reality and which is in itself ultimate reality.

Yoga ("adaptation") is a specifically Indian means of self-control. The conception of it, both as the theory of psychological reactions and a practical method of self-discipline, implies the belief, current in Indian philosophy, of an indissoluble relationship between matter and spirit, between physiological and psychic existence, both of which are conceived as being of a pneumatical nature, and animated by a kind of breath *(prana),* but which can be influenced by regulation of the breathing, by physical postures, and by the manipulation of thought. The Classical Yoga, reputedly founded by Patanjali, also known as *Rajayoga* ("Royal Yoga"), aims at arresting the movement of the mind to free the psychic being of all that is extraneous to its sheer reality and to pose it in perfect stability. There are eight stages: curbing the instincts; disciplinary preparation; postures *(asana);* breathing control *(pranayama);* a withdrawal of the senses and movement *(pratyahara);* fixation of thought *(dharana);* meditation *(dhyana);* and the final goal, *samadhi* ("fixation of the psychism").

Another form of Yoga, the *hathayoga* ("forced yoga") is more complex in its theoretical conception and requires an even harder physical training. It is generally practised as a collective or individual exercise in communities like those

◀ *Yoga postures (Sivayogamandir)*   *Attitude of meditation* ▶

of the Saivistic monks, particularly the Lingayats, who are dedicated not only to ontological speculation but also to a direct experience of the Self, the Absolute.

Though certain realizations of Yoga are reputed to confer miraculous powers, such as levitation, far beyond the normal reach of man, it is strictly forbidden to seek them, as the result would be that the subject became a prisoner of worldly achievements and thus cut himself off from the quest of the Absolute. By training in certain exercises, however, physical achievements are attained that are far beyond the scope of the average man. It is thus possible for certain Hathayogi deliberately to stop for a time their breathing and their perceptible heart-beats, to dissociate the normal synergy of muscular contractions, to contract or dilate at will hollow organs, such as the bladder or rectum. Psychic reactions, which are difficult to describe for those who experience them and which are partly subconscious, are recognizable only by the accompanying exterior signs and by their repercussions on images consciously perceived and the mental attitude of the subject. Thus in India the subjective philosophic conscience is offered an additional and excep-

tional instrument through the experiences of Yoga. The technique is one that cannot be mastered haphazardly, and Yoga practised by the individual is of limited use and not without danger. It requires a long period of supervision by a master to learn progressively the technique of the exercises before the student reaches the stage of personal mastery. Yoga therefore consists of a steady, systematic progress towards fixed themes of meditation and the contemplative states corresponding to philosophic ideas learnt, rather than a free method of research into ideas. It does not, however, completely exclude the possibility of divergence in experience on the part of the master and his disciples, and consequently of differences of opinion. In any case Yoga tends to complete the intellectual conceptions of discursive and logical thought by a direct apprehension of the object of them, and to fix the psychic being, with its sensitivity and its understanding, on the concept taken as object, in order that the two may be fully adjusted. Thus the *yogi* can ultimately judge his being in unison with the Absolute. The early stages of the technique at least develop the patience of the student, give him powers of attention and concentration

Hermit living in a cave

of thought, and he also benefits from increased suppleness of the body. Thus Yoga is sometimes practised as a mere physical and mental exercise.

The English school of classical philosophy is a widely taught form of Western philosophy. Marxism and existentialism are also known, but many students and philosophers who compare the philosophic ideas of their country with those of the West make their comparisons almost exclusively with the ideas of Locke and Hume, with the positivists of another age, and with the modern materialists. The result of this is a current belief in a radical opposition between the West which is a slave of materialism and mechanism and an India which is unique in possessing a liberating spiritual outlook. But better-informed thinkers can compare the philosophies of similar nature that can be considered as counterparts in India and in the Western countries, and realize that India has, in addition to the metaphysical rationality which she holds in common with the West, a further means of metaphysical experiment provided by Yoga.

By confronting philosophical ideas one arrives at new conceptions linking Western and Indian ideas. As far as religious philosophy is concerned, this can achieve a spirit of compromise, which admits that there is a general convergence of theological and metaphysical ideas in the conception of an Absolute Being, transcending any image or appellation which is given to him. In this way all religions may be said to aspire towards a Supreme Reality, at which each aims according to its own lights. The higher conception of this Reality, and the convergence of the different religions towards it, would be the dominant motive behind their individual

efforts, which they now believe to contend with each other. The various religions would find their ultimate common goal in a " theosophy ". The Theosophical Society, which was founded in India by Europeans at the end of the last century, and the headquarters of which is at Adyar, near Madras, has spread throughout India, Europe, and America and has adopted the general principles of Vedantic metaphysics and of the techniques of Yoga. Apart from this, many Indian intellectuals follow the syncretic ideas of the mediæval Hindu and Moslem sects, and believe in a general theism rising above sectarianism and founded on Vedantic metaphysics.

In modern times other schools have been founded that are characterized by their development of ancient philosophical traditions. Among these mention should be made of the *ashram* (retreat) at Tiruvannamalai of Ramana Maharshi, who died in 1951; that of Sri Aurobindo, who, on account of his nationalist activities, emigrated from Bengal to Pondicherry, where he founded and directed for many years, in collaboration with his principal helper, The Mother, an *ashram,* of which she alone has been the leader since his death in 1950. The doctrine of Aurobindo, whose initial education was exclusively English and classical, links the conceptions of evolution according to which man, the highest evolution so far reached, is not at the summit of his development, with the Indian conceptions of the universal divine presence and of the possibilities of attaining divine existence by means of an " integral " Yoga. It also includes study in the technical, artistic and even sporting fields in its spiritual quest for a superhuman state.

Painting on fabric

Rabindranath Tagore, whose centenary was in 1961, is famous for his poetry, songs, novels, short stories, and plays. His works are the most widely known abroad of all modern Indian literature, as most of them have been translated into English, and even rewritten by the author himself in that language, and then transposed into a large number of European languages. Some of the translations have been made by famous authors, such as the French writer André Gide, who published a version of one of his short stories under the title of *Amal et la lettre du roi*.

Hindi writing may be said to rival the Bengali; many novels have been written in this language, and one of the most famous authors is Premchand. Increasing numbers of books are also being published in Marathi and Gujarati. An important place in Marathi literature is occupied by scientific writing and the views on tradition published by the leading nationalist B. G. Tilak.

The authors write increasingly in the language in current use, and, as they bring their works within the scope of a vast public, they are gradually making this everyday language the normal mode of literary expression. This progress is more notable in Bengali and Marathi than in Hindi, with its different dialects. In Hindi, and to a lesser extent in other languages, there are some authors who prefer a more learned vocabulary taken directly from the immense wealth of Sanskrit literature; while others remain closer to the spoken tongue, using many of the words of Arabic or Persian origin that make up the Urdu vocabulary. They are thus creating a literature in Hindi that can easily be transposed into Urdu, while Urdu literature can readily be translated into this style of Hindi.

Tamil is the leading Dravidian literary language, both traditionally and in its present-day development. Its modern literary works of all types are characterized by their strength and fervour.

Modern Tamil literature has its origin in the Press of the last century. It has broken with the traditional, rhetorical, versified style with its erudite clichés and, deeply influenced by English literature, it has achieved a means of conveying descriptions of the exterior world, nature in all its beauty, and of revealing the inner world of the heart and its passions, as in the traditional literature known as *Sangam*. Among the modern poets and prose-writers whose work has remained as a model after their death, special mention should be made of Suppiramaniya Baradi, a

MODERN LITERATURE

Daily papers, numerous periodicals, and large numbers of books are published in each of the many literary languages of India. Classical Sanskrit is still used in the publication of periodicals and independent literary works in both prose and verse. Bengali is the Indo-Aryan language that has shown the greatest development in the realm of *belles-lettres* and, indeed, in all branches of literary work. Bankim Chandra Chatterjee is one of the well-known Bengali novelists.

Painting by Jaimini Roy

THE ARTS TO-DAY

nationalist patriot who died young, and in whose work modern ideas are linked with courage and patriotism.

A development parallel to that of Tamil may be seen in the original literary works which are now being written in the Malayalam of Kerala, the Kanarese of Mysore, and the Telugu of Andhra Pradesh.

Indian art as a whole belongs to that vast tradition of the past which has made Indian civilization what it is to-day. Modern Indian art has kept some elements of this tradition, but has been considerably influenced by modern artistic developments in other countries of the world. Here technical considerations are particularly important. Because of constructional techniques and

Bharatanatya dance pose : shooting with bow and arrow

materials used, the latest buildings are in the modern universal uniform style, and unadapted to the Indian climate, though this defect can be overcome by air-conditioning. There are some recent buildings in granite, marble, or sandstone that still present some traditionally Indian architectural characteristics. They are composite in style, and elements of Hindu, Mogul, or even Victorian Gothic architecture are intermingled. Modern private houses, though constructed in an austere style with large windows, as in any other country in the world, are often characterized by particularly striking geometrical dispositions, and by the inordinately large number of balconies and terraces. They are made more attractive by the lay-out of their gardens, as are public buildings, universities, institutes, and schools.

There is a flourishing school of modern paint-ing. Indian artists follow the styles and techniques of modern European painters, particularly the French. They depict the landscape and people of their country in a manner which, though similar, is nevertheless original, and often more poetic. They are little influenced by traditional Indian pictorial art, in spite of the fact that they frequently use in decoration themes and sketches reminiscent of the ancient frescoes of Ajanta, "modernizing" the legendary images or figures of divinities. One particular group is employed in illustrating editions of works of ancient litera-ture. Their illustrations are characterized by the sumptuous manner in which gods and men are portrayed against a background of fantastic cosmic landscapes.

Dancing and music continue in the old tradi-tions with modifications, except for the schools of which the aim is to preserve the old techniques

Manipuri dance pose ▶

Bharatanatya dance pose : Krishna playing the flute

and the classical themes. The modifications are due to the influence of the radio and gramophone records popular in other countries, which are adopted and spread by means of the Indian cinema, in which songs and dancing play a considerable part. Modern Indian musical compositions have retained their national character, in spite of a number of adaptations of Western technique, by the use of the classical musical instruments. These include string instruments such as the *vina* and the *sitar,* wind instruments such as the flute and the *nagasvaram,* and a whole series of percussion instruments: drums, long drums beaten at each end, low drums beaten in pairs, known as *tabla.*

Dancing is held in high esteem, and traditional displays often consist of tribal, martial, or folk dances, and the religious festival dances, a frequent theme of which is Krishna playing among the cowherds. Several classical styles of dancing are still practised, the most famous of which is the *Bharatanatya,* the art of dancing following the rules of Bharata, who is believed to be the author of the most ancient treatises on music, dancing, and acting. Another well-known classical style, considered to have originated in Assam, is the *Manipuri.* These classical dances are not ballets, but figures executed by one dancer or a small group. The typical *Bharatanatya* costume worn to-day by the women dancers includes trousers, over which hang from the waist an accordion-pleated flounce. For the *Manipuri* they wear a skirt mounted on a stiff, polygonal frame. Traditionally the poses of the various dances indicate certain feelings. They are completed by very precise movements of the hands, the *mudra,* which form a language of their own, expressing passion or attitude of mind; they cannot be understood by anyone who has not studied them, and are often completely unintelligible to the members of the general public, who are able to appreciate only the graceful movements and the rhythm of a dance.

A specialized form of theatrical entertainment is the *Kathakali* of Kerala, the presentation of the major episodes of the *Ramayana* by actors dressed in conventional costumes, and made up to such an extent that they appear to wear masks.

Some companies of young dancers present ballets that have their inspiration in the traditional folk dances, and alternate them with revues and satirical sketches on modern Indian life, following the style popular in Europe and North America.

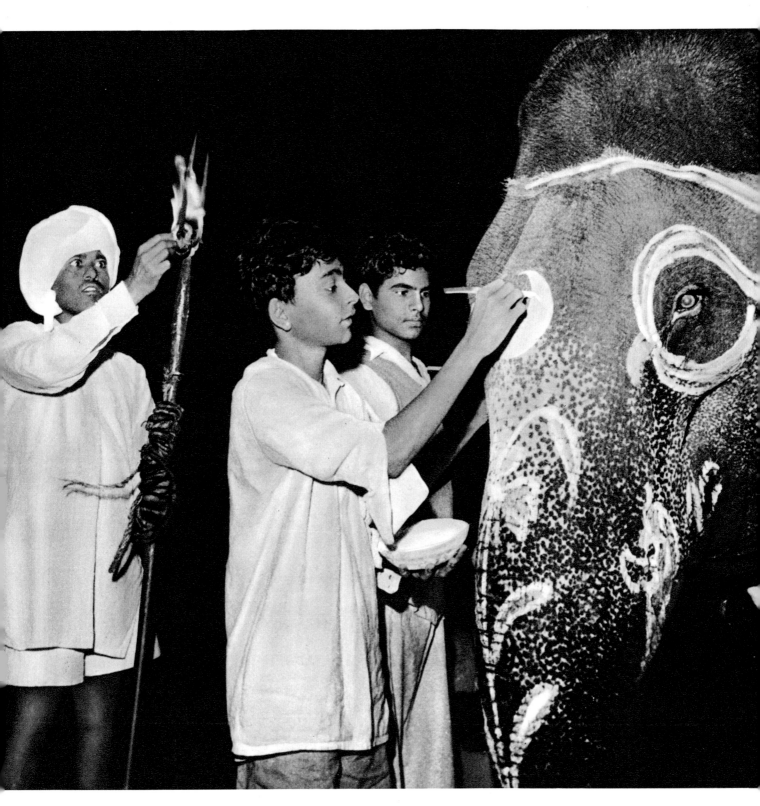

Making-up an elephant for a torchlight procession

Actors of the Kathakali

Kathakali dance gestures (mudra)

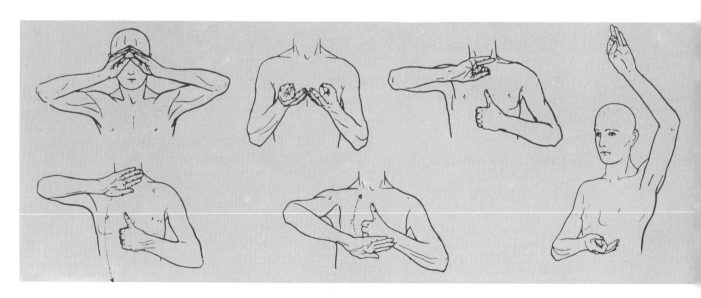

Scene from the Indian film of Aladdin and his Wonderful
Lamp

THE CINEMA

The characteristic form of modern entertainment is the cinema. Cinemas are to be found even in country districts in areas where electricity is available, and Indian films are popular not only in India itself but in a number of countries in South-east Asia, such as Indonesia, Siam (Thailand) and Cambodia. There are at least four principal categories of film. In the first three, those with mythological, legendary, or modern subjects, the convention is that the action should be separated by intervals of dancing or singing, with the result that the complete performance generally lasts three hours. The ending is traditionally a happy one, with virtue triumphing over repentant vice. The décor is of little importance compared with the standard of the acting and the feelings expressed. The films in this group with a modern setting are often moralizing in tone, and set out to reform, showing, for example, the injustices of caste discrimination or social prejudices, the cruelty of egoism or the greatness of virtue.

The fourth category of film is sentimental and deals with social reform, and can be very moving when it depicts noble characters against the background of the hard struggle of life. It is characterized by the adoption of forms and techniques similar to those internationally in vogue in the Western world. This type of Indian film is the one best known in international film circles, but not the one most successful in India itself, or even, when dubbed, in the countries of South-east Asia. It is films of the first three categories that are the most popular in India, and they are available in the different regional languages.

India's adoption of film techniques to make the cinema one of her main national industries, at the same time adapting it to the various languages and cultural backgrounds of the different regions, gives a picture of the country as it is to-day—a country which has united vastly different lands and peoples, a country with a rich heritage, a country which can find a place in the modern world without losing its individuality.

Advertisement of the Tamil film Parttipan Kanavu (The King's Dream)

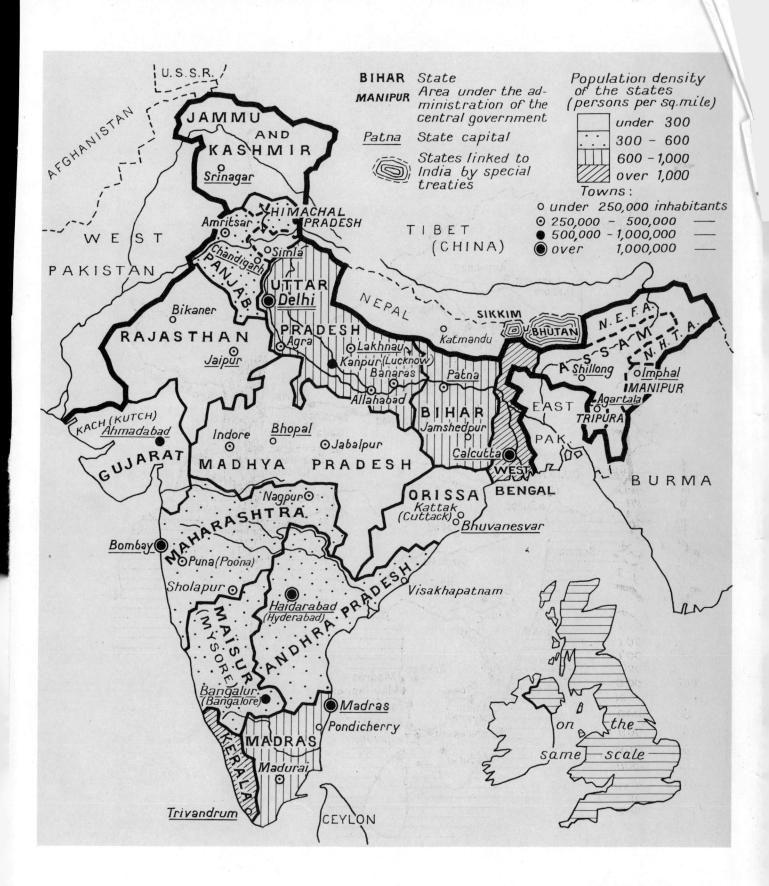

BIHAR State
MANIPUR Area under the administration of the central government

Patna State capital

States linked to India by special treaties

Population density of the states (persons per sq.mile)

under 300
300 – 600
600 – 1,000
over 1,000

Towns:
○ under 250,000 inhabitants
◉ 250,000 – 500,000 —
● 500,000 – 1,000,000 —
◎ over 1,000,000 —

AFGHANISTAN

U.S.S.R.

JAMMU AND KASHMIR
○ *Srinagar*

WEST PAKISTAN

HIMACHAL PRADESH
Amritsar
○ *Simla*
PANJAB
Chandigarh

TIBET (CHINA)

UTTAR
● *Delhi*
PRADESH

Bikaner ○

RAJASTHAN

NEPAL

Agra ○

Jaipur ○

○ *Lakhnau*
Kanpur (Lucknow) ●
Banaras ◉
Allahabad ◉

SIKKIM

○ *Katmandu*

BHUTAN

N.E.F.A.

ASSAM
○ *Shillong*

N.H.T.A.

○ *Imphal*
MANIPUR

Patna ◉

BIHAR

Jamshedpur ●

EAST PAK.

Agartala ○
TRIPURA

KACH (KUTCH)
Ahmadabad ●

GUJARAT

Indore ○
Bhopal ○

MADHYA PRADESH

○ *Jabalpur*

Calcutta ◎
WEST BENGAL

BURMA

ORISSA
Kattak (Cuttack) ○
Bhuvanesvar ○

Nagpur ◉

MAHARASHTRA

Bombay ◎
◉ *Puna (Poona)*

Sholapur ◉

Haidarabad (Hyderabad) ◎

ANDHRA PRADESH

Visakhapatnam ○

MAISUR (MYSORE)

Bangalur (Bangalore) ●

Madras ◎
○ *Pondicherry*

MADRAS

KERALA

Madurai ◉

Trivandrum

CEYLON

on the same scale

India : Political

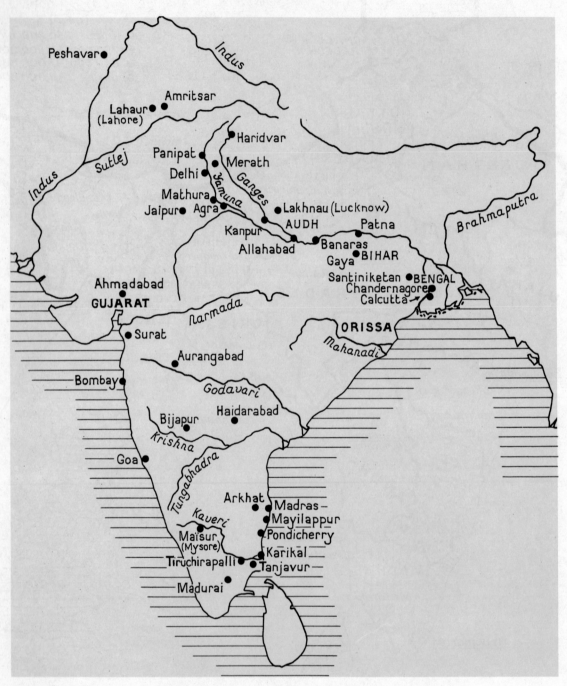

India in the eighteenth and nineteenth centuries

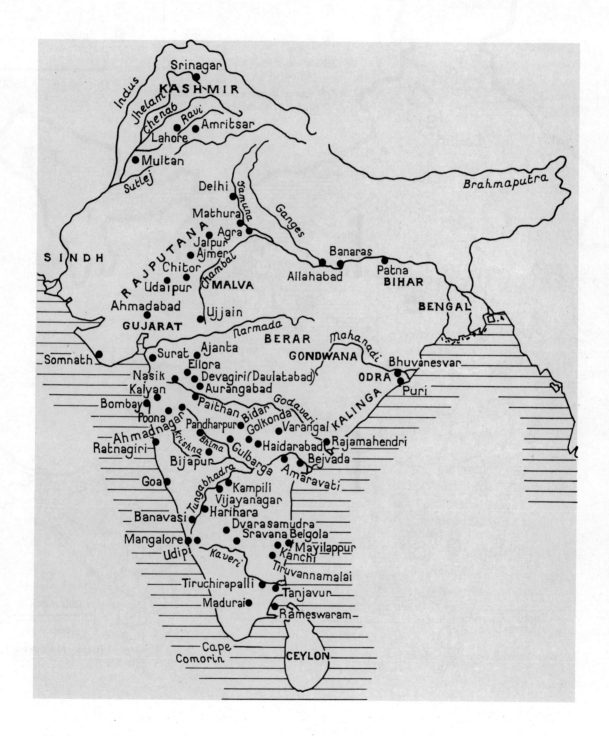

The India of Vijanagar, the Bahmanis and the Moguls

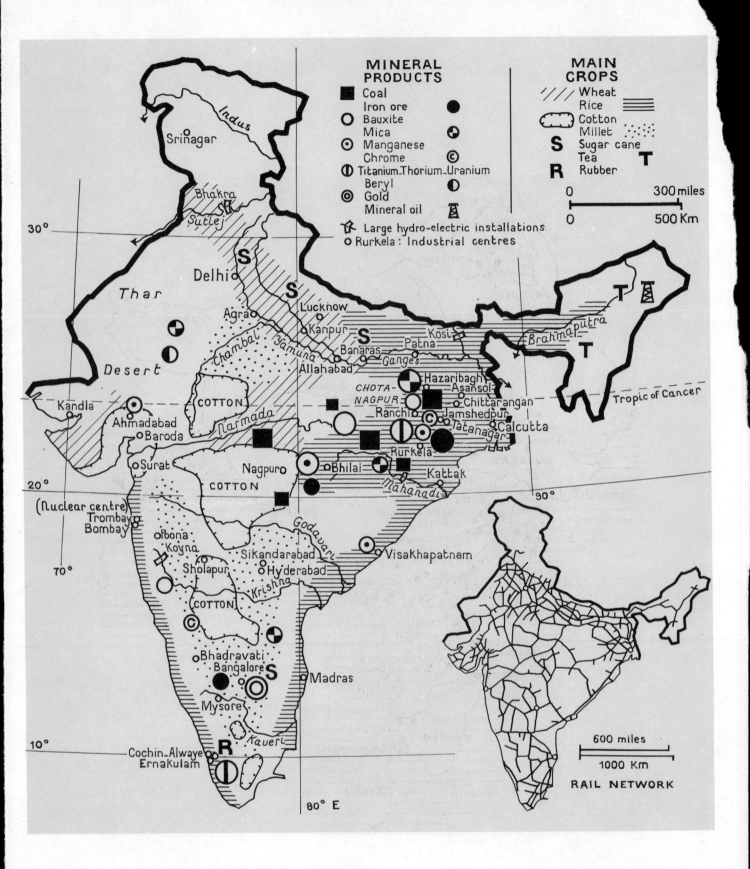

MINERAL
PRODUCTS
Coal
Iron ore
Bauxite
Mica
Manganese
Chrome
Titanium.Thorium.Uranium
Beryl
Gold
Mineral oil

🏭 Large hydro-electric installations
○ Rurkela : Industrial centres

MAIN
CROPS
Wheat
Rice
Cotton
Millet
S Sugar cane
    Tea
R Rubber   T

0   300 miles
0   500 Km

Srinagar
Indus
Thar
Bhakra
Sutlej
30°
Delhi
Agra
Chambal
Yamuna
Lucknow
Kanpur
Banaras
Patna
Kosi
Ganges
Allahabad
Brahmaputra
T
Tropic of Cancer
Desert
Kandla
COTTON
Narmada
CHOTA-
NAGPUR
Hazaribagh
Asansol
Chittarangan
Ranchi
Jamshedpur
Tatanagar
Calcutta
Ahmadabad
Baroda
Surat
Nagpur
COTTON
Bhilai
Rurkela
Kattak
Mahanadi
20°
90°
(Nuclear centre)
Trombay
Bombay
Poona
Koyna
Sholapur
Sikandarabad
Hyderabad
Krishna
Godavari
Visakhapatnam
70°
COTTON
Bhadravati
Bangalore
S
Madras
Mysore
Kaveri
10°
Cochin.Alwaye
ErnaKulam
R
80° E

600 miles
1000 Km
RAIL NETWORK

India : Economic

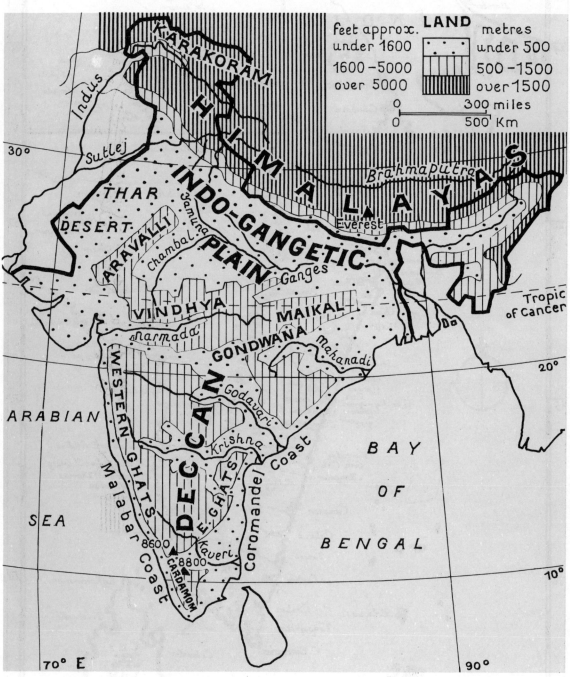

India : Physical

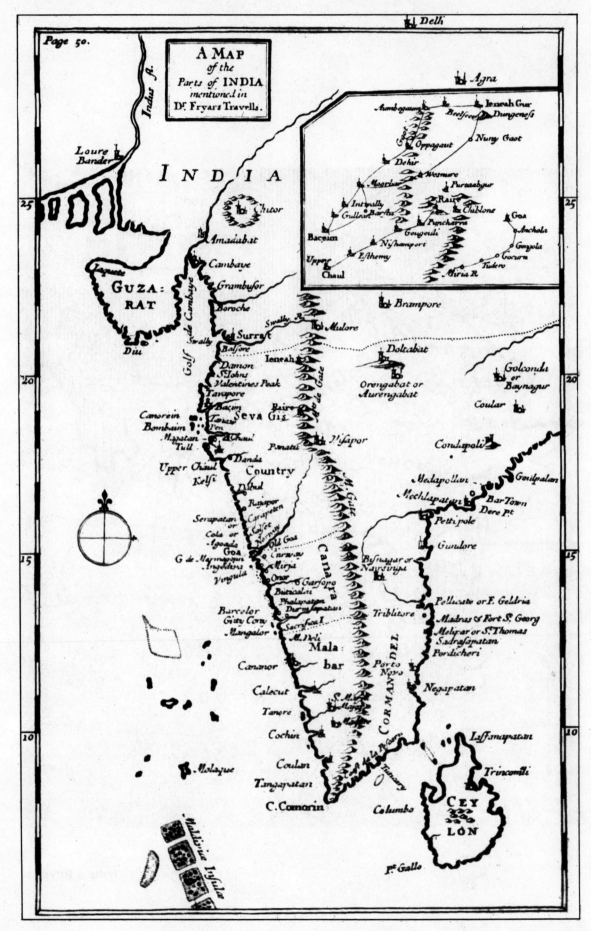

John Fryer's map of India (*A new account of East India and Persia*. London, 1698)

THE PAST
AND ITS TRADITIONS

1 INDIA UNDER BRITISH RULE

The present marked diversity of the Indian scene, of its inhabitants and their outlook, can in the first place be attributed to the variety of peoples who have lived there from prehistoric times and then to the mixture of races and civilizations which subsequently invaded the country and became established there, sometimes intermingling with the previous inhabitants to form new social entities, sometimes remaining as communities apart. Finally, the diversity is heightened by the way in which physical or climatic conditions have influenced the life of the people in the various regions. It has been in the past and still is a matter for wonder that India, a land of so many differences, some of them more deep-rooted than those that separate the countries of Europe, should have achieved a political unity that is quite unknown in Europe. Some people consider this unity artificial and liable to disruption. They believe it to be a survival of the unity achieved under British rule, temporarily strengthened by the struggle for independence, and think that there are irreconcilable elements at present joined together which are destined ultimately to break away from each other. They do not take into account the fact that such a union, though complex, can be stable, and can possess in its unity specific characteristics in no way equivalent to the sum of the different elements of which it is composed. They are, moreover, particularly forgetful of the fact that, in spite of certain autonomistic movements, political unity in India has increased since independence by the absorption of the former princely states into the nation as a whole, and that British policy was one of unification of its authority over the country as a whole, but of division of the country itself into a number of separate units.

The existence of an Indian nation and Indian unity must not therefore be considered as ephemeral. It represents strong traditional bonds between the outlook, feelings, and relationships of widely differing peoples set against the same background. The mutual antagonisms of these people are common features, but they may be considered as reciprocal positions in a stabilized entity rather than cracks in its surface.

Throughout its known history the Indian scene has presented a stage divided into compartments, but which is nevertheless a unified whole. This unity is to be found neither in racial ties nor in historical events, and there is no common background of religious beliefs or philosophic opinions. There have been in the course of history frequent encounters between native races and foreigners, the country has known constant upheaval, and different systems have clashed time and again, bringing nothing but division ; but behind these differences there has always been a unifying conception of the world which has dominated and organized all the varying elements. This general conception of the world, cosmic, final, physical, physiological, and social, founded on learned conceptions, has nevertheless always had an element of simplicity and has been within the grasp of the nation as a whole, not merely of the intellectual element. The beliefs of the intellectuals were by no means exclusive ; they were adopted on broad lines not only by the people of India as a whole, but by other nations beyond its boundaries, whether near or far, peoples who had become familiar with these beliefs and who were the first to appreciate the political unity of India. Chinese Buddhist pilgrims of the seventh century would often speak of the " five Indias, " but they considered India as an entity, and some of them learnt of Indian civilization before ever reaching the country, in Sumatra, which lay on the sea route from China, and where Indian culture was regularly taught.

The Sanskrit language, stabilized by its gram-

The temple of Minakshi-Sundaresvara at Madurai (seventeenth century). Gate tower (gopura) ▶

162

matical tradition and classical literature, was the means of propagation of Indian knowledge, whatever may have been the origin or the religious beliefs of the teachers. Sanskrit was certainly known only by small minorities, but these minorities were to be found in each different region, and therefore could interpret to the people of the different areas the same fundamental conceptions, the same legends, the same popular tales, the same theoretical or practical scientific ideas, whether in the field of astronomy or medicine or of astrology and magic.

Indian culture was unified and broadcast by means of Sanskrit very much in the same way as Hellenic civilization by means of Greek. The various empires in which India was incorporated favoured this, just as the empire of Alexander the Great helped to spread Greek civilization. At the same time it is largely because of their essential nature, and not merely because of favourable historic or political circumstances, that Indian and Greek thought have become formalized and have spread throughout wide areas of the globe.

Indian unity has been remarkable for much more interior diversity than was ever found within the sphere of Greek civilization, and it has been even more threatened by the domination of foreign powers and invaded by the influence of powerful civilizations which might have shaken the authority of Indian culture ; moreover, in modern times it has had to withstand the threat of being eclipsed by the efficiency of technical progress. The breadth and vitality of Indian civilization cannot, however, fully explain its resistance to the influences that have threatened to dissipate it. The resistance can be attributed to the structure of Hindu society, which may be considered as the source and mainstay of Indian civilization, a society which has retained its existence in spite of foreign contacts and the domination of powers from outside. Though the division into castes has never been a social phenomenon moulded in an unchangeable fashion, as is sometimes believed, the theoretical division of the nation into closed communities which were mutually complementary has had the effect of making Indians consider that they are members of social groups which are not limited by regional boundaries, and they have thus arrived at a conception of unity going beyond the bounds of local geography and politics, cutting as it were across the currents of invasion. The Brahmins, for example, were associated not only with their local compatriots of different classes,

with whom they formed a social unit on a regional basis, but also with other Brahmins in other regions. If political events disrupted their region and forced them to emigrate, they did not break their links of rank, customs, and education with their fellow-Brahmins elsewhere. They could even strengthen the feeling of group unity by gathering together men of their caste from other areas to work together for the common defence of the group.

In order to understand India to-day it is necessary to follow her long history, and see how in the course of centuries she has absorbed different human and intellectual elements, to realize the basic knowledge and conceptions that have for so long a period characterized her outlook and made possible the influence that she has had over an area extending from Iran to the Pacific Ocean.

INDIA SEEN THROUGH WESTERN EYES

Until comparatively recent times the Western countries had only intermittent contacts with India and, being ignorant of her history and civilization as a whole, could judge her only superficially through the outward appearances presented at any particular time. They did not see her development in the course of history, and finally conquered her for a period without understanding her. The conclusions reached about her had repercussions on India throughout the period of British rule; she reacted according to these conclusions, being anxious to justify approval and to invalidate scorn or reproach. Her outlook was in this way a prelude to her present-day attitude, which is to adapt herself to modern internationally accepted ideas and activities without renouncing her fundamental specific national characteristics.

The European idea of India was traditionally based on travellers' observations, prejudices inherited from former travellers or the historians of Alexander the Great, mingled with the current conception of foreigners in general, and the true picture of the races of India and their civilization played but a very minor rôle in the general conception.

Before Alexander the Great's expedition to India the country was known to the Hellenistic world only through a few products, such as pepper and cotton, and the legendary tales of the curious things which were said to be found there.

Jewellery of an Indian dancer.
From the top: earring, nose-clip, necklace;
bottom right: pendant;
bottom left: hair ornament ▶

There is evidence of scientific and philosophic relations between India and ancient Greece, made through the Persian Empire, which at that time included the Basin of the Indus, in the writings of Plato, Hippocrates, and possibly also Heraclitus. But these were not sufficient to form a general idea about India in public opinion. People thought of it vaguely as a country inhabited by " Ethiopians "—that is to say, people with " burnt faces ", various tribes with strange customs, including also some learned men.

Alexander the Great's expedition to take possession of the Basin of the Indus, after his conquest of the Persians, brought the Greeks face to face with an Eastern empire before the strength of which they were obliged to retreat. Alexander died in 323 B.C., and his successors had to yield to this Indian empire the extensive territories of the Indus basin which the Persians had held since the time of Darius. The empire in question was the ancient empire of Magadha, where the Maurya dynasty had become established and expanded under the leadership of Chandragupta, known as Sandrakottos to the Greeks.

Through Alexander's expedition the Greeks also learnt of the division of Indian society into closed professional classes, of the Brahmins who were often champions of the resistance against the foreign aggressor, of the Samanes, philosophers and practical scientists, and of the " naked philosophers " who practised amazing asceticism.

The ideas about India spread by the historians of Alexander the Great were repeated throughout the world of Græco-Roman antiquity. A precise and accurate synopsis of the Brahmanic doctrine had spread at the beginning of the third century to Christian Rome, but it was available only incidentally to the general public by the *Refutation of All Heresies* attributed to St Hippolytus or one of his followers. In the meantime, geographical knowledge and commercial interests had developed on account of the trade in luxury goods between the Roman Empire and India and South-east Asia. But the Western world did not know that, in the third century B.C., King Asoka, the grandson of Chandragupta, had sent envoys to five different Greek kings of the period, in order to attempt to establish a universal order of peace and toleration, an aim that has been through the ages one dear to the Indians, and one for which modern India still strives. Nor did the Western public know of the relations between their scholars and artists and those in India at the beginning of the Christian era, when North-west India borrowed from Greece and Rome designs for her sculpture and general knowledge in the field of astrology. Greek and Latin writers have left us very little information about the Greek colonies in Asia, which nevertheless gave rise to Indo-Greek kingdoms in India. To Europe of classical antiquity India remained a country of fabulous wealth and extraordinary sages.

Mediaeval Europe, cut off from India by the rise and expansion of Islam, knew even less about it. It merely retained some notion of the wonders recounted by the storytellers of antiquity about the fantastic beings who were reputed to have inhabited it, such as the Cynocephali, or dog-headed men, and the Skiapodes, men with one single foot, large enough to shelter their heads. At the time of the Crusades some doubts were entertained about these strange creatures. Were they really human, and should they be baptised if they were encountered ? When St Bernard preached in 1146 at Vézelay in favour of the Second Crusade, sculptors represented Cynocephali among the people to whom the mission of the Apostles was addressed. Bestiaries and lapidaries described the fantastic creatures and the fabulous jewels to be found in India.

The first great European travellers were the missionaries or merchants who began to travel extensively in Asia at the end of the thirteenth century, and their accounts tended to confirm the established impression that India was a land full of wealth and strange things but not a country with an important civilization. Men such as Giovanni di Monte Corvino and Marco Polo, who were conducted around by Moslem merchants who despised Hindu culture, saw only vague idolaters wherever they went. Its vast circulation made Marco Polo's book largely responsible for the idea that India was a country full of great wealth in the hands of men of little account.

From the time of Vasco da Gama, who reached India in 1498, the fleets which sailed east from Europe landed in the peninsula with this false impression. It was the time of the Renaissance, and the rediscovery of Greek and Latin manuscripts, including those that dealt with India, but they brought no light on living humanity. Until the seventeenth century, scholarly travellers sought things described by the ancients rather than making an attempt to get to know the Indians of their own time. The latter, for their part, showed little willingness to confide in foreigners whose customs and bearing offended their sense of strict methodical purity.

The importance, originality, and value of Indian civilization was discovered in the seventeenth century by the Italian Jesuit Roberto di Nobili, and he was followed by other members of his order, and also by Protestant missionaries, such as Ziegenbalg, in the eighteenth century ; but current prejudices were against Nobili, and the work of none of these missionaries was appreciated by anyone except scholars. For a certain time the West had been impressed by the power and extent of the Mogul Empire, but the fact that it was Islamic did much to hide from the public the importance and vitality of Hindu India. In the eighteenth century, after the brilliant reign of Aurangzeb, this empire collapsed into anarchy, though it continued to have an official existence. India therefore appeared to the trading companies that came to make their fortunes there as a disorganized country peopled by idolaters and Moslems, an easy prey and a source of great wealth ; and it was the British company that was destined to receive this prize.

In addition to the work of isolated missionaries, important studies of Indian civilization were undertaken during the eighteenth century. In 1719 the Bibliothèque royale in Paris undertook a systematic research on Indian books ; Joseph Deguignes made a study of Persian and Chinese documentation on India ; Anquetil-Duperron carried out investigations in the country itself ; then there was finally the work of a group of British scholars in Calcutta—Wilkins, William Jones, and Colebrooke—and the foundation of the Asiatic Society of Bengal in 1784. From the point of view of the general public, all this was in vain. The idea of the inferiority of India, a country twice conquered, first by the Moslems and then by the Europeans, continued to prevail. The greatness of Hindu civilization had been revealed, but it was not present greatness. It belonged to primitive times, and had degenerated. Was it even original ? Did not the India of ancient times simply retain traces of primitive revelation ? Did its civilization not represent the teaching of the Hebrews and the Greeks ? Was not Sanskrit a secret language invented by the Brahmins to conceal their thoughts from their Moslem conquerors ? Though the authentic texts of the *Veda*, the most ancient sacred books of the Brahmins, had been catalogued in Paris since 1739, many people refused to believe that they

Indian Cynocephali shown among those who were to receive the Mission of the Apostles. Vézelay, interior portal (twelfth century)

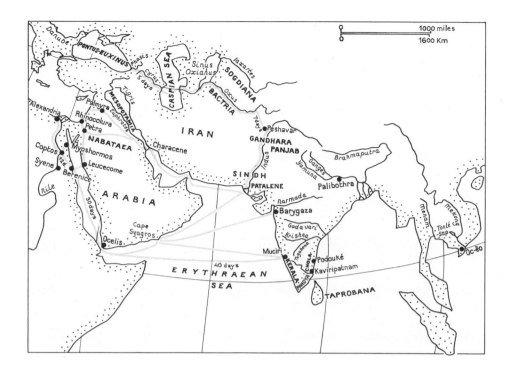

Trade routes to India in the early centuries of the Christian era

existed. Contemporary India was dissociated from a great civilization believed to be dead, and it was customary to pour scorn on scholars who found in it a source of admiration. Some of them, particularly those whose knowledge of the country was limited to books, yielded to the pressure of public opinion, acclaiming the monuments of the past, but despising the Indians of their own time, who they were led to believe were degenerate. Such was the situation at the beginning of British rule. India's political division, prevalent ignorance about her real genius and her position among the civilizations of Asia, together with the interests at stake at the time, all combined to make people consider her as a heterogeneous mass of weak and superstitious peoples who had to be dominated as soon as possible and who could be gradually enlightened.

INTELLECTUAL REACTION IN INDIA

In order to rise above this scornful attitude and to become finally a proud, independent entity India had to undergo a patient struggle that was primarily psychological rather than political. It was a struggle intensified by the fact that Hindus were conscious of a very real eclipse of their former greatness. The arguments of their critics were not entirely unfounded at the time when they were first expressed. The Hindus were obviously powerless from a political and military

point of view. Though their cultural tradition had survived, it had no longer its former greatness, and orthodox Hindu society was becoming increasingly strict in the maintenance of its customs, because it felt them being threatened or overwhelmed. They were practised with an exaggerated strictness on account of the fear of having to relinquish them completely, and therefore the Hindus gave the impression of being blind

A Skiapod. Sens Cathedral (twelfth century)

Harvesting pepper in the Malabar Coast area. From the Book of Marco Polo

followers of superstitious beliefs. This state of affairs had been current ever since the time of the Islamic domination, which nevertheless had shown itself to be tolerant at times. This unhappy situation was held to be one of the misfortunes of the Kaliyuga, the present era in world history when *Dharma* had become degenerated in accordance with the cosmic rhythm accepted by cosmological theory.

It was therefore necessary, in spite of the unfortunate period through which they were passing, for the Hindus to revive their decadent civilization and to make prejudiced foreigners appreciate it. In fulfilling these tasks India had the particular advantage of that mastery of self and imperturbability which were traditional in her religious and intellectual attitude, and which have always been one of the essential characteristics of her ideals. The Hindus did not rise up in an attitude of irritation in the face of wounding judgments; they worked silently and steadily to make them of no account; and gradually, under the officials of the East India Company, who were disorientated by suddenly having to govern Bengal, they managed to re-establish their authority, which had dwindled under the rule of the Moslem princes.

It was, indeed, in Bengal that the East India Company first established British domination in India, particularly after 1765. Events leading up to this included a whole series of successes and reverses in conflict with the different European companies and with the local authority, the Nawab (Nabob), who came nominally under the rule of the Mogul emperor in Delhi. Clive's victory at Plassey in 1757 was a decisive factor.

The caste of the clerks *(kayastha)*, which had already been employed under Moslem administration, found that its functions increased under the British, who had no experience of the laws and customs of the country. The educated Brahmins *(pandit)* achieved an important position because of the recourse which the British were obliged to make to their knowledge. When Warren Hastings, who was Governor from 1772 to 1785, was in need of a code of Hindu laws in order to adminster justice the Brahmins of Calcutta presented them to him in a form that followed the classical text of the *Dharmasastra* ("treaties of Right Order"), which defined the Brahmin ideals of social conduct, in this way seizing the opportunity to have their principles made legal by the new authorities. They also legitimately profited from the need to acquire practical knowledge of the benevolent or intellectual curiosity of some of the company's officials; they taught them about Sanskrit literature and were not long in undertaking research into the study of Sanskrit themselves, reviving an interest in it in their own circles. From 1822 onward a large Sanskrit dictionary, the *Sabdakalpadruma,* which was full of quotations, was published under the direction of Radhakant Deb. Shortly before that a group of pandits had supplied the Sanskrit scholar H. H. Wilson with the documentation for the first Sanskrit-English dictionary, which appeared in 1819.

Hindu activity was at the same time encouraged by English scholars such as Wilson and others in different countries of Europe who were specialists on Indian questions. Wilkins's translation of the *Bhagavadgita,* which appeared in 1785, had already shown certain enlightened Europeans that India had a sublime conception of the Supreme Being and of the duty of man to carry out the acts of his life in a spirit of unselfishness and serenity. From 1879 onward, when William Jones began the publication of a translation of the principal works of the Sanskrit theatre, India's classical literature, moving in its appeal, became known, and the romantics were soon to be attracted by Indian heroines, and to revere the anchorites meditating in their tranquil woodland retreats. The publication in 1801 of the monumental translation by Anquetil-Duperron of fifty *Upanishads,* the *Oupnek'hat,* had

The goddess Kali, copied by a European from a popular Indian picture. (Thomas Maurice, Indian Antiquities, *London, 1794)*

How the King of Malabar wears his jewels. From the Book of Marco Polo

revealed to philosophers the scope of Indian metaphysics, and Schopenhauer had given it further publicity. The book had established the existence and value of the *Veda* and, as it had been translated from a Persian version of the Sanskrit text made by Dara Shukoh, a Mogul prince, it offered a proof that even the adherents of Islam appreciated the value of Vedic thought.

From that time onward, the tradition of the Brahmins, which had always quoted the *Veda* as

Portrait of an English gentleman in India. The Earl of Denbigh, attributed to Van Dyck (1599-1641)

its authority, was able to take advantage of European criticism, but it was also imperative to repudiate ideas and customs condemned by these critics. This could be done in all good faith, as the philosophy of the *Upanishads* did not influence custom and the organization of society. The more recent conventions, which bound the Hindus with their detailed recommendations, could be set aside as representing a deterioration of the primitive Brahmanistic outlook. Moreover, these regulations were not generally speaking as binding as narrow interpretations of them might lead one to believe.

Under the influence of European ideas, a movement advocating the reform of the Hindu religion, destined to bring it back to the primitive state of purity that its adherents believed was to be found in the *Veda*, sprang up in Bengal, where Ram Mohan Ray founded in 1828 the Brahmasamaj ("the Brahmanical Society"). Ram Mohan Ray was a distinguished scholar, well versed in Brahmanic, Arabic, and European culture, and he found in the *Veda* a liberal theism. He strongly denounced ideas and customs not sanctioned by the *Veda*, such as the sacrifice of the *satis* ("good wives") on the funeral pyres of their husbands. He was a Brahmin of fairly elevated rank, in a hierarchy which existed only in terms of current local opinion. His visit to England, where he died in 1833, gave rise to sharp controversy in Brahmin circles about the right of a Brahmin to live in a foreign country among *mleccha* (barbarians without Brahmanic culture). His work was continued by a number of influential and educated men who did not belong to a class of society whose rank was founded on strict observance of traditional customs. One of his most notable followers was Dvarkanath Tagore, one of the eminent members of the important Tagore family, which had been degraded in the eyes of the most orthodox Hindus by the compromising attitude adopted by one of its ancestors towards the Moslems, but which was powerful and respected by the remainder of society. Dvarkanath's son, Debendranath Tagore, founded in 1839 the movement known as the Tattvabodhinisabha ("the Society of the Awakening to Reality") and subsequently merged it with the Brahmasamaj. He was deeply religious and was known as *maharshi* ("the great seer"), like the Vedic and legendary sages. His son was the poet Rabindranath Tagore, whose centenary was celebrated in 1961. Rabindranath Tagore made known to the whole world the

*The Mosque of Asaf-ud-daula, Lucknow (end of the eigh-
teenth century)*

Goa. From Souchu de Rennefort, Mémoire pour servir à l'histoire des Indes Orientales, *1702*

sensitivity of an India advancing towards independence, a nation which in its spirit and its art was progressing towards an all-embracing humanism, leading man to a realization of beauty and of the infinite. His works, written in Bengali and English, and translated into many other languages, won him the Nobel Prize. He was also an educationist, and founded at Santiniketan in 1921 the "Abode of Peace", an international university for intellectual and artistic studies, by which his memory is still kept alive. Another Bengali, Aurobindo Ghose, or Sri Aurobindo as his followers call him, founded an *ashram* at Pondicherry, from which he preached the evolution towards a "Life Divine", going beyond Tagore's conception of the full development of humanism.

These and many other developments were quite independent of the Brahmasamaj, which was the first of a series of important movements for the reform of Brahmanism. The evolution of the Brahmasamaj itself prospered for a time under the leadership of Keshab Chandra Sen, a member of the *vaidya* ("doctors"), a caste that included physicians and scholars. He was the descendant of a friend and scientific assistant of H. H. Wilson, and aimed at reconciliation between the educated Brahmanistic India and the Christian Western world. In close contact with Lord Lawrence, who was Viceroy from 1864 to 1869, he appeared to come very near to Christianity, was a strong opponent of Hindu customs such as child marriage and the ban on the remarriage of widows, and he spent some time in England. But later in life his semi-Christian theism took on a more strongly Hindu aspect. In 1878 he found a husband for his daughter when she was only thirteen. In 1880 he found justification for the worship of a number of divinities representing the various manifestations of the one God, and in 1881 he founded a new movement, the "New Dispensation Church," which found favour with neither Christians nor Hindus.

The reform of Hinduism, in the sense of a return to its original sources and the foundation of movements towards reconciliation with other religions, was not limited to Bengal, but was propagated or grew up more or less independently in many parts of India. Europeans became involved in it, and even led movements, such as the Theosophical Society, founded in 1875 at Adyar, a town near Madras at the mouth of

Moslem tomb at Lucknow (end of the eighteenth century)

the river of the same name, by a Russian spiritualist, Mme H. P. Blavatsky, and an American, Colonel H. S. Olcott. At a later date a leading member of this society, which has branches in many countries of the world, was Annie Besant, who founded the Central Hindu College. This establishment finally became, under the Pandit Malaviya, the Banaras Hindu University.

There were also other movements that believed in a return to the original sources, but they were less conciliatory, and consisted of the reaction of Hinduism influenced by other religions, but in a more exclusive spirit. Among these mention should be made of the Aryasamaj ("Aryan Assembly"), founded by the Gujarati monk Dayananda Sarasvati. It had its earliest centres

in Bombay and Lahore in 1875. Dayananda aimed at a return to the *Veda* itself and to the *Veda* alone. He interpreted it in such a way as to discover in it the principal beliefs of Hinduism, but not the forms of worship nor the social customs. He condemned idolatry and caste distinctions, admitted the equality of the sexes and the remarriage of widows, and advocated education for girls.

The Ramakrishna Mission, founded by Vivekananda, showed less partiality in favour of the *Veda*; its creed was based on the *Vedanta* and the use of Yoga, and it borrowed from Christianity little more than a method of proselytism. It was one of the forms of Hinduism best adapted for presentation to the Western world. At the

Collège La Martinière, Lucknow. This was a palace bequeathed as a school by Claude Martin (1735-1800) of Lyons, a general in the service of the Nawab of Audh. Martin's tomb is in the crypt of the palace

Parliament of Religions held in Chicago in 1893, and in numerous writings, Vivekananda showed the value of classical philosophic Hinduism, together with the deep mysticism of his master Ramakrishna.

The Indian Moslems, for their part, followed the lead of the militant Hindus in their dual effort for revival and adaptation. Their revival movements came at a much later date, as there was opposition to any innovation by the strictly orthodox groups. In 1877, thanks to the initiative of the Sayyid Ahmad Khan, the Muhammedan Anglo-Oriental College at Aligarh was founded and subsidized by Moslem princes: this was the first concession made to the modern outlook. Other institutions subsequently came into being, and Moslem intellectuals profited from general scientific research, even for their interpretations of the Koran. The *Maulana* (doctor) Abul Kalam Azad showed the way by his commentary in Urdu on the Koran. He was a strong partisan of collaboration with the Hindus in matters outside the domain of Moslem law, and he became the first Minister of Education in the Indian central Government after independence.

Thus during the nineteenth century a class of intellectuals developed in India, possessing differing outlooks and religious beliefs, but characterized by the common desire to maintain their fundamental differences and yet to adapt their secular activities to the needs of modern life. This group of men served the British Government, taking over most of the administrative and technical posts, and proved itself fitted to take over the reins of government.

ECONOMY AND POLITICS IN INDIA UNDER BRITISH RULE

The section of the population which received a European-style education played an ever-increasing part in the administration of the country, while the people of India and the work

Travellers' resting-place and pavilion on the road from Delhi to Agra (Indo-Moslem style) ▶

which they carried out made the main contribution to the economy of the country and to the armed forces. A very important characteristic of British rule in India was, indeed, the way in which a very small number of Englishmen as compared with the population and the extent of the country exercised their influence through the intermediary of the Indians themselves.

It was not true that the people of India as a whole welcomed subjection to a foreign trading company, the East India Company, which was the origin of British domination. The fact of the matter is that British power was established without the Indians really becoming aware of it, without its appearing as a revolution or even a novelty, in a country where the independence of the Hindu majority had been overcome long since, or had been compelled to withdraw. The country's economy had already been disturbed before the advent of the British. There was also the essential factor that the British made no frontal attack on the social structure of India.

The conditions of the establishment of British rule and its later experiences explain both its essential nature and why it finally came to an end.

The situation brought about by Islamic domination itself explains these conditions.

The British first made their appearance in India as traders, after the Portuguese and the Dutch. A trading company that started in 1600 obtained in 1613, through James I's ambassador accredited to the court of the Great Mogul, the right to trade in Surat (Gujarat), and then established agencies at a number of points along the coast, in spite of the activities of the Portuguese and the Dutch. On account of attacks and pillage by them, forts were constructed and troops maintained, in spite of the opinion of Sir Thomas Roe, second ambassador of James I at the court of the Mogul Emperor, who in 1616 had obtained the right to trade anywhere in the country. But the company had already since 1613 established a policy of armed support for the various sovereigns and princes in order to gain privileges by helping the King of Persia, Shah Abbas, to conquer the town of Ormuz on the Persian Gulf. The trading-post of Madras was founded and Fort St George built there in 1640. Fort William at Calcutta was constructed in 1696, after the company had first been installed there in 1690. Bombay was acquired for the

Presumed portrait of Anandaranga Pillai, an agent of the Compagnie Française des Indes at Pondicherry. About 1740

British Crown in 1661, as part of the dowry of Catherine of Braganza, wife of Charles II.

After a few attempts the French settled in India, and the Compagnie des Indes Orientales was founded by Colbert in 1664. A trading-post was first established at Surat, and then hostilities broke out with the Dutch, with whom Louis XIV's armies were at war in Europe. In 1672 the French seized San Thomé (Mayilappur), which the Dutch had already conquered from the Portuguese, but it was soon afterwards besieged by the Sultan of Golkonda. The French asked help of another prince, Sherkhan Lodi, who owed allegiance to the Sultan of Bijapur and who, in order to create a trade rival for the Dutch, ceded Pondicherry to the French company in 1672. These spheres of influence of the various European countries therefore corresponded to the divisions of India between different rulers, and the mutual help of the European traders and the Indian princes in their struggles against each other brought the country into a permanent state of unrest.

The claims made on either side were to act not only for the prosperity of local agriculture, industry, and commerce, but also to enhance the power of the local sovereigns. The European agents, or *feitores* as they were called in Portuguese, were the managers of European establishments which prepared the cargoes for the ships belonging to the different companies, sold the imports that they brought, speaking in the name of their sovereigns. The latter, who had given the trading companies their privileges and often subsidized them, gave them substantial diplomatic and military aid and could frequently change their status by treaties concluded in Europe. Pondicherry in particular had an eventful history; it was taken by the Dutch in 1693 and restored to the Compagnie des Indes Orientales in 1697 under the Treaty of Ryswijk; it was taken by the British in 1761, 1778, 1788, and 1793, returned under the Treaty of Paris in 1763, the Treaty of Versailles in 1783, and the Treaty of Paris in 1814; and it was only after the capture in 1788 that it was restored to the French by virtue of a treaty concluded in India itself. In the same way Madras, which was captured by La Bourdonnais in 1746, was returned to the British under the Treaty of Aix-la-Chapelle in 1749.

The Indian princes and rulers exercised authority for their part either in the name of the Emperor (Padshah) at Delhi (the Grand Mogul, as the Europeans called him) or on behalf of his governors *(Subadar)* who were the viceroys of large regions *(subah)*, or his Nawabs (Nabobs),

who were subordinate to the viceroys. Delhi exerted only nominal rule over the chieftains in distant areas, and they refrained from paying their tribute when the emperor was too weak to send troops to insist on his rights. Aurangzeb, who died in 1707, was the last of the emperors who maintained any effective rule from Delhi; he, indeed, succeeded in increasing his domination by the annexation of the lands of the Sultans of Bijapur and Golkonda, in 1686 and 1687 respectively. But the imperial power was already beginning to decline before his death, and the final blows to it were dealt by Nadir Shah's expedition from Persia in 1739 and by the campaign of the Afghan chief Ahmad Shah Durrani in 1757; both of these were pillaging expeditions which led to the sacking of Delhi. It was nevertheless in the interest of the local rulers to continue to recognize the sovereignty of the emperor, for it was from him that they held the only titles to power to which they could lay claim. They held their positions not only on account of services rendered, but also through intrigue and by gifts made at Court, and were ready to take up arms to secure the lands thus allotted to them. Some of them merely applied to the emperor to legitimize their titles to territories that they had acquired by force of arms. The Nawabs acted in the same manner with regard to the Subadars.

Gold medal of the Compagnie Française des Indes, 1750, from the trading-post of Masulipatam (Andhra)

The foundation of the Compagnie des Indes Orientales by Louis XIV
in 1664. From Souchu de Rennefort, Histoire des Indes Orientales, 1668

Hindu rulers who were still unconquered, and who held the Moslem princes in check, were not always unwilling to accept official titles from the Mogul Empire, which represented, at least as far as the Moslem authorities were concerned, the established order of things. The Marathas had become powerful in the seventeenth century under the leadership of Sivaji (1627-80), a Hindu of the Bhonsle family, a member of the Rajput clan and the noble class of the *kshatriya*, though he did not belong to the highest rank. The Maratha prime ministers, who held the title of *peshwa* ("guides"), which was of Persian origin, were Brahmins from Konkan, belonging to the caste known as *Chittpavan*. Thus the Maratha Confederation, whose cavalry was a force to be reckoned with throughout India, represented Hindu power. Though it had on countless occasions waged war against the Empire, it sometimes sought a position of honour in it, even when the power of that Empire had become no more than a fiction. In this way the Maratha chief Mahaji Sindia gave himself the title of Wakil-i-Mutlag ("Regent of the Empire") in 1785, and restored to the throne the unfortunate Emperor Shah Alam, whom the Rohilla chief Ghulam Qadir had captured, blinded, and deposed; and in 1794 he made the Emperor, whom he had in his power, confer Mogul dignities upon the *peshwa* whose vassal he declared himself to be.

The heads of the European trading companies had entered into this competition, and had intrigued to obtain the position of Nawab and other favours. Dumas, who was Governor of Pondicherry from 1735 to 1742, had entered into relations with the Nawab of Arkat (Arcot), and through him had obtained from the Emperor in 1736 the right to mint money. After the death of the Nawab, who was killed by the Marathas in 1740, he gave asylum to his widow and daughters and refused to hand them over to the Marathas. He received the congratulations of the Subadar of the Deccan, the Nizam ul-Mulk ("the Administrator of the Kingdom"), and the Emperor conferred on him the title of Nawab.

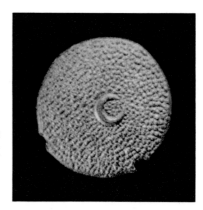

Gold pagoda (coin) known as " the three svamin," Vishnu and his two wives. Currency of Yanaon, minted at Pondicherry (eighteenth century)

He accepted this, not as a personal honour, but in his office as Governor of Pondicherry, so that it passed to his successor Dupleix in 1742. Dupleix would have liked Chanda Sahib, the son-in-law of the former Nawab of Arkat, to succeed to his father-in-law's title, but the Subadar appointed another man. When the Subadar died in 1748 Dupleix upheld as claimant his grandson, Muzaffar Jang, who was in favour of Chanda Sahib. He supplied his two allies with troops, and the Nawab of Arkat was killed in the battle of Ambur in 1749. Muzaffar Jang proclaimed himself Subadar of the Deccan on the battlefield itself, and declared Chanda Sahib to be the Nawab of Arkat. With great ceremony Dupleix recognized in Pondicherry the titles which his two allies had just secured for themselves. As a recompense they awarded him lands from which he could draw the revenues. It then remained for the three of them to take possession of the lands and titles thus acquired. Dupleix was able to levy the taxes on the lands assigned to him in areas near his existing concessions, but Muzaffar Jang and Chanda Sahib were powerless to do anything. Nasir Jang, a brother of the dead Subadar, had proclaimed himself Subadar of the Deccan, and Muhammad Ali, a son of the Nawab killed at Ambur, claimed that he was his father's heir, and retired to the Fort of Tiruchirapalli (Trichinopoly). The British in Madras took the side of these two claimants, who appeared for a time to be victorious, as Nasir Jang had captured his rival. But Nasir Jang was assassinated by conspirators in 1750, and Muzaffar Jang was once more proclaimed Sudabar by his supporters. Dupleix again acclaimed him with great ceremony in Pondicherry, and was as a consequence nominated as Governor of the territory extending from the river Krishna to Cape Comorin.

Dupleix accepted the title, declared that he would delegate the office to Chanda Sahib, and believed himself to be master of India. He placed Muzaffar Jang, who was leaving to take possession of the throne of the Deccan, under the protection of Bussy, but the conspirators who had assassinated Nasir Jang attacked and killed Muzaffar Jang. Bussy immediately had Salabat Jang, the third son of the Nizam ul-Mulk, proclaimed Subadar by the army, and installed him on the throne at Aurangabad in 1751, obtaining from him the renewal of the former concessions and an extension of the territories, together with a substantial personal recompense in exchange for the protection offered by his troops. At the same time, while the armies of Dupleix and Chanda Sahib were about to attempt to overcome Muhammad Ali, who was supported in Tiruchirapalli by the English, Clive captured Arkat. In 1752 Chanda Sahib was taken at Tiruchirapalli and executed, and the army capitulated. Dupleix, in making himself the protector of the Indian claimants and taking part in their wars, had contravened the orders given to him more than once by his company, which

Pathan (Afghan) chieftains from Peshavar

Vue d'une Tour de Pagode

had enjoined him to restrict his activities to commercial affairs, as France was not seeking territorial domination in India. He was recalled in 1754, but his dismissal did not put a definite stop to the hostilities between the English and the French, which continued until the beginning of the nineteenth century, as a consequence of the wars between the two countries. Many historians writing about Dupleix have accused the Ministers of Louis XV of incapacity, because they would have refused to support him to retain the Indian Empire that he would have acquired for France. They base this assumption on the fact that Clive and his successors, with similar means at their disposal, gave England effective mastery not long afterwards; but they forget that in the time of Dupleix the power acquired was really fictitious, and it was dependent on the decisions of sovereigns who had no real sovereignty. Although the acquisition of the title of Nawab, which brought the heads of the trading-posts into the hierarchy of the Mogul Empire, was made by

Dumas and not Dupleix, it has often been attributed to the latter, as well as the intervention in the disputes about the succession of the Indian princes. British historians have also magnified the importance of Dupleix, who was indeed a man of much more than average capacity, on account of their pride in their country's victory over him. Few authors have taken into consideration the feelings and reactions of the different peoples of India in their accounts of the intrigues and struggles to gain supremacy.

However, the East India Company rid itself of the competition of the French, the Portuguese, the Dutch, and the Danes, who had also established trading-posts in India, and, benefiting from the decadence of the Mogul Empire, established sovereignty in Bengal, just as Dupleix and Bussy had hoped to do along the Coromandel Coast and in the Deccan.

The history of British domination, however, had followed a different pattern. In order to extend its position the East India Company, at the end of the seventeenth century, had resorted to the use of force against the local authorities, with the campaign of Child in the west coast area and an expedition in Bengal against Chittagong. It was during the reign of Aurangzeb, so these attempts to gain power were quickly repressed. Aurangzeb, who wished to develop foreign trade, had accepted the submission of the English, who agreed to restrict themselves to commercial activities. In 1696 the East India Company had even managed to obtain the post of *zamindar* ("land holder") for the territory around Calcutta, and in 1717 this position was confirmed and extended and freedom of trade granted. The company was then in a prosperous position, as were the Hindu merchants who traded with it. The same was true for the other European establishments, especially the French trading-post of Chandernagore, where Dupleix had shown his talents as a businessman before becoming Governor of Pondicherry in 1742. But in 1756 an officer of Siraj-ud-daula, Nawab of Bengal, had taken refuge with the British; they refused to surrender him, so the Nawab attacked and captured Calcutta. Clive recaptured it, and forced the Nawab to restore the privileges of the company and to authorize it to fortify the town and to mint its own coinage. At this time hostilities had broken out in Europe between England and France. Clive therefore attacked Chandernagore and captured it. That was when he began to intervene directly in Indian politics.

In conspiracy with the great Hindu merchants

A young horseman. Mogul painting of the beginning of the eighteenth century ▶

and bankers in relation with the East India Company who were dissatisfied with the Nawab, Clive negotiated with one of the Nawab's grand officers, Mir Jafar, who was ready to betray the Nawab. He then attacked the Nawab at Plassey (Palasi) in 1757. The Nawab's army disbanded and fled. Clive installed Mir Jafar as Nawab, and he was awarded the rank of *umra*, grand officer of the Mogul Empire. From that time onward the East India Company played a leading rôle in the politics of Bengal, by alliances with the rulers whom it had put into power or whom it upheld, and by paying outward allegiance to the Emperor, and having him legitimize its claims, even though it might fight him if the occasion arose. In 1764 Hector Munro won a victory at Baksar over Shuja-ud-daula, the Nawab of Audh, who had the Emperor Shah Alam II virtually in his power. Munro was then nominated *vazir* (prime minister) of the Nawab, and the victory was considered as one gained against the Empire, even though the Empire was maintained. Clive returned to India in 1765 after a period in England, and was nominated Governor and Commander-in-Chief. He opposed General Coote, who wished to march on Delhi and take possession of the Empire, albeit in the name of the Emperor. Clive was content for the East India Company to be officially granted the *divani*, a ministerial office for the collection of taxes in the provinces of Bengal, Bihar, and Orissa. This gave the company full power, and at the same time maintained the fiction of the respect due to the régime. This apparent respect was primarily destined as a reply to the opposition that existed in both England and France to military conquest. As a consequence the East India Company conquered a large part of India in stages, notably under Wellesley,[1] Governor-General from 1798 to 1805, whose costly conquests of Mysore, the greater part of the Maratha states, and other territories incurred disapproval. But the conquest was carried out with the policy of continuing the existence of a number of princely states and controlling them by means of Residents rather than taking direct control of the administration, a task more difficult in itself, and more compromising in the eyes of the populace.

For a long time this policy was no direct concern of the peoples of India. They had little interest in the identity of men who, unknown to them, gave mutual recognition to each other's claims to be their masters at various levels, or who fought

[1] Richard, Baron Wellesley in the peerage of Great Britain, Earl of Mornington in the peerage of Ireland, elder brother of Arthur Wellesley, later Duke of Wellington.

An employee of the East India Company in Bengal

each other to substantiate their claims. These masters paid no attention to social conditions, but were interested only in receiving the taxes, which in any case were inevitable. Certain groups even found the situation advantageous. Trade with the foreigner helped the artisans, merchants, bankers, brokers, and forwarding agents. The army gave employment to a large number of men and thus supported also their families. A whole host of servants, small shopkeepers, and carriers formed vast moving bazaars around it as they do around the crowds of pilgrims at a religious festival. The dangers of warfare were not negligible, but the recruits were either members of castes with a traditional background of military honour, who would fight bravely, or else they were soldiers of chance, who were ready to flee at the least alarm or desert to the enemy, their only allegiance to their chiefs being in respect of their pay, which was often in arrears. Some of them were attracted to the army by the hope of pillage. In any case, there was no question of national wars, even for the Europeans who were dispatched to uphold the power of foreign princes or commercial interests, and among whom desertion was not infrequent. Many of these European soldiers, moreover, were mercenaries drawn from the ranks of adventurers or ne'er-do-wells.

But the people suffered indirectly from the situation in a very serious manner, either by pillage in times of war, from the way in which passing troops of infantry and cavalry devastated their farmlands, or by the serious aggravation of the general economic position.

The trade of the European companies had in the early days helped the country, for it imported very little from abroad, but exported its spices and materials to Europe and the Far East in exchange for silver ingots; but the agents of the companies carried on large-scale trade on their own account in the interior of the country. Only part of the money accrued from this trade remained in India, as much of it returned to Europe. But the price of the exports which was paid to the producers brought additional wealth to the country, together with the profits of the Indian middlemen and the expenditure of the Europeans living in the country.

The intervention of the companies in political matters changed this state of affairs. To the positions granted to the agents, in exchange for help given to claimants to a position or to overlords, must be added considerable gifts in money and *jagir* (lands), the income of which was made over to Europeans. Corruption and exaction were frequent among junior agents, who were anxious to become wealthy like their superior officers, and this also considerably impoverished India.

The systems of tax-collection put into operation by the East India Company also had the result of greatly impoverishing the countryside. The two most important of these systems were the one instituted in Bengal by Lord Cornwallis, who was Governor-General from 1786 to 1793, and the one applied in Madras, first by Reid and then by Sir Thomas Munro.

In Bengal, as in the greater part of India, the taxes were levied by the *zamindar*, and the quota to be raised by the farmers of each village was fixed by agreement with the *panchayat,* or village council, according to the harvest. The office of *zamindar* was virtually hereditary. Lord Cornwallis considered the *zamindars* as proprietors, and instituted a fixed amount of tax. As a penalty for non-payment, the *zamindar* could lose all or part of the lands for which he was responsible for tax-collection, and the office was sold by auction. If a peasant were bankrupt his

case could be taken before a tribunal. The East India Company received in principle 45 per cent of the tax and the *zamindar* 15 per cent. Very little remained to the farmer when deduction for the expenses of running the farm had been made. Such an exorbitant tax frequently remained unpaid, the tribunals were overwhelmed with work, and the *zamindars* frequently lost their offices, which were sold in Calcutta to speculators, who took their place without any experience of the lands in question, and without any interest in them on a long-term basis. Under these conditions land was left uncultivated by peasants who could not make a livelihood from it, though finally a certain balance was found between the fiscal claims and the possible capacity for payment of the *zamindars* and the farmers.

In Madras a system was instituted under which the tax was collected directly from the *ra'iyat* (ryot), or farmers, by agents of the East India Company who toured the countryside and imposed taxes according to the reports made by their employees.

The economy of the country suffered finally from a cause completely independent of the actions of the company—namely, the decrease in exports and the difficulties of the craftsmen that arose on account of the Industrial Revolution in England and the expanding economy of America. Indeed, the production of raw materials such as cotton and sugar cane in America created competition for the East India Company that was even more to be feared because America is nearer to England than India is, and the American imports had less tax to pay on their arrival at the British ports. At the same time, the mechanized production of American cotton materials in the Lancashire mills enabled imitation Indian fabrics to be produced at low prices, and, moreover, tariffs protected this output against the import of the Indian goods. Finally, English fabrics were imported into India. Many Indian weavers were forced to abandon their looms. The silk industry was maintained, and indigo from India continued to be more important than the American. The production and export of opium compensated the company for the reduction in other exports. But the fact that most of the indigo plantations were in British hands, and that the East India Company had a monopoly for the cultivation of opium, which it produced cheaply and smuggled into China, meant that only the company and its agents were compensated in

Banaras, by W. Daniell (nineteenth century)

any way for the loss of trade. So India as a whole changed from a country important for the production of valuable raw materials and manufactured goods into a dumping-ground for industrial products made in Britain.

The activities of the East India Company and conditions of overseas trade combined during the second part of the eighteenth century and the beginning of the nineteenth to decrease considerably India's economic wealth. The political power of the Mogul Empire had dwindled, but the country, which had been in the grip of bitter struggles, now acquired an administration which was of great benefit to it after the recent general

disturbances. The control exercised by the British Government over the East India Company was gradually rendered more effective. The first step in this direction was Pitt's Act of 1784, which followed the financial difficulties, scandals of plundering, and peculation that had for a long time been a source of anxiety and disapproval to part of the British public. Public disapproval had already been one of the factors which provoked Clive's suicide in 1774, and in 1786 it gave rise to the impeachment of Warren Hastings, who had been Governor from 1772 to 1785. During this trial, which resulted in an official acquittal, Burke's eloquence in denouncing the crimes of

Shuja-ud-daula, Nawab of Audh (Gentil)

the accused, which went to excesses in its severity against Hastings, at the same time was such an expression of a desire for justice and honesty that Burke is still considered in India as the originator of the British liberal tradition so often to be seen in England's later dealings with Indian problems.

The principal organizers of the administration of the East India Company brought it in line as much as possible with those features of the British system that seemed to them the best. They carried out their work well, in that they were competent and energetic, but they did not always act opportunely, as they did not understand the institutions and customs that they were trying to reform. They ended by raising a barrier between a British colonial society that was exalted as something of a superior nature, and an abased native society. The administrative reforms of Lord Cornwallis withdrew all high posts from the Indians, and a series of measures for the reorganization of the army placed the Indians in a permanently subordinate position, whatever their capacities or their former ranks were. In the early days the companies of sepoys recruited by the European trading companies or by the Mogul princes had been commanded by their own Indian officers, who were in close touch with the Europeans. The need to train the sepoys in European methods of warfare certainly required the appointment of European instructors, but there was no necessity to make it impossible for Indians to reach the

higher ranks, once their capacities had been proved. The measures taken by the East India Company in favour of British civil servants and officers, and even also those of junior rank, allowed the whole British colony to maintain a luxurious standard of living, and they were even instructed to do so. Allowances were given to prisoners of other nations captured in India, so that no European should appear poor in Indian eyes, though these same prisoners were treated in a very different manner when on English soil.

These prejudices in favour of prestige would have had a foundation only if the Indians had been incapable of judging the qualities of a man by anything beyond his outward appearance. They founded a spirit of inequality based on origin and, in particular, European origin, far more effective than that of the Brahmins and the Sudra which found so much disfavour in European eyes.

As far as legal institutions were concerned, the reforms made during the governorship of Warren Hastings may have suppressed some incoherency and certain abuses, but in their desire to respect local custom and religion they served to resuscitate and stabilize the theoretical divisions of society of the ancient Brahmanic tradition, and thus presented India as a country wedded to that tradition.

At a later date the work begun by Macaulay in 1834 gradually gave India a legal system applicable to all persons whatever their status, and in accordance with the universal evolution of legal principles. But Macaulay, who was narrowly prejudiced in favour of the inherent excellence of European civilization, had declared in 1833 that the greatest day in British history would be the one when the Indian public, educated in the European way, would demand European institutions. In 1835 he obtained from the Governor, Lord William Bentinck, a decision that public funds appropriated to education should be employed on English education alone. This decision proved too rigorous for full application, but, in its misunderstanding and scorn of true Indian public opinion, it made the Indians oppose the plans of the British rather than attract them towards the goal of acquiring an English outlook. The tendency which was fostered and which finally triumphed, in spite of the opinion of men like H. H. Wilson, who had a true understanding of Indian problems, was moreover harmful to the general development of learning. Limiting Government responsibility to the propagation

Indian painting of the nineteenth century from Orissa. In the centre, British officers and sepoys

of a foreign system of education meant renouncing any education at all for the mass of the population. The Government was unable to offer an English education to any beyond those whom it needed to fill the posts in its administration, and it deliberately abandoned the greater part of the population to the generous but necessarily restricted initiatives of missionaries and philanthropists. The maintenance of institutions like the Sanskrit College at Banaras, which were aided by men like J. R. Ballantyne, continued or was in some cases renewed; these institutions aimed in theory at perpetuating the existing classical teaching, modifying it by the introduction of modern scientific ideas, but the policy of adaptation was not implemented. It was not, moreover, until 1854 that any measures were taken in favour of primary education.

It was at this period that the East India Company undertook a certain number of measures in favour of the material and intellectual equipment of the country. It was known that India had always been characterized by its good road system and its irrigation works, and it was felt that

the British could do no less. The Public Works Department was created in 1854, and the construction of railways was begun. The great Ganges canal between Haridvar and Cawnpore (Kanpur) was built, and an important road constructed linking Calcutta, Delhi, and Peshavar (Peshawar). These extensive works were carried out under the governorship of Dalhousie (1846-56). Lord Dalhousie was a convinced supporter of the policy of annexation, and considered that domains in which the ruling family left no heir should automatically revert to the East India Company; he moreover believed that in the interests of the people any badly administered lands should also be taken over. Thus the well-being of the people was made a justification for the East India Company's dictatorial measures; in the early days of the establishment of trading-posts and military campaigns, Europeans of different nations had claimed that they were intervening in India on account of national prestige and for the renown of their own sovereigns. Thus a certain consciousness of the rights of the conquered people was appearing, though it still

189

served as a pretext for the annexation of lands and revenues. On the other hand, the undertaking of public-works schemes of use to the country as a whole really necessitated a unification of power; and it should be noted that independent India to-day still benefits from work undertaken at that period, work that she is in the process of expanding.

But at the time the policy of annexation and Europeanization that the East India Company was applying with increased resolution gave rise to an increasing muted opposition, all the more so because it came at a period when Indian trade and industry were declining and when a powerful administration had rigorously imposed higher taxes. Foreign writers on India, and even some English ones, revealed this. In 1844 Barchou de Penhoën had shown the dangers in his book *L'Inde sous la domination anglaise,* and underlined the possibility of the outbreak of a major revolt due to discontent among the soldiers. He saw the seriousness of the situation for England, especially if Russia, then extending her activities in Turkestan, should intervene. The Swedish General Biornstierna, although a great admirer of the British Empire in India, had already seen as early as 1839 that the system could not be maintained indefinitely, and had been insistent on the matter of the Russian menace. The British authorities showed some anxiety on the Russian question, but neither Dalhousie nor his successor,

Canning, realized the possibility of a large-scale revolt. This revolt broke out, however, on May 10, 1857, under the conditions foreseen by Barchou de Penhoën, with the mutiny of three sepoy regiments at Merath (Meerut). They marched to Delhi, which fell to them without resistance, and proclaimed Bahadur Shah emperor. He was already nominally emperor, but had been pensioned by the British, and Canning had declared that he would have no successor. The revolt spread throughout the valleys of the Ganges and the Yamuna, and into central India, though it did not gain the whole country. At the end of a struggle marked by acts of heroism and atrocity on either side the revolt was quelled by the British with the help of considerable numbers of Indian troops who had remained loyal to them. Its end marked the consolidation of British domination. But in 1858 the Mogul Emperor was deposed and the East India Company deprived of its political rights, the power passing into the hands of the British Crown, which governed through the intermediary of a Secretary of State for India. Canning was maintained in power and appointed Viceroy. The policy of annexation was officially abandoned, and Indian princes were guaranteed their sovereign rights under the British Government, whose vassals they became in 1877, when Queen Victoria was proclaimed Empress of India.

The nature of the 1857 revolt has given rise

Dancer and musicians playing the tabla and cymbals. Woodcut by Rani Chanda, Santiniketan, 1938

Siege artillery of the Anglo-Indian army in the nineteenth century. Capt. G. F. Atkinson, A History of the Indian Campaign

to much discussion. The English have shown themselves eager to consider it as no more than a mutiny, but Indian nationalists later described it as a war of independence. The British view may appear to have been confirmed by the loyalty of part of the Indian army to British command, and even on the Indian side it has been suggested that if the English had been dispossessed the result would have been not independence but anarchy. Neither of these views is conclusive; the movement was none the less real because it was not a unanimous rising and was destined to fail. Nevertheless some modern British historians tend to see in it Indian conservative reaction rather than a movement towards independence; this point of view, though one of the more recent, is also one of the least founded. Leaders such as Lakshmi Bai, the heroic Rani of Jhansi in Bundelkhand, and Nana Sahib at Kanpur indeed fought for independence, at a time when annexations were increasing and the East India Company was denying them their rights. The Hindu or Moslem sepoys revolted not so much to acquire political independence as to achieve independence in the social field of their customs and religions which they believed to be threatened.

It was not, however, a general uprising of the people. The populations of the different provinces were not united by a common feeling and they could not all of them at the same time hold the company responsible for their suffering or even resent its domination, as it still acted through the intermediary of local princes and tax-collectors, making no direct contact with the people. It is also to be noted that it was especially the latest victims of the annexations who rose up, following the example of the sepoys, who had revolted against military measures which they considered were attacking their customs, and also on a question of honour, after their resistance to orders had provoked brutal and infamous repression. But a large percentage of the population living under the rule of the princes and *zamindars,* and which was also ill treated, took part in the insurrection. Insufficient preparation and lack of co-ordination in the command of the insurgents, who, in spite of relative union among themselves, belonged to both the Hindu and the Moslem communities, gave the British

191

time to collect their forces and quell the attempted revolt.

Marx and Engels, who watched closely the events of the Mutiny, saw in it neither a real uprising of the people nor a reactionary movement. They noted, in common with most non-British observers, the relative union between Moslems and Hindus against their common masters, the rapidity with which the uprising spread, and the way in which it coincided with the withdrawal of large numbers of British troops from India.

The positivist followers of Auguste Comte, P. Laffitte, and the Englishman Richard Congreve, advocating the subordination of political consideration to moral ones, condemned British imperial policy in no uncertain terms. They emphasized the uselessness of a so-called duty to promote civilization that would justify the idea of conquests while, according to them, the doctrines of the different peoples were adapted to the state of their differing civilizations, which would gradually evolve towards a rational state and which should not be replaced in an abrupt manner by European civilizations which were far from having reached final perfection.

Indeed, the psychological result of the uprising and the suppression of it was the broadening of the gulf between the British community and the peoples of India. This separation had the final result of allowing Indian society to maintain the specific structure of its intellectual background, even when it was anxious to acquire knowledge of British science, culture, and organization, having realized their power and practical efficiency.

On the English side, in spite of the victory, the memory of the Mutiny gave rise to a more circumspect and liberal policy, and this allowed the Indians to take an increasingly greater part in State administration, and finally to take over the reins of government of a State which was modern in conception, though it had been retarded by a long period of administration that had not in the beginning been conceived for its benefit.

In 1858 the political situation was put into order by the reconquest of the towns and provinces that had revolted. The economic, social, and psychological conditions had yet to be dealt with. The economic situation was of direct interest to Britain, who controlled or influenced production and trade, and was responsible for financial organization. The other matters came within the scope of local customs and ideas that she professed to respect, but which, since the uprising, she had mistrusted, customs she considered as inferior and which she hoped, through her own example, gradually to reform.

Contacts between British and Hindu and Moslem society were therefore mainly restricted to official, administrative, and business relations. This was attributed to the closed nature and the prejudices of Hindu society, and principally of the Brahmins. Indeed, relations had been smoother before the conquest and the subsequent tension which it had produced. The official exclusiveness of the British in their parties, clubs, and even in railway carriages was far more rigid than that of the Brahmins, who drew no racial distinctions but who judged bearing and education in relation to their own standards of purity. The gulf between the two nations did not, however, prevent matrimonial alliances, legal or otherwise, and these gave rise to a small class of Anglo-Indians, who showed a tendency to be prouder of their British than their Indian blood, and who were often unjustly despised by both sides, in a situation where they might have formed a bond, had not either side been so full of disdain and bitterness with respect to the other.

Under these conditions, with no contact with the peoples of India, the British administration after the Mutiny tended to favour a class which was intermediate between them and the mass of the people—that is, the landowners or *taalluqdar* and any others who could lay claim to their right to hold land. This was particularly true in Audh, an area recently annexed. Most of the holders of land could show no legal rights to their claims, and therefore, if they were not evicted, they became tenants with a very precarious tenure. Through the course of years many different measures were taken to make the status of tenant farmers more secure by fixing rents for a certain period. But the security of the farmers, always at the mercy of climatic catastrophes which could bring about terrible periods of famine, was not in all districts guaranteed by legislation. On the other hand the English civil servants undertook or organized a considerable amount of research work and compilation of statistics on the country and its resources, studying it district by district. Manuals and gazetteers exist that are still valuable sources of information about the state of India in the second half of the nineteenth century and the beginning of the twentieth.

The Government paid less attention to the study of the inhabitants than to that of the country. A certain number of civil servants and

An elephant of the temple of Vishnu Varadaraja at Kanchipuram

Army officers, mainly undertaking private research, made studies of archæology and inscriptions. These included James Prinsep, who was working as early as 1837, James Ferguson, and General Cunningham, who founded the Archæological Survey, in which the name of Sir John Marshall was to figure in the twentieth century. History was studied under similar conditions. Elliot and Dowson undertook research into Moslem sources; Colonel Tod made a study of the local chronicles of Rajasthan; George Grierson studied peasant life in Bihar; Crooke, local customs and traditions; while linguistic studies were represented by the work of Grierson and the foundation of the Linguistic Survey. But research into Indian civilization received comparatively little encouragement in England. Indian studies at Oxford in the second half of the nineteenth century were dominated by the work of a German, Max Müller, and it was in Germany and in France that research in this field was most active. Franz Bopp inaugurated a scientific study of the comparative grammar of Indo-European languages, which established the relationship between the majority of European languages on the one hand and Persian and the Sanskrit of India on the other. Vedic studies were undertaken in Germany by Rudolf Roth, Albrecht Weber, Hermann Oldenberg, and Karl Geldner, and Frenchmen such as Abel Bergaigne also made considerable contributions to this research. Roth, working in collaboration with Otto Böhtlingk, published the most important of the Sanskrit dictionaries. The study of Buddhism was particularly active in France, where the leading scholars were Eugène Burnouf, Emile Senart, and Sylvain Lévi, and also in Belgium, where the work of Louis de la Vallée Poussin was noteworthy. The historical study of the grammar of the modern Indo-Aryan languages was started in Paris by Jules Bloch. Dutch scholars such as Hendrik Kern, or Frenchmen, such as Auguste Barth (a particularly competent Indian scholar), Bergaigne, and Louis Finot, opened the field of research into the expansion of Indian civilization into Indonesia and Indochina; and the Ecole française d'Extrême-Orient was established in 1900. Alfred Foucher described the artistic relationship between India and the Hellenistic world, while the cultural relationships between India and China were studied particularly in France, first by Joseph Deguignes in the eighteenth century and subsequently by Abel-Rémusat, Stanislas Julien, and Edouard Cha-

vannes in the nineteenth and twentieth centuries. Even in British India itself the principal scholars of the human element of the civilization were mainly Germans or Austrians, such as Kielhorn, Bühler, Hultszch, and Aurel Stein. The work undertaken by Englishmen, which was no less considerable in its scope, was of an essentially practical nature. In the period between that of the early pioneers and more recent times it consisted mainly of studies of modern languages and of modern aspects of the country itself. Especially after the events of 1857, the gulf that the British felt separated them from the Indians doubtless prejudiced many minds against the country.

For a long time there was a prevalent idea that though a legendary India might at one time have had a brilliant civilization, England had saved it from the state of anarchy in which she found it, and had restored peace. India was a country incapable of ruling herself, and would fall back into a state of disorder and devastation if her protector did not exert strict control over her. Thus access to the higher grades in the public services was only gradually made open to Indians, even when they had an English education which fully qualified them for such posts, though the subordinate positions were filled mainly by Indians. From 1858 onward Indians were theoretically eligible for the entrance examination for the higher grade in the Indian Civil Service, but the examination was held only in London, and it was not until 1893 that it was decided in the House of Commons to hold a simultaneous examination in India, though even that resolution was not carried out. In 1888 the Viceroy, Lord Dufferin, expressed his opinion that greater use should be made of the capacities and possibilities of co-operation of the Indians, but emphasized the fact that it was essential for England to retain her control of public administration, as only she could keep the peace between the various Indian communities. It was not until 1926 that impartial recruitment really came into force with the Public Service Commissions which were created or adapted with this end in view.

Nevertheless the spread of English education throughout the country gave rise to an increasingly large group of Indians of all backgrounds who had a similar education and a means of communication in common, replacing the Sanskrit of former times, and this training gave them a means of carrying on activities in the European manner and made it possible for them to unite.

STEPS TOWARDS INDEPENDENCE

A number of Englishmen finally came to realize that it was not only unjust but impossible to continue to underestimate the true value and the competence of the Indians ; they were in direct opposition to the over-sensitive European element, which, for example, reacted violently against the decision of the liberally-minded Lord Ripon, who was Viceroy from 1880 to 1884, to recognize the competence of Indian judges who were as well qualified as English ones to pronounce judgements in cases affecting Europeans. With the approval of Lord Dufferin, these broader-minded Englishmen helped in the constitution of the National Indian Congress, which met for the first time in Bombay in 1885.

Other groups destined to attract the attention of the authorities towards Indian interests had already been organized on a local scale. The Parsee community, which, though small, was energetic and worthy of respect, had founded as early as 1852 the Bombay Association, under the leadership of Naorozji Furdunji and Dr Bhau Daji. Another Parsee, Dadabhai Naorozji, had founded in London in 1867 a society with

The Hindu University at Banaras

Rabindranath Tagore

similar aims, and in 1876 he denounced in *Poverty of India* the economic policy that had caused the increased poverty of the country. Hindu groups sprang up in Calcutta, Poona, and other centres. Dadabhai, who was president of the second session of the Congress, held in Calcutta in 1886, became a Member of Parliament in Britain in 1892. In the early stages the delegates to the Congress were nearly all members of the middle classes. The princes and the great land-owners, who owed their positions to the fact that they were established or maintained in them by the British, and the large-scale businessmen, whose affairs depended on current circumstances, played no part in it. The Moslems at first held themselves aloof, as they feared that, if the claims to power sought by the Congress came to fruition, India would have a Hindu Government, and that Islam would be subjected to the rule of infidels, instead of having the temporal as well as religious domination that was its due.

The Congress, in agreement with the English liberals, fully recognized the benefits that British rule had brought and was continuing to bring to India, but did not spare its criticism, and claimed for the competent interested parties the right and the power to intervene on behalf of the progress of the country as they understood it. Part of the British administration was unwilling to see in them anything more than a group of agitators hostile to progress made on English lines. Some of the actions carried out by the nationalists supported this thesis, for example the attitude of Bal Gangadhar Tilak, who, in spite of his broad intellectual outlook and many other aspects of his activities, opposed in the name of tradition the medical measures taken during the cholera epidemic in 1897. But others, such as Gopal Krishna Gokhale, who founded the Servants of India Society in 1905, were working in favour of an Indian parliamentary system with practical and moderate views.

Lord Curzon's term of office as Viceroy (1899-1905) was characterized by a series of measures destined to help the peasants after the great famine of 1899, but also by decisions in matters of authority that rode roughshod over feelings that had been clearly expressed by the Indians. One of these was the administrative partition of Bengal, made in spite of the unifying bond of language. The language was not, indeed, threatened, but the partition cut across a feeling of Bengali national unity that Curzon failed to understand, seeing only in the opposition to his plans a coalition of local and personal interests. The result was a campaign not only of protests but of acts of violence and the boycott of British imports. The latter was by way of reaction against the advantages given by the Government to British industry for the import of its products, at the expense of Indian native production; it was, indeed, a reaction in favour of the products of the country itself (*svadesi*). At the same time, the prospects of success of a movement in favour of independence were increasing. The Japanese victory over Russia in 1904 had demonstrated that the Europeans and their arms were not invincible. The numerous wars and expeditions in which the British authorities had made use of Indian troops, in Afghanistan, Burma, Malaya, Egypt, the Sudan, South Africa, China, and Tibet, had made the Indians aware of their military prowess. Finally, the example of an independent Japan, where maintenance of traditions went hand in hand with modern progress, showed that European domination was no requisite for modernization, and even retarded it, as India was unable to follow a policy of industrialization, but had been maintained for a long time as a dumping-ground for foreign products, to the detriment of the prosperity of its craftsmen. The movement known as *svadesi* was therefore by no means the simple manifestation of a blind policy of xenophobia. It was accompanied by a growing

An Indian carnival. Krishna is using a syringe to squirt women with coloured water (eighteenth-century painting) ▶

The Mahatma Gandhi

pressure on the part of Indian interests for the building of power installations and the creation of a heavy industry, and it led in the first instance to the construction of a hydroelectric power plant in Mysore in 1903 and the establishment in 1907 by the Tatas, a Parsee family, of the Tata Iron and Steel Company. In 1906 the Congress formulated a claim for self-government (*svaraj*). But the Muslim League was founded in the same year, and this institution worked against the Congress in its struggle against the British, by taking the British side over the question of the partition of Bengal.

In 1906-7 a Moslem delegation led by the Aga Khan obtained from the British Government in India a promise that the Moslems should vote separately for their own candidates for the representative assemblies that were to be created. This was the beginning of the division that was to end, at the time of the establishment of independence in 1947, in the creation of the independent state of Pakistan, distinct from India, allocated to the Moslem party, and consisting of the Indus Basin in the west and Eastern Bengal in the east. Eastern Bengal had already been separated from Western Bengal by Curzon, and united with it again in 1912. A great Moslem poet, Muham-

mad Iqbal, sang the praises of the potential force of Islam, and revived people's consciousness of it, while on the Hindu side Rabindranath Tagore, whose writing was more universal in scope, drew on nature and the popular traditions of Bengal to produce works of an artistic and emotional value hitherto unknown, which were to bring him the Nobel Prize in 1913, and to make him known far beyond the boundaries of India. At the same period international science benefited from the discoveries of Indian scholars, such as the botanist Jagadish Chandra Bose, the mathematician Ramanujan, and the physicists C. V. Raman and S. N. Bose.

The Moslem and Hindu movements were capable of concerted action, though not of unification. They worked together at times, when groups of Moslems joined the Congress, as happened under the leadership of Muhammed Ali Jinnah, who was to become the first Governor-General of Pakistan ; this alliance was principally after 1916, when the Moslems of India were aroused by the hostile attitude of the British towards the Turkish Caliphate, and incited to join the Hindus in their struggle against British domination.

After the beginning of the 1914-1918 war this

Jawaharlal Nehru, Prime Minister of the Republic of India

struggle was carried on under the leadership of Mohandas Karamchand Gandhi, who became the Mahatma ("great personality"). He was a member of an orthodox Hindu commercial family from the Gujarat, and after receiving an English education had become a barrister; he believed in self-mastery and moral justice, finding his inspiration in the *Bhagavadgita*, the Gospels, and the writings of Tolstoy, and had worked self-lessly and efficiently in South Africa to help to improve the conditions imposed on Asiatics there. When he returned to India in 1915 he adopted an attitude of calm resolution amid the confused mass of movements which had arisen in the country, and had the power to transmit his attitude to the crowds, in a way that paralysed the authorities without making them resort to repression. This was the *satyagraha* ("clinging to truth"), which consisted of passive resistance and civil disobedience. This attitude was characteristically Indian. The Brahmanic attitude had for centuries considered *satya* (truth) the absolute power against which in the long run nothing could prevail. Holding obstinately the conviction that one was in the right, without allowing oneself to be led into the hazardous and cruel path of violence, practising non-violence (*ahimsa*) meant ensuring ultimate success, and that is why the motto of the Republic of India today is *Satyam eva jayate*

("Truth alone triumphs"). Gandhi often linked with this attitude, in addition to general strikes (*hartal*), protest through fasting, an ancient traditional method of restraining creditors and authorities. The use of this method was also characteristic of the struggle for independence that was being carried on at the same time in Ireland, where fasting was also an ancient tradition. To these demonstrations Gandhi added the personal example of spinning cotton, to symbolize and encourage the struggle of Indian handicrafts, which he wanted to see revived, against the import of foreign goods.

Gandhi's principles were not universally followed. Some of the partisans of independence resorted to violence, assassination, and conspiracy, sometimes helped, both before and during the War, by the Germans, who were eager to weaken England. Generally speaking, however, the Indians wanted their independence but not the defeat of England, with consequent risks to India itself, and so they supplied without hesitation a force of 1,200,000 men, of whom 800,000 were active combatants, and also provided considerable financial aid. Part of the country, moreover, was in favour of the maintenance of the *status quo*.

The transfer of the Government to Delhi, the ancient Mogul capital, in 1911, and the great Durbar, conducted with magnificent display in the presence of George V as Emperor of India, with its solemn assembly of the vassal princes around the British throne, had given rise to promises of importance. India was therefore expecting a policy of liberal reform after the victory of 1918. But as a consequence of the wartime disturbances, the upheavals on account of the quarrel with the Caliphate, and the impatience that had too long been restrained, there were measures of repression which were both violent and humiliating, as happened also in Ireland in 1920. The most serious events in India took place at Amritsar in April 1919, when a number of Europeans were massacred and public buildings burnt down; the military subsequently fired on an unarmed crowd, which had collected in defiance of a ban, killing 379 and wounding 1,208.

From then onwards, in spite of numerous conferences, resolutions, and partial reforms, the Indian independence movement was carried on irrevocably, sometimes with outbreaks of violence, but essentially by means of campaigns of non-co-operation and civil disobedience, and thanks to the realization of an increasing section of British public opinion that it was neither just nor feasible to maintain imperial rule over a country which was ready for self-government. The Constitution of 1935 already accorded to India provincial parliaments and ministers, but this was not carried out without clashes, disturbances, and frequent imprisonment of Indian leaders. It was then that a group of patriots, who were to be the first leaders of the independent India, grew up ; it included men such as Nehru, the son of Motital Nehru, who was already one of the leading figures of modern India, Vallabhai Patel, Rajendra Prasad, and Rajagopalachari.

The whole question was raised again at the time of the 1939 war. In 1940, the Congress proposed a policy of co-operation in the war effort if the demand for independence were accepted, and so India once more participated valiantly in the campaigns that were to lead to victory. Her collaboration was nevertheless constantly accompanied from 1942 onwards by the demand, "Quit India ! " and she did not condemn the activities of Subhas Chandra Bose, who armed a force of "Free Indians" to fight with the Germans and the Japanese. Subhas Chandra Bose, known as *Netaji* ("leader"—a translation of Führer), who was killed in 1945, is still a popular hero of the independence movement.

Between the two wars the purely Indian political parties were augmented by some influenced by English politics or world movements, and the most significant of these to come into being was the Indian Communist Party.

After the end of the War the question was no longer whether India should achieve independence, but the form that the independence should take. The price of the decision was the division into the two Dominions of India and Pakistan. The co-operation of Lord Mountbatten with the Congress leaders brought matters to a swift conclusion, and independence was declared on August 15, 1947.

But the partition effected was not without its tragic element. Between the two parts of Pakistan and the stretch of Northern India that separates them population movements were immediately carried out which may be described as battling currents of frantic emigration, involving massacres on both sides, reciprocal reprisals on the part of both Hindu and Moslem communities on emigrants who had, moreover, generally lost all their possessions. The riots in Calcutta and Delhi in August and September 1947 made it appear for a moment that India would revert to anarchy and atrocities now that the British protection was withdrawn. But the Moslems were not systematically banished from India. Those of the south,

Dr Rajendra Prasad, first President of the Republic of India

and those who were not influenced by the fear (instigated by the Moslem League) of a Hindu Government, realized that they were dealing with a tolerant Government and did not emigrate. Under the influence of moral authority, and in particular that of Gandhi, the massacres ceased. But Gandhi was shot on January 30, 1948 by a nationalist who accused him of supporting too accommodating a form of Hinduism.

Though violence had come to an end, the situation of the refugees remained desperate for a long time. To this other serious problems were added, such as how the population was to be fed, how unity should be achieved, social questions solved, necessary equipment obtained, or international relations carried out. But most of these problems were not new, and independence removed some of the obstacles or causes of delay, though it also gave rise to ill-considered aspirations. India retained the public services which were already manned by Indian civil servants. Her leaders had already studied at length, as members of the opposition or even in prison, affairs of state and the economic situation. They were therefore ready to carry on the work that Britain had begun, not independently of them, but with their criticism and protests, and also with their assistance. It was a difficult task, but one with which they were familiar.

2

HINDU AND MOSLEM INDIA

BEFORE BRITISH RULE

The unfortunate clashes and political differences between the Hindus and the Moslems which were characteristic of the period of British rule and which cast a shadow over the early days of independence do not represent in any way the normal and inevitable state of their mutual relations. Not only did Southern India remain undisturbed by these troubles but, before the European conquests, Hindu and Moslem communities managed to live peaceably side by side for centuries, even when their princes were at war with each other. Though the land was frequently ravaged by these conflicts, they were rarely religious wars, and differed very little from the clashes that occurred between two Moslem or two Hindu princes.

Except during the initial period of invasion, when the Moslem kings showed intolerance, Hindus and Moslems frequently lived side by side in India in a spirit of compromise. The division of Hindu society into castes implied formal limitations in matters of outside contacts, and had the effect of forbidding private and family relationships, and thus prevented infringements of privacy and causes of conflict. But it left the Hindus free to pursue normal relations in matters of business, politics, administration, and, even though such contacts were less frequent, in the scientific and cultural fields. Moreover, men who owed no allegiance to any social group, or to the orthodox beliefs of their family background, had for a long time discovered themselves to be of the same mind in matters of religion and mystique, were they Hindus or Moslems. Finally, Hindu society had already acquired the art of living in the traditional manner on the fringe of Moslem domination, as it was to do later under the British Empire. It even retained its full characteristics to a higher degree under the Moslems, for it was more influenced in less than two hundred years by European civilization than it was by Islam over a period of seven centuries.

The Hindus had been humiliated, persecuted, and impoverished by the Moslem conquest, and the expansion of their civilization had been curbed, but the long periods of calm that were established on different occasions brought about eras of peace and prosperity to which many travellers bore witness. The state in which the European trading companies found India in the eighteenth century, when the Emperor at Delhi no longer had any real power and various claimants were disputing the right to rule the different provinces, was not the normal state of the

Avudaiyarkovil (Tanjavur district): King Arimardanapandya

Madurai: the marriage of Minakshi and Sundaresvara, with Vishnu playing the part of the bride's father (seventeenth century) ▶

Stucco decoration on a temple in Tiruchirapalli (eighteenth century)

country, though the situation was by no means a new one.

The European companies arrived at a time of crisis, when the Mogul Empire was disintegrating, and this crisis was prolonged by their interventions.

The Hindu or Moslem kingdoms between which India was divided, and particularly the Mogul Empire, had presented a very different picture to foreign travellers in the preceding centuries. There had been continuous wars, but they were waged between great powers that were firmly established. Chroniclers and travellers had been particularly interested in the lives of the princes, which were greatly disturbed by rivalry, intrigue, treachery, assassinations, and military expeditions, and they described the strength of these princes and sometimes the atrocities committed by them, but generally speaking they dealt in a more summary fashion with the life of the people. They give the impression that there was perpetual disorder everywhere. But it must be observed that in fact the disturbances they describe were scattered over several centuries and over vast areas of the country. Many regions enjoyed extensive periods of peace, and in some of them the disturbances were practically nonexistent. The political situation therefore allowed the administrative authorities of the villages full exercise of their powers, and agriculture, industry, and trade were carried on normally. Moreover, even the writers who give detailed descriptions of the struggles are in agreement over the immense wealth of the country. They even give an exaggerated estimate of this wealth in the emphasis they place on the actions that were ruining the country as compared with the reasons they advance for the prosperity.

An even more valid witness to this prosperity is the enormous intellectual and artistic output of the whole country in the course of these centuries, both in Hindu and in Moslem circles. The most notable evidence is provided by the architecture and sculpture carried out in the period in question. It is, however, true that this is often considered as a manifestation of the ostentation of the princes, and that this external magnificence was perhaps a reason for the impoverishment of the people rather than an indication of the wealth of the country. But it must be observed that these monuments are to be found in all regions, and that, whether Moslem or Hindu, they are equally imposing and present the same high standard of execution; this implies the availability of a labour force not only extensive but also highly skilled, and one that existed throughout the period and in all parts of the country. These workers had to be paid and maintained, and the necessary materials and tools provided. All this suggests that in all the kingdoms in which these extensive projects were undertaken means existed that would be inconceivable in a state of anarchy, and which necessarily imply that the activities of the farmers and the craftsmen were maintained at a high level.

Tiruvadavur (Madurai district): bronze statue of Manikkavasagar, a saint of the Saiva sect

HINDU RULERS AND TRENDS IN SOUTHERN INDIA

The two principal powers in India in the period extending from the fifteenth to the seventeenth centuries were the Hindu Kingdom of Vijayanagar, which dominated the South with its brilliant civilization, and the magnificent Mogul Empire, which extended over the North, after having conquered the previous Moslem kingdoms that had for long been established there, and the emperors of which considered themselves not only the sovereigns but the heirs of the former rulers.

The Kingdom of Vijayanagar, which took its name from its capital, "the city of Victory", the ruins of which may be seen to-day at Hampi, on the Tungabhadra river, was founded in 1336, and for more than two centuries united the Hindu forces of the South against the opposition of the Islamic conquerors.

Even before the formation of this kingdom Hindu civilization and religion flourished throughout Southern India, and its art, science, and literature had been important for a long period, and were characterized by their constantly renewed activity. Sanskrit was the common language of learned circles, but each of the spoken languages had its own literature, each in its own domain, and these different literatures exerted a reciprocal influence on each other. In this way the Indo-Aryan Sanskrit civilization of the North and the Dravidian of the South came together and enriched each other. Philosophic and religious movements had been springing up for centuries in this region, in rivalry with each other and at times in conflict. One of their aims was to preserve the ancient sacred texts of the *Veda* and *Brahmana* which were striving after *bhukti*, the enjoyment of an ordered world; and with this they associated *bhakti*, the love of the unique Supreme Being who manifested himself in a whole host of divine forms. This philosophy proved through reason, finding the idea in the *Upanishads* which were attached to the *Veda*, the absolute essence of this Being. It was strongly monotheistic, and relegated any idea of polytheism to the worldly sphere. As far as the *bhukti* was concerned, it admitted the existence of gods of nature, but it taught how man might free himself from them through the ultimate *mukti* (liberation), thanks to the *bhakti* of devoted worshippers and the knowledge (*jnana*) taught

*Pallavanesvaram
(Tanjavur district):
bronze statue
of the goddess Uma
and her child Skanda*

by the philosophy itself. These ideas and this out-look were nowhere else more fitted to combat Islam and to refute its common accusation of gross idolatry. It was, indeed, in Southern India that the great Dravidian philosophers of the *Vedanta,* the final crowning realization of the *Veda,* had successively formulated their doctrines. It was there, too, that Hinduism was kept constantly alive, through fierce controversy as well as by study and piety.

Literary activity had long flourished, especially in the Tamil, Kanarese, and Telugu languages, as well as in Sanskrit. There was also considerable literary activity in Marathi and in regions bordering those in which Marathi was spoken, where the local dialect was akin to Gujarati. An example of this was the coastal area of Konkan, one of the important centres of which was Ratnagiri, later the home of the Brahmanic caste of the *Chitpavan,* who were important in the Ma-

ratha country from the seventeenth century onwards. A work written in Marathi as early as
1290 was the *Jnanesvari*, named after its author,
Jnanasvar; it was a work which exemplified the
monistic teaching of the *Bhagavadgita*. At the beginning of the fourteenth century another Marathi writer, Namdev, sang the praises of Vitthal,
Vishnu worshipped in Pandharpur, where the
poet was born.

In the Tamil, Saivistic literature included the
ever-popular hymns in honour of *bhakti* and collections of the legends of devout worshippers,
such as the *Periyapuranam* composed by Sekilar
(Chekizar) in the twelfth century ; and side by
side with them the development of the traditions
of Meykandar ("He who has seen the truth")
and of the master of Saivistic thought, Arunandi
("Fortunate through grace"). These two philosophers had founded at the beginning of the thirteenth century the *Saivasiddhanta*, a doctrine that
still remains one of the major currents of the traditional philosophy of the country. They established a conception of man as a sheep (*pasu*) held
in the grip of a bond (*pasa*), the world, from
which the shepherd (*pati*)—that is to say, God
—will deliver him. In Vaishnava literature the
school of Ramanuja was particularly significant,
and one of its important works, which is still considered authoritative, was that of Vedantadesika,
who was born at Kanchi in 1268. The hymns and
poems of the devout Tamils, known as *Alvar*,
were the object of detailed expositions in Tamil,
Sanskrit, and a technical language in which
Sanskrit terms and grammatical forms were
mingled with Tamil phrases; this language is
known as *manipravalam* (pearl and coral), symbolic of the union of the two jewels of the Sanskrit and Tamil languages.

In the Kanarese-speaking territories there was
a flourishing Jain literature, comprising the lives
of the great religious sages, and Jain versions of
the Brahmanistic and Hindu legends and epics,
such as the *Ramayana* composed by Pampa in
the twelfth century. The literature of the Virasaiva or Lingayats had also been important since
the foundation of the sect by Basava, also in the
twelfth century. The *Vacana* ("utterances"),
popular texts in a very simple language, had
from the earliest times begun to constitute a literature of exhortation to the devotion to Siva that
was within the grasp of all.

In addition to the Lingayat movement, which
broke away from the customs of caste and ritual
observances, there was the royal traditional Saivism, for which an ever-increasing number of
sanctuaries were built. At Dvarasamudra, the

*Twentieth-century imitation of a temple pillar
of the Vijayanagar style*

207

capital of the Hoysala dynasty, on the site of the
present-day Halebidu ("the ancient abode"),
the temple of Siva Hoysalesvara ("Lord of the
Hoysalas") bears witness to the strength and the
delicate style of the architecture and sculpture of
the Kanarese country. The intricacy of the carv-
ing of the stone, treated by the artists as if it were
wood or ivory, make it rank as a masterpiece.
Vaishnavism had also in the twelfth century been
a source of inspiration for the construction of
monuments of similar style, such as the temple of
Kesava at Somnathpur and the temple of Cen-
nakesava at Belur; it experienced a period of
renewed fervour when Ramanuja was expelled
from Srirangam, near Tiruchirapalli, in the
Tamil country, by an intolerant sectarian Saivistic sovereign, and went to stay at Melukote in the
Kanarese country. In the thirteenth century
Madhva had founded at Udipi the Vedantic
school that was called by outsiders *dvaita* (dua-
lism), because it taught a belief in the dual existence of God and the world, though at the same

time it gave full power and supremacy to the one
and only Vishnu.

In the Telugu-speaking country (Telingana or
Andhra) the Lingayat movement had gained
rapidly, and among the earliest manifestations of
Telugu literature was a life, written partly in
Sanskrit and partly in Telugu, of Panditaradhya,
one of the precursors of Basava. Another early
Telugu work was a *Basavapuranamu*. Both of
these were written by Somanatha, who was active
at Kakati (Varangal) in the second half of the
twelfth century, during the reign of King Prataparudra I, of the Kakatiya dynasty. In the preceding century Nannayya Bhatta had already
composed a Telugu version of part of the *Mahabharata*. Prataparudra himself had either written
or ordered the composition of the *Nitisaramu*, a
collection of rules of conduct. Another Prataparudra, who reigned at Varangal from 1294 to
1323, had been a patron of Sanskrit letters, and
his praises had been sung in the *Prataparudriya-
yasobhushana* ("the ornament of the fame of
Prataparudra"), a treatise of rhetoric which
Vidyanatha had dedicated to him. But Prataparudra also encouraged Telugu poetry, and Raga-
natha, the principal author of the Telugu *Ramayana*, was his friend.

*Vyaghrapada, " the tiger-footed,"
one of the mythical sages of Chidambaram
(twentieth century imitation of
Vijayanagar style)*

Thus intellectual and artistic activity flourished in similar yet distinct forms in the Tamil, Telugu, Kanarese, Marathi, and even the Gujarati areas, forming altogether a cultural entity strong enough to oppose Islam, even when the hazards of warfare gave the Moslems the advantage.

It has also become a tradition in India to group together men of these regions which are called the five Dravidas after their languages, even through Marathi and Gujarati belong to the Indo-Aryan linguistic family and not to the Dravidian. But this group, which lived to the south of the Vindhya Mountains, was in contact by way of the east coast route with another Hindu group, known as the five Gaudas, living in five regions to the north of the Vindhya Mountains. They were the Sarasvatas of the region to the west of the Yamuna basin; the Kanyakubjas farther east in the Ganges valley; the Maithilikas of the area farther east still, to the north of the Ganges; the true Gaudas or Bengalis; and the Utkalas of Odra or Orissa. This classification covers the total extent of the Hindu areas at a time when the Moslem conquests had overrun the whole Indus Basin, West and North-west India north of the Vindhya Mountains, part of the Ganges Basin,

and probably even areas included in the region of the five Gaudas, where Hindu civilization was still tolerated.

The area linking the region of the five Dravidas with that of the five Gaudas was Kalinga, where the principal language was Telugu. This region extended from Telingana and the river Godavari in the south to the lands of the Mahanadi Basin in the north, known as Odra or Utkala, where Oriya, an Indo-Aryan language, was spoken. The country inland, the upper valley of the Mahanadi, formed the Gondwana, the forest lands of the Gonds, an area that still remains outside the general currents of Indian civilization. At the beginning of the fourteenth century, when the Southern forces were about to be grouped together under the Vijayanagar Empire, Hindu civilization had flourished in Kalinga and Odra as much as in the lands of the five Dravidas. For several centuries the adherents of the cults of Siva and Vishnu had vied with each other to build temples throughout an area in which there were countless sanctuaries and holy places dating back to very ancient times. The present temple of Jagannath ("the protector of the world") at Puri was constructed in the

209

*Vishnu in his incarnation
as the child Krishna
(twentieth-century imitation of
Vijayanagar style)*

twelfth century on the site of a former sanctuary. It is dedicated to Vishnu under the names of Jagannatha and Purushottama ("supreme man"). The principal statue contrasts greatly with all other manifestations of Indian art. It consists of a block of wood, roughly carved in the form of a human bust, with two stumps of arms. According to legend, a divine artist, Visvakarman, had undertaken to carve the holy image out of wood washed up by the sea, on the condition that nobody should watch him while he was at work. The King was overcome by curiosity, with the result that the artist abandoned the work when it was scarcely begun. In the twelfth century the temple of Purushottama was visited by Ramanuja, whose unfulfilled wish was to reform the worship there according to the rules that he himself had instituted at Srirangam. But the sanctuary of Jagannath clung jealously to its own conception of orthodoxy, and still remains, after all the vicissitudes of its history, one of the main centres of pilgrimage of the Vishnu cult. The chief manifestation that attracts pilgrims is the annual procession of the divinity in a monumental chariot. There is a legend still spread abroad by travellers that devout worshippers throw themselves under the wheels of the chariot in order to be crushed by the god; though it is nearly a hundred years since W. W. Hunter pointed out that these were accidents, due to the size of the chariot and the closely packed crowd.

A dancer: sculpture in the temple of Chidambaram

Sun-worship, later abandoned, was allied to the cult of Vishnu. To this sect we owe the masterpiece of architecture and sculpture of the Temple of Konark (Konarak) in Orissa, built by King Narasimha I (1238-64), who for a time repelled the Moslems of Bengal.

Odra and Kalinga, ruled by various dynasties, had no political link with the southern union of Vijayanagar. They were in equal conflict with

*The pool and one of the towers at the entrance
to the temple of Chidambaram* ▶

Chidambaram: Nagas
(mythical creatures, half human, half serpent)

then the Kakatiyas of Varangal, to the south of the Godavari; then the Hoysalas of Dvarasamudra, in the land to the south of the Krishna and the Tungabhadra; and finally the Pandyas of Madurai. These conquests brought him as far south as the island of Ramesvaram, which lies opposite Ceylon. But a series of revolts, the death of Ala-ud-din, Malik Kafur's *coup d'état* at Delhi, and the final collapse of the Khalji dynasty gave a moment of respite to the kingdoms of the South, where the invasion had brought about upheaval among the rulers, and had given rise to strife and disorder. It was not long before Muhammad Tughlak, founder of the Tughlak dynasty, marched south. In 1323 his son captured Prataparudra II at Varangal, and renamed the city Sultanpur. Muhammad Tughlak then transferred his own capital from Delhi to Devagiri ("the mountain of the gods"), calling it Daulatabad ("the abode of happiness"). The transfer was unfortunate and short-lived, for by 1329 Muhammad Tughlak was already returning to the North.

Before this, in 1327, he had taken Kampili,

the Vijayanagar Empire and with the kingdoms and expeditionary forces of the Moslems, and were nominally absorbed into the Mogul Empire only in 1578. It was the Kanarese, Telugus, and Tamils, the true Dravidians, who, though linked by religion and civilization to this Hindu kingdom, grouped together within the Vijayanagar Empire to make a stand against the assaults of Islam. The Moslem attacks came first from the Sultanate of Delhi and the kingdoms that paid tribute to it, and later from the Mogul Empire.

The Sultanate of Delhi first attacked the South at the end of the thirteenth century in the reign of Ala-ud-din Khalji. Gujarat and the Yadavas of Devagiri were forced to pay tribute, and in 1297 the Vaghela dynasty of Gujarat was conquered. But it was in 1309-10, at the time of the violent campaign of Malik Kafur, the general of Ala-ud-din, that the Moslem armies for a time disturbed the whole of the South and began to arouse a spirit of reaction. Kafur first conquered the Yadavas of Devagiri, reputedly the descendants of the race among which Vishnu was incarnated in the form of Krishna, at the time of the war described in the *Mahabharata*;

A dancer: sculpture in the temple of Chidambaram

chaos that marked the beginning of the present cycle, a column of fire appeared to Brahman and Vishnu, who were fighting for supremacy; neither Brahman, who had taken the form of a bird (*hamsa*), nor Vishnu, transformed into a wild boar, could reach the top nor root to the bottom of it, and it was in this way that they came to understand its infinite nature. This column of fire was was the first *linga* (sign) of Siva, the true Supreme Being. The huge fire lit there every year at the festival is symbolic of the *linga* of fire, and still attracts pilgrims. It is also in this holy place at the foot of the mountains that in recent times the Maharshi Ramana lived in meditation.

It is not a fortified place, but legends recount the miracles wrought by Siva on behalf of the armies of his worshippers, and it was therefore probably not sheer chance that led Ballala to retire to Tiruvannamalai. In any case, the Saivistic faith, and the Lingayat cult in particular, led the inhabitants of the Kanarese and Telugu areas to offer a prompt resistance to the Moslem invaders; and it was this same faith that in modern times inspired firm opposition to the British in Karnataka. Kampili and the coastal region were soon reconquered by Ballala and two zealous Lingayat chieftains, Prolaya Nayak and Kapaya Nayak. In order to meet the situation the Sultan of Delhi sent as envoys two Hindu princes who had been captured in Kampili and converted to Islam. But they promptly returned to the Hindu faith, inspired by the stand that it was making against Moslem ascendancy.

These two princes, the brothers Harihara and Bukka, founded the city of Vijayanagar in 1336, guided by Vidyaranya ("Forest of Knowledge"), one of the sages of Saradapitha ("the Seat of Wisdom"), the centre of a movement started by the philosopher Sankaracarya at Sringeri. The sage was in meditation at a temple near the Tungabhadra, dedicated to Virupaksha, a terrible form of Siva. It was there that he counselled them to found the city, at first named Vidyanagar ("City of Knowledge"), which was planned in order to bring good fortune in the form of a *shrichakra* ("Circle of Fortune"). Harihara was named king, and the dedication ceremony took place in the temple of Virupaksha. The two brothers joined with the men who had already taken up the struggle and succeeded in emancipating the country, but the Hoysala king was killed in 1342 in an expedition against the Sultan who was established in Madurai. In 1344 the Hoysala succession fell to Bukka, and shortly afterwards he conquered the

after an heroic resistance on the part of the Raja, and had then laid waste the Kanarese country of Dvarasamudra; but the Hoysala King, Ballala III, had retired farther east to Tiruvannamalai in the Tamil country. In this place there is a mountain similar to Kailasa, the home of Siva; and, according to a religious tradition that is still current, it is the place where, in the midst of the

Chidambaram: a dancer ▶

Tulu-speaking country around Mangalur. In 1346 Harihara, Bukka, and their three brothers went to Sringeri to celebrate the victory in the presence of Bharatikrishnatirtha, the representative of Sankaracarya at the Seat of Wisdom. The kingdom of Vijayanagar, which was an empire consisting of several kingdoms, was thus placed under the spiritual leadership and given the benediction of the *jagadguru* ("preceptors of the world"), the sages of the *Vedanta*.

The Vijayanagar Empire was henceforth pledged not only to establish the Hindu *dharma* from a political point of view, but also to protect the sacred literature. It was the duty of the princes as temporal guardians of the *dharma* to develop ritual and to promote the study of the *Veda*. Bukka did this by giving his patronage to several Vedic scholars, including Sayana, the best-known commentator of the *Veda,* and his brother Madhava. Bukka thus acquired the title of Vaidikamargapravartaka ("promoter of the Vedic way"). He also was a patron of the Saivistic tradition of the Agama, the ritualism of which was less naturalistic, and emphasized the importance of adoration and devotion. He appointed as minister another Madhava, who was a commentator of another important Saivistic work, the *Sutasamhita*. His *rajguru* ("royal preceptor") was Kashivilasakriyasakti, a master of this minister; he was a devout worshipper of Siva, and followed the Saivistic doctrines of Kashmir. Through this official leadership, which was in harmony with public opinion in general and particularly with the ideas of the Lingayats, there was a real renaissance of Vedic studies, particularly among the Brahmins of the *smarta* ("traditionalist") group; at the same time there was a development of all the forms of Vedantic doctrine, and Kanarese, Telugu, and Tamil literature acquired an increasing amount of Sanskrit terminology and rhetoric.

The Tamil country, with its own traditions and its adaptation to Northern or Sanskrit civilization, continued, as it had done for a number of centuries, to provide the Telugu and Kanarese countries with strong sources of inspiration through its religious literature, and its tendency towards the contemplation of the Absolute, personified as the dispenser of grace and the object of adoration. The new movement in favour of Vedic and classical erudition, which received the patronage of the court, came from the North. A material witness to this fact was the increasing use in royal inscriptions and official charters in Sanskrit of a script used only in the Vijayanagar Empire, the Nandinagari script, derived from the Nagari of the

The Fort of Jingi near Tiruvannamalai

West, itself closely linked with the Nagari of the North. Nevertheless in the Tulu country, where the language, which belonged to the Dravidian group, had no literature of its own, the Vedic texts were written and preserved in a script allied to the *Grantha* of the Tamil area. The *Veda* had existed throughout the educated and Brahmin circles of the South long before the foundation of the Vijayanagar Empire; with the renewal of this study, encouraged by the rulers, they were transliterated into all the different scripts in use in the area, and were by no means solely an import from the North.

The Telugu element appears to have been favoured for the appointment to official positions throughout the Empire, on account of its foundation by a Telugu dynasty. The village with its local assembly was the basis of the administrative organization. Territories consisting of a certain number of villages grouped round a main one, or sometimes a more extensive area, constituting a *rajya* (kingdom), were administered by a *Nayaka* (governor).

The *Nayaka* collected the land taxes and taxes on commercial transactions, which formed the basis of the finance of the local area and the Empire, and he also maintained troops which were held at the disposal of the central authorities. The activities of the *Nayaka* were supervised by agents of the central Government. Many of the *Nayakas* and the landowners came from the Telugu country, and in this way a caste of owners, the *Reddi*, was often established outside the Telugu territory; they were, moreover, accompanied by Telugu castes of traders and artisans. Servile castes also sometimes joined the little Telugu colonies set up in the Tamil country and considered by the inhabitants as intruders.

The cohesion and organization of the Empire was favourable to steady activity in agriculture, trade, and industry. According to the descriptions given by various travellers, and by the Portuguese who had settled along the coast, the capital was one of the largest cities in the world. Most people were impressed by its buildings and its great festivals, one of which was the festival of Durga, where great hosts of buffaloes and goats were sacrificed, and by the sacrifice of the *sati* on the funeral pyres of their husbands.

Important building projects carried out, which included not only the construction of temples and palaces but also public works, were a source of wonderment to foreigners. Examples of this are the building of a dyke along the banks of the Tungabhadra and the construction of a great aqueduct at Vijayanagar.

But the Empire never experienced a long period of peace. The unity of the princes who founded it was remarkable, and contrasted strongly with the rivalry and treachery that prevailed at this period among feudal princes, whether Hindu or Moslem. But this unity did not stand the test of time, especially in the numerous periods of wars between the rival kingdoms seeking to usurp the central power.

On the Hindu side, the kingdom of Kalinga and Odra went to war against Vijayanagar several times, principally in the fifteenth century, and there were numerous frontier changes in the eastern coastal area between the rivers Godavari and Kaveri.

Hindu civilization did not cease to flourish on either side ; its manifestations were on the whole different in the two areas, though in no way exclusive. Generally speaking, Vijayanagar followed the Saivistic cults, and Odra the Vaishnavistic. Prataparudra Gajapati of Odra (1497-1540) became a disciple of Chaitanya, important for his revival of the cult of the love of Krishna ; Chaitanya travelled or sent his disciples throughout the Vijayanagar Empire and a great part of the remainder of India.

MOSLEM POWERS
IN THE SOUTH

The common enemy of the two great Hindu powers was Islam, represented by the kingdom of the Bahmanis, which became established in 1347, a little after the Vijayanagar Empire, and which dominated the whole territory from the lands north of the Godavari to the Krishna. It was supported on the west by the Moslem powers of the west coast area, and limited on the east by the Vijayanagar Empire, which extended over the rich area of the deltas of the two rivers.

The kingdom of the Bahmanis came into existence after a secession of the Moslem powers of the Deccan, which had in the first place been established in the name of Muhammad Tughlak, Sultan of Delhi. Abul Muzzafar Ala ud-din Bahman Shah, the ruler who founded it, and who had himself proclaimed Sultan in 1347, claimed descent from the Persian epic hero Bahman. He set up his capital at Gulbarga, and appointed governors in the other territories that constituted his domain, at Daulatabad and Bidar, and in Berar. He was succeeded by his eldest son, Muhammad I (1358-77), who consolidated the new kingdom and began a series of struggles with the Vijayanagar Empire, which was frequently attacked by the subsequent Sultans of the same dynasty. These Sultans made a great effort to introduce as much Persian civilization as possible into the country, by constructing large numbers of magnificent buildings in the Persian style, and by giving encouragement to the production of Persian literature in the kingdom. Hafiz of Chiraz, the greatest of the Persian lyric poets, was even invited by Muhammad II (1378-97). It is related that he set sail, but was forced to turn back by a tempest in the Persian Gulf. But it was not the arts, literature, and the ordered conduct of public affairs which characterized the Kingdom of the Bahmans. It was, like most other states, founded by reason of the ambition of intriguing rulers, torn by rivalry, revolts, assassinations, and every form of court intrigue and revolution, in spite of the efforts of administrators of real worth like Mahmud Gavan, who was sacrificed by the Sultan Muhammad III in 1481 on account of slander.

The dynasty came to an end in 1527, and by then the division of the kingdom into five sultanates had already taken place. Berar appears to have seceded about 1484, the territory of Ahmanagar had declared its independence in 1490, and was to absorb Berar in 1574. The Kingdom of Bijapur, which was the most important, had been founded in 1489-90 by Yusuf Adil Khan, a Georgian slave of Mahmud Gavan; he is alleged by some to have been a Turkish Sultan who had escaped from a massacre and had taken refuge in Persia. Golkonda was made a kingdom in about 1512 under the leadership of a Turk, Kuli Kutb Shah, whom Mahmud Gavan had made governor of the Varangal region. The Bahmani dynasty came to an end at Bidar, where the rulers had established their capital after leaving Gulbarga, and it was Bidar that became the fifth sultanate until it was absorbed by Bijapur in 1619.

The adventurers who established kingdoms in this way came from all the different countries which owed allegiance to Islam. The lands conquered from the Hindus were subjected to a continuous stream of immigration of Moslems and of slaves from Negro Africa and Asia, and the immigrants even included Genoese and Venetians converted to Islam. These foreigners sometimes came into conflict with the Moslems who already occupied the country. Some were Sunnites, others Shiites, and they practised varying degrees of orthodoxy. Some professed exceedingly rigid principles and showed complete intolerance of "idolaters", which often led to massacre or plunder. But others lived peaceably with the Hindus and respected their faith, acknowledging its high worth in the ultimate impulse towards the Supreme Being. Hindus were employed in the administration. Moslems married Hindu women, and a quite considerable number of their leaders had Hindu mothers. Yusuf Adil Khan of Bijapur had married a Maratha woman, had Marathas in his service, and authorized the use of the Marathi language for conducting business. But in his kingdom at that time it was the Portuguese Albuquerque who exemplified intolerance and violence. Incited and helped by a Hindu chief whom the Portuguese called Timoia, Albuquerque seized Goa by a surprise attack in 1510, promising to respect the laws of the people and to reduce by one-third the tribute paid to the Moslem prince of Bijapur. He was expelled shortly afterwards, but recaptured the town in the November of the same year; this time the victory was followed by pillage, massacre, exile, and

confiscation, and the tribute was maintained at the former level. Moreover, in order to establish stability in the colony, Albuquerque forced baptism upon young women who were mainly Moslems, and compelled them to marry Portuguese. He thus treated the conquered country very much in the same way as the Moslems did on other occasions.

Whatever the religion of the conquerors was, many of them used it as a pretext for abuses, claiming to humiliate and slaughter the Hindus in the name of a faith of which the latter had no knowledge, and from which they were repelled by the harsh treatment and injustice committed in its name. Even the most peaceable among the conquerors were marked by a spirit of partiality; Muhammad II Bahmani, for example, a great lover of Persian literature, confined State aid dur-

The siege of a fortress.
Mogul painting of the seventeenth century

ing the famines of 1387 and 1395 to Moslems, though it is true that his resources were not sufficient for him to be able to help a vast population. But it is correct to say that the Bahmanis and the later Sultans were typical rulers of a conquered country, and their régime was characterized by the pomp of the rulers, maintained at the expense of the people. Athanasius Nikitine, a Russian merchant who visited Bidar between 1470 and 1474, was struck by the contrast between the luxury of the ruling classes and the poverty of the farmers.

Excesses, however, were not inevitable, as there were some Moslems whose outlook was liberal and conciliatory, and they found that they could live in harmony with the Hindus, who practised exclusiveness within the group, but who were tolerant to foreign communities. Moreover, the armies recruited to uphold the authority or claims of rival princes, often brothers or members of the same family, passed from one to the other, motivated by questions of pay or booty, without any consideration of nationalism. Outbursts of nationalism, like movements of religious solidarity, happened only on rare occasions. An example of such an outburst on the Hindu side was the concentration of national forces in opposition to the foreigner which gave rise to the creation of the Vijayanagar Empire. And in 1565, more than two centuries later, a coalition of Moslem Sultanates vanquished this same Empire. It was then, indeed, that Ram Raya, who exercised his rule under the nominal authority of King Sadasiva, was conquered and killed in a fierce battle in which he had been unwise enough to engage in his service two Moslem contingents, who turned against him during the action. The city of Vijayanagar was then captured and systematically destroyed as a result of five months of vandalism.

A princess receiving a painter, who is presenting her with her portrait, and a musician.
Mogul painting of the eighteenth century

The strength of the Moslem armies was in their artillery and more particularly in their cavalry. Horses do not prosper in the Indian climate, and the steady import of Persian mounts, one of the major aspects of trade at the time, and one in which the Portuguese competed with the Moslems, gave the latter considerable advantages in warfare. The elephants of the Hindu princes were difficult to control in combat, and were subject to panic, which sometimes made them turn against the army that they were supporting, so that they were far from being a compensation for lack of cavalry.

The destruction of Vijayanagar came very shortly before the weakening of the Sultanates that conquered it. The development of the Mogul Empire throughout Northern India was already threatening the South, and began by undermining the power of the Moslem rulers in the areas nearest to it, though the southern elements of the Vijayanagar Empire held firm. Thanks to them, a new dynasty, the Aravidu, extended the power

A girl reading and smoking a hookah.
Mogul painting of the eighteenth century

of the earlier Vijayanagar dynasties until the middle of the seventeenth century. But the kingdoms of which the Empire had been composed became independent one after the other. The principal ones were Mysore and the Nayaka kingdoms of Madurai and Tanjavur (Tanjore).

Tirumala Nayakkar (1623-59) was distinguished by the construction at Madurai of the great temple of Minakshi and Sundaresvara, to-day one of the most famous temples in the whole of India. The legendary history of the city is still celebrated there, as are the miracles of Siva, performed in his incarnation as Sundaresvara, or, in Tamil, Sokkanadar ("the Handsome Lord"), superb husband of Tadadagai ("the Irresistible"), born, through the grace of Siva himself, as Queen of the Pandya country. This *kumari* ("young girl") was the virgin warrior who gave her name to the most southerly headland of the peninsula, known to Europeans as Cape Comorin. She could be conquered in love only by Sundaresvara, for she was the incarnation of his eternal wife, Parvati.

Tanjavur had been taken over and governed since 1674 by a Maratha dynasty, which remained in power until the British annexation in 1799, though it was allowed to rule nominally until it became extinct in 1855. The Maratha

princes collected in this city, which has a famous temple, one of the most important libraries existing in India to-day. It is housed in the Maratha palace, where the principal collection of Tamil bronzes in existence is also to be seen.

Mysore acquired autonomy under Raja Odeyar (1578-1617), a descendant of a branch of the Yadava of Devagiri. The dynasty that he founded was overthrown by the Moslems, and two of their well-known rulers were Haidar Ali and his son Tipu, who during the eighteenth century were allies of the French against the British until the time of the defeat and death of Tipu in 1799. The Hindu dynasty was subsequently re-established, and its present representative is the Maharaja Sri Jaya Chamarajendra Wadiyar Bahadur, who became Governor when his kingdom became part of the Indian Republic.

ISLAM OF THE NORTH AND THE MOGUL EMPERORS

The Moslem invasions of India began as early as the first century of the Hegira, which started in 622 (the beginning of the Islamic era), the year marked by the journey of Mahomet from

A combat on fantastic elephants.
Mogul painting of the eighteenth century

Akbar. From Manucci, Histoire du Mogol ▶

A girl and an antelope.
Mogul painting of the eighteenth century

mathematician came to Baghdad with a *Siddhanta,* or treatise on astronomy. It was at this period that the Arabs learnt of the trigonometrical sine, which was an Indian invention, and the numerical system using the figures 9 to 0; this system, which was current in India, was borrowed by the Arabs and transmitted to Europe, where the signs that are in reality of Indian origin are referred to as Arabic numerals.

Indian medicine was studied in a similar way by the Arabs in their early thirst for knowledge as well as for fresh territories. For their part, the Hindus from the beginning entered into relations with the Arab scholars without reticence. But from the tenth and twelfth centuries onwards their relationships became rarer and more difficult because of the armed attacks on the Hindus by the Moslems, and also because the Arabs and the Persians at this time were turning increasingly towards the acquisition of Greek knowledge, as it was more accessible, belonging to the civilization of countries nearer their own, and being in part translated into Syriac, a Semitic language like Arabic. Moreover, Indian science was presented in the form of mnemotechnic compilations

Mecca to Medina. At first they took the form of attacks on the west coast and momentary incursions. But in 712 the Arabs seized the Sindh territories of the lower Indus Basin and then advanced as far as Multan. Their rule in the Sindh appears to have been lenient. They encouraged conversion to Islam, but restricted themselves to imposing on non-Moslems a capitation tax known as *jizya* ("compensation"). They managed to recruit in India troops which they used in 767 against the Byzantines. From this time onward they played an increasing rôle in the overseas trade of the Indians and even of the Chinese, and right up to modern times trade was considerably developed by them and by the Persians between the Persian Gulf, Arabia and Africa on the one hand, and India and the Far East, including China, on the other. They were, moreover, doing no more than continuing the tradition of merchant shipping that Herodotus had already attributed to them in the fifth century B.C.

The Arabs of the Sindh were responsible to the Caliphs of Baghdad. It was during the reigns of two of these rulers, al-Mansur and al-Mamun, that the greatest efforts were made to acquire Greek, Syriac, and also Indian scientific knowledge and to transmit it into Arabic. In about 772, during the reign of al-Mansur, an Indian

A bird-catcher.
Provincial school of the eighteenth century

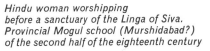

*Hindu woman worshipping
before a sanctuary of the Linga of Siva.
Provincial Mogul school (Murshidabad?)
of the second half of the eighteenth century*

difficult to tackle. Finally, it belonged to a race of people considered as idolaters, against whom the Moslems were engaged in active struggle, while the "idolatry" of Aristotle, Ptolemy, or any of the other Greeks of antiquity belonged to a forgotten era.

The clashes with the inhabitants of India began with the invasions of the Afghans (known as Pathans in India), who came under Turkish authority. Ghazna was attacked by Alptigin in 962 and then by Sabuktigin in 977. The latter attacked Jaypal, the Hindu ruler of Lahore, and defeated the coalition of Hindu princes formed to withstand him. His son, Mahmud, led the first of the great invasions that became progressively destructive from the year 1000 onwards. In 999 Mahmud had made a vow to lead a holy war (*jihad*) against the Hindus every year, and he partially fulfilled this vow, though he acquired more treasure for himself than Moslem converts. But, by declaring themselves converts to Islam,

Hindus could have access to any post. Islamic exclusiveness has, indeed, always been religious and never racial. This fact is of great significance, for, aided by the Indian spirit of religious tolerance, Hindus have often, in the course of the centuries, found it easier to live on amicable terms with Moslems than with certain Europeans who despised them. Mahmud himself, having converted Sukhpal, the grandson of Jaypal, made him a ruler, though Sukhpal betrayed him by returning to Hinduism. On the other hand Anandapal, the father of Sukhpal, made an alliance with Abdul Fath Daud, the Moslem ruler of Multan, against Mahmud, and then offered his aid to Mahmud against the enemies who were attacking him in the rear in central Asia; and he finally rallied a coalition of the Hindu kingdoms of the West to attack Mahmud again. In spite of the fundamental religious barrier, the Moslem and Hindu princes, from this onwards and throughout the course of

*Akbar at a combat
between two black antelopes.
Mogul painting of the eighteenth century,
copy of a work of the school of Akbar*

history, made a general practice of changing their alliances and attitudes according to the political opinion of the moment, very much like the rulers of mediæval and modern Europe.

Mahmud succeeded, by a series of expeditions, in breaking up Indian resistance, whether it was that of the Moslems under the command of Daud or the Hindus of Anandapal and his allies. These expeditions ended in the capture of the Panjab, the destruction of the temples at Mathura, a holy place dedicated to Krishna, the overthrow of the Pratihara dynasty of Kanauj, a passage across the desertic regions of Rajputana to elude Hindu resistance, and the destruction of the temple of Siva at Somnath, a famous place of pilgrimage in the Gujarat, in 1026.

These invasions, which were accompanied by terrible violence, aroused hatred in India against Islam, as is recorded by the Persian scholar al-Beroni (973-1048), who had settled in the Panjab and made a serious study of Sanskrit and Indian civilization. But, in spite of the hatred spread by the Turkish conqueror, Indian scientists did not hesitate to give information to this

Jahangir with a portrait of Akbar (seventeenth century) ▶

شبیه حضرت جهانگیر پادشاه که شبیه حضرت اکبر پادشاه را می‌بیند

scholar, who was one of the greatest Arabic writers, and he was thus enabled to compile an important work on Indian civilization, the *Tarikh al-Hind*.

In 1173 Muhammad Ghori, the Afghan prince of Ghor, seized Ghazna from the Turks, and from 1175 onwards led attacks against the Moslems of Multan, who belonged to the Ismailian sect, though he fought without success against the Hindu Gujarat. In 1191 he was beaten once

more by Prithviraj, the king of Delhi and a hero of Rajput chivalry, but in 1192 Prithviraj fell in a second battle, and this left open the whole of the Ganges valley to the Afghans. The onslaught of Prithviraj and the Rajput warriors was not an isolated impulse. Its praises were sung in a vast poem in Western Hindi, the *Prithviraj rasau*, composed by Chand Bardai of Lahore, and it has never failed to inspire the proud courage of Rajput leaders who followed the epic tradition of the heroes of the *Mahabharata* and the *Ramayana* of ancient India.

The conquests were continued by Kutb-ud-din Aibek, one of the Turkish *mamluks* (slaves) of Muhammad Ghori, whom he made viceroy, and by Muhammad ibn Bakhtyar Khalji, who reached Bengal in 1199, after fighting his way through Audh and Bihar.

The conquest of Bihar and Bengal spelt disaster for the Buddhism that flourished there under the influence of numerous monasteries, for it was suppressed by the death or dispersal of the monks. Many of the monks emigrated to Tibet or Indochina, and in this way the Moslem invasion had the unforeseen effect of helping to spread Buddhism, if not in Tibet, where it was already deeply rooted, at least in South-east Asia. Hindu temples were destroyed, but the faith survived among the people, as it is a religion which, unlike Buddhism, is not separated from the life of the people by the organization of a community separate from the ordinary society of laymen. The invader was eager to continue his conquests and his destruction of Buddhism by attacking Tibet, but he failed completely and was assassinated soon afterwards. Muhammad Ghori was also assassinated in 1206 by another Moslem. Kutb-ud-din became Sultan, and he in his turn was succeeded by another *mamluk,* his son-in-law Iltutmish, the chief ruler of the dynasty known as "Slaves" according to the real meaning of the word *mamluk,* though the status of these rulers was rather that of vassal princes. Moreover, it was only at the beginning that they were really vassals or slaves.

Under their rule Islam was established throughout Western and Northern India, from Gujarat to Bengal, though the main centre was Delhi, which became their capital. Many temples were destroyed, and the materials used to construct

Agra: The Red Fort

mosques. Among the most remarkable monuments of the Delhi region is the Kutb Minar, begun under Kutb-ud-din and completed by Iltutmish. It stands near an ancient temple, the nucleus of an ensemble completed by the tomb of Iltutmish and by the addition of a famous ancient iron pillar bearing a Sanskrit inscription of the fourth century.

After the reign of Iltutmish, a series of outbreaks, the short reign of his daughter, Raziyat ud-din, and further uprisings, the dynasty was strengthened by Balban, who resisted the first Mogul invasions, which were signalled by the sacking of Lahore in 1241.

In 1290 the Mamluk dynasty was replaced by the Khalji, who were Afghan, though probably originally of Turkish descent. Their first ruler was Jalal ud-din Firuz Shah; he was succeeded by Ala-ud-din, who was responsible for the expeditions of Malik Kafur to Southern India. This Southern movement came in the period which followed the Mogul threats from the North, but it encountered Hindu resistance. The resistance was fierce, but it was quelled in Rajputana, and one of the notable suicides that marked this time of struggle was that of Queen Padmavati of Cittaur (Chitor), who in heroic despair threw herself into the flames with her companions, in order to escape from the conquerors.

The Khaljis were succeeded by the Tughlaks,

Decorative detail from the tomb of the Itmad ud-daula

Agra: The Taj Mahal

among whom was Muhammad Tughlak, who wished to extend his rule to Southern India, but who was forced to return to Delhi. In 1339 he saw Bengal achieve its independence from the Sultanate of Delhi, and his successor, Firuz Shah (1351-88), was able to rule in comparative peace, except towards the end of his reign of thirty-seven years. In 1359 he founded Jaunpur, which became a great centre of Persian civilization, an "Eastern Chiraz". He established the system of *jagir* (fiefs), the revenues of which were accorded to their holders, and the practice of slavery, but was also known for his buildings and public works and irrigation schemes.

In 1398 the Mongols came on the scene again, under the leadership of the Turko-Mongol Timur, the famous Tamerlane. They vanquished the Rajput and Afghan forces of Mahmud Tughlak near Panipat, sacked Delhi, massacred their prisoners to prevent any later revolt, destroyed and pillaged. Sharaf ud-din, the Persian panegyrist of Timur, justified all this in the name of religion, which he claimed to have inspired in Timur a desire to punish the Moslems of India for being too tolerant towards the Hindus. Timur in fact attacked under any pretext all the powers which refused to submit to the rule of the Empire that he had founded in the Samarkand area of Sogdiana, north of the Oxus. He had conquered Samarkand and made it his capital. Though his invasion of India was marked by atrocities, it directly affected only a small area of the subcontinent, but it destroyed the central Moslem power of Delhi, and left the Moslem and Hindu rulers to stand alone in their many kingdoms and principalities at a time when the Moslem and Hindu peoples were uniting against a common peril and the excesses of their temporal leaders

229

*Shah Jahan in ceremonial procession.
Mogul painting of
the eighteenth century, presumably
a copy of a seventeenth-century work*

who prided themselves on their religious orthodoxy. The horrors that accompanied the invasion
were even more significant by the way in which
the reports of them were spread throughout the
country than by the actual atrocities perpetrated
in any locality. They helped to bring about new
alliances between Moslems and Hindus in India,
and this was finally of benefit to the Mogul
Emperors when they ultimately became established in the North.

Conditions among the peoples of Northern
India were, moreover, favourable at this period to movements of reconciliation between
the two communities. They both lacked unity,
as each was divided into numerous sects. Moreover, the Moslems included not only powerful lords and foreign rulers, but also humble
people who had settled in Hindu towns and villages, and in addition Hindu converts to Islam

or descendants of converts of varying origins and
circumstances of conversion. They were governed
by numerous rulers who made alliances or fought
irrespective of religious background, with the
result that they had no policy, either national or
foreign, to defend or fight against. They could
undergo the disasters of war and pillage caused
by powerful attacks from without only in the
same way as they bore the upheavals of drought,
floods, famine, or epidemics. Whether they were
caused by man or by nature, the disasters deprived many people of their means of living in the
fields or in the workshop, and they were forced
to seek a livelihood in the armies of the princes
or the services that supplied them, and this meant
that, though great armies could easily be recruited,
they were very weak from a military standpoint.
But these disasters were never on a national scale,
and the people, whether Hindus, Moslems, or

Shah Jahan as an old man.
Mogul painting of
the seventeenth century (?)

converts to Islam, ended by forming one Indian nation, the unity of which resided in the common background of living conditions. They also came to draw closer together in the general conceptions of their religion, which transcended the servitude and misfortunes of this world, and to lose the distinction between the *Sadhus* and the *Fakirs*. The Persian *Sufi* joined with the mystics and the Hindu *yogi*.

This explains why, apart from Islamic literary circles where Arabic and more particularly Persian were used, and the Sanskrit Brahmin milieux, throughout the whole of North and Western India in the fifteenth and sixteenth centuries there arose in popular circles an intellectual movement which had many facets and no co-ordination, but which was always characterized by the fusion, with varying degrees of importance, of Hindu and Islamic inspiration. The movement included poets who sprang from among the ranks of the simple

people, who were in search of God and who repudiated the world and its conventions. Among these poets was Kabir, the Banaras weaver, the spiritual heir of Maratha saints such as Namdev, venerated by Moslems and Hindus alike; Nanak, the founder of the great Sikh community; the great host of those who were known in Hindi as *Bhakt* or *Bhagat* (" devout men ") or *Sant* (" saints ") ; or again those who in Persian were called *Pir*. These religious leaders held no particular dogma, and little is known of their lives; some of them are legendary figures and may be transformations of the native genii, like Zindapir, the " Living Saint, " who represents the God of the Indus ; others include the revered healer Saki Sarvar, who lived in the twelfth and thirteenth centuries, and whose main followers were the Jat, Hindu peasants of the Panjab, and also some Moslems ; and a sage known only by the name of Satyapir (" the True Saint "), whose cult was founded in

Bengal in about 1500 by Husain Shah; the name Satyapir is half Sanskrit *(Satya)* and half Persian *(pir)*.

These material conditions and this general outlook prevalent in Northern India at the beginning of the sixteenth century paved the way for both conquest and unification when the Mongols came back in force. After the departure of Timur the Sayyid dynasty had contrived to reign in Delhi by dealing diplomatically with the Mongols; Sikandar Shah, the principal ruler in the next dynasty, that of the Lodi, managed to regroup some of the provinces under his authority, but he treated the Hindus with cruelty. The dynasty came to an end in 1526 with the defeat of Ibrahim Lodi in the plain of Panipat, an ill-omened place for the rulers of Delhi.

The Mongol conqueror, Babur, who was a descendant of Timur, had lost Samarkand to the Uzbeks; he was now about to conquer the new kingdom that was to become the Mogul Empire.

On this occasion Delhi was not destroyed. Babur settled at Agra, founded by Sikandar Lodi, but he still had to overcome, with the aid of his son Humayun, a considerable amount of resistance. He established his rule in the East as far as the frontiers of Bengal, and died in 1530 at the age of forty-seven, leaving his memoirs, which were written in Oriental Turkish. After his death, struggles and intrigues broke out among his sons, as generally happened with Moslem princes; and, although Humayun had been named as his successor, he did not achieve final possession of his throne until 1555, having been obliged to seek exile in Iran in 1540. Humayun died in 1556, and it was his son, Akbar, who really established the Mogul Empire. He achieved this after a hard struggle, but he owed his success chiefly to his tolerant and even sympathetic attitude towards the Hindus and their civilization.

Akbar's outlook was in harmony with the movement of reconciliation between Hinduism and Islam; the two communities had found a common bond in their horror of the first Mongols, and the new Mongol ruler united them even better by treating them on an equal footing. The capitation tax formerly levied on Hindus was suppressed, and the highest posts were now open to them without their having to renounce their faith. One of these Hindus to reach a high position was Todar Mall, who was a general, a Minister, and a remarkable administrator; he reorganized the country, and instituted a regular tax-collection system, while at the same time he was the compiler of vast volumes in Sanskrit on Indian traditional knowledge. And a Moslem,

Abu'l Fazl Allami, compiled an epitome of the State of India, the *Ayin-i Akbari* ("The Institutes of Akbar"). It was also during the reign of Akbar that Chaitanya, the great Bengali reformer of the Krishna sect, through the efforts of his disciples rediscovered the holy places dedicated to Krishna in Maratha and the district around it, destroyed by Mahmud of Ghazna nearly five centuries before, and re-established worship there. In 1573 Akbar made a personal visit to the disciples of Chaitanya at Vrindavan, and a poem in Hindi in honour of Chaitanya is attributed to him. Akbar was no less interested in Christianity. He took pleasure in the comparative study of religions, and would listen to discussions

by representatives of the different cults ; and with Abu'l Fazl and other helpers he attempted to create a new religion, which was to be the synthesis of all existing ones.

This attitude remained, however, far from conciliating all the Hindus, and annoyed the strictly orthodox Moslems. The serenity of the Emperor's lofty religious speculation was troubled by numerous campaigns led in search of further conquest or to quell revolt, but this did not prevent the Empire from extending its territories and becoming more stabilized in the course of an enlightened reign which lasted nearly fifty years, from 1556 to 1605.

Akbar's heir, Jahangir, had already tried to seize the throne during his father's lifetime, and had had Abu'l Fazl assassinated. Jahangir was soon in his turn to struggle against one of his sons. He restored Moslem orthodoxy to favour, and was himself under the influence of his Persian wife, Nur Jahan ("the Light of the World"), who was famous for her intrigues.

In spite of Nur Jahan, Jahangir was succeeded by his son Shah Jahan ("the King of the World"), who reigned from 1627 to 1658 ; he administered justice with care, but also had to repress a number of revolts among the princes. It is he who, inconsolable at the death of his wife, Muntaz Mahal, had constructed in memory of her one of the most elaborate mausoleums in

New Delhi:
*Astronomical instruments in stone
at one of Jaysingh's observatories
(eighteenth century)*

the world, the Taj Mahal at Agra. He was buried there beside her when he died in 1666 in the Red Fort at Agra, where he was being held prisoner by his son Aurangzeb, and from where he was able to gaze upon the magnificent tomb of his beloved.

The heir presumptive of Shah Jahan had been his eldest son, Dara Shukoh, who shared Akbar's liberal and considered outlook. He was interested in Sanskrit literature, and had had Sanskrit works translated into Persian. It is he who wrote the Persian version of the principal *Upanishads,* which were made known in Europe by Anquetil-Duperron. Shah Jahan became ill in 1657, and the ultimate succession was disputed among his four sons; the victory went to the clever but hypocritical Aurangzeb, who seized his father and proclaimed himself Emperor, putting one of his brothers to flight and killing the others.

The detailed history of the contentions between these refined monsters has been recounted many times by European visitors to their courts who marvelled at their magnificence as well as at their crimes. The mosques, forts, tombs, and other monuments still bear witness to their splendour. It was possible to maintain this magnificence because of the productive power and the artistic development of this vast empire, where wealth changed hands in the course of wars but never left the country.

Aurangzeb was both conqueror and administrator, and a fanatically orthodox Moslem, whether by conviction or by policy; from the military point of view he managed to hold the empire together until his death in 1707, but he destroyed the balance achieved in the relationship between Moslems and Hindus, and thus unwittingly paved the way for the anarchy precipitated by the Persian invasion in 1739.

3

ANCIENT INDIAN CIVILIZATION

In spite of the two superficial layers superimposed on Indian civilization by the British in more recent times and here and there by Islam, it still retains the essential characteristics of its own national heritage. It can be understood fully only through this heritage, which is not always easily discernible. The foreigner who visits nothing but the great cities of the North will not readily suspect its existence. Ancient monuments are not to be seen in Delhi and Calcutta like those of the ancient Greeks and Romans in Athens or Rome. The outward appearance presented by Indian cities is either Mogul, English, or hybrid. The splendours of ancient India have been reduced to a few vestiges remaining in gardens and mutilated statues in the museums. In the holy places without any ancient grandeur, such as those of the modern Banaras, there are many things to bear witness to living Hinduism, but it seems strange and poor. The traveller generally has to leave the main roads to find the great pre-Islamic temples such as those of Khajuraho, where the artistic splendour contrasts strongly with the bare or over-decorated sanctuaries of the present day. Even in Orissa, in the East, throughout the South and West, in Gujarat, and, indeed, in all regions where the pre-Islamic monuments stand in their magnificence among those erected at a later period by the followers of Siva and Vishnu and by the Jains, the ancient heritage of India appears to the stranger to perpetuate an archaic life apart.

Nevertheless, whatever the impressions of the visitor may be, India's essential possession is the remains of her ancient civilization, which she preserves sometimes with full knowledge, sometimes in a chauvinistic spirit, and sometimes subconsciously, as a natural inheritance of the minds and customs of her ancestors. This inheritance consists of the psychological outlook of her main social groups, not merely the memory of past historical greatness. Historical recollections, indeed, play a minor rôle, except on occasions when there is a question of pride involved with respect to other nations. It is a tradition in India inevitably to adopt the attitude of being less interested in world events themselves, with exact details and location, than in their significance and their possible consequences. Thus history is not a detailed and explanatory account of the state of world affairs; it is a treasury of examples of the fame, prosperity, or misery arising from the way in which kings in their sport spread Order or Disorder among the peoples.

When considering the world the Indian mind is striving after this idea of *Dharma,* a normal, natural state of law and order; though it can also look beyond the world and find exaltation in the ideal of the Absolute. It is of little import that these ideas are understood by only a minority, and that the great mass of the people has never even thought of them; for they have built up religions and traditional laws that govern the whole nation, whether the people accept them or are ignorant of them.

The development of the Indian spirit, which had already acquired full maturity long before the Islamic invasions, survived all historical events, and was not dependent on the political power of the ancient empires that had been founded on Indian soil. Their rôle was limited to helping the diffusion of the Indian outlook during a restricted period. They cannot, however, be considered as essential factors, as the Indian outlook spread throughout Eastern Asia without any military or political conquest. Conceived by the Indian mind, it was spread by commercial contacts. There was scarcely any question of political influence except in the later period when the Moslems

Bhuvanesvar: Temple of Lingaraja

is not one of attachment to a definite line of thought. On the contrary, it consisted of the absorption and assimilation, in a continuous process, of many different ideas, by a major genius in quest of a high standard and of achievement of greatness, profoundly rational and essentially radiant.

It was, indeed, a whole world, vaster than the India of present times, unstable, and consisting of many political divisions, yet united by its knowledge and its outlook, which had attained maturity and was in full expansion when Islam arrived to confront it and share its territories, at first in the seventh century and increasingly from the eleventh century onward. At that time Indian civilization had spread beyond the country itself to the whole of Central, Eastern, and Southern Asia, where its influence was felt side by side with regional civilizations which were more localized, but some of which, like the Chinese, were more powerful. The Indian civilization was characterized by its science, technical developments, magic, and art. It did not lack unity, as it was based on a state of knowledge and techniques that were uniformly taught through the medium of the classical Sanskrit education. At the same time several of the great Indian religions flourished in those same countries to which the general Indian civilization had spread, encouraging its development, which was also helped by trade relationships. Indian Buddhism spread throughout Central Asia, to Tibet, China, Japan, Indochina, and Indonesia, teaching a method of retiring from the world and society into the disciplined life of monastic communities. The cult of Siva, and sometimes also the worship of Vishnu, offered to the people of Indochina and Indonesia a concept of the way in which the world should be governed and a means of salvation through worship, rites, knowledge and love of the essence of the world, of God.

Such an important and far-reaching civilization, characterized by vast literary works and imposing monuments, could survive the onslaughts of Islam and Europe, undergo temporary eclipses, and even lose part of its greatness, but it could never disappear. This is why its tradition still strongly influences the people of India to-day, though the main element is now the Hindu, the Buddhist elements of the mediæval period having been eliminated. The Buddhist influence still survives outside India, sometimes as a principal force, sometimes in a weakened form, in countries such as Tibet, Mongolia, China, Korea,

invaded the heart of the country, and subsequently when Islam became a rival outside the boundaries of India itself. The development and expansion of this traditional Indian spirit came to a halt at the stage which it had reached and in which it deliberately maintained itself in an attitude of reaction against foreign pressure. But during its long period of development it had always been receptive to outside influence. And it had gleaned many treasures from classical antiquity, from the Mesopotamians, Persians, and Greeks, to use in its own way and to spread to different parts of the world.

The history of the formation of this tradition

Japan, Burma, Thailand, Laos, Cambodia, or Vietnam. In many of these lands, and also in Indonesia, the Indian tradition of art has survived, as did the Greco-Roman in Europe of former days, in spite of all the religious changes and complete adaptations to the national genius of the peoples concerned.

In the full knowledge of this tradition, and the broad influence that it has had without resorting to force, India does not consider herself as a young nation, newly emancipated. Her autonomy does not date from independence, but it is a political sovereignty which she has recovered, and from which she had never spiritually abdicated. The history of her ancient civilization shows us this, and justifies her national pride.

Khajuraho: Temple of Vamana, south side

THE EARLY ELEMENTS
OF INDIAN CIVILIZATION

The origins of Indian civilization, like those of all ancient civilizations, are obscure. The oldest-known witness to it is a book, the *Rigveda,* which was not written until much later, but which was handed down by recitation from antiquity, and which was greatly venerated at all periods. Rigid mnemotechnic methods were employed so that it could be recited faultlessly, and the rarity of the variants encountered, in whatever region it was written down, and the archaism of the Vedic-Sanskrit used, bear witness to extreme accuracy of transmission. The essential meaning of *Veda* is knowledge, and of *Rigveda* "knowledge in sacred verse". The *Rigveda* is a series of hymns in honour of divinities which represent mainly the elements and forces of nature. These hymns were first considered as representing man's earliest adoration of the beauty of the world. But a compilation so full of masterpieces must be a collection of learned texts, not by any means all contemporary, designed to be recited as the accompaniment to a complicated liturgy. They represent the product of a forgotten period of considerable length, and are full of poetic art, speculation, and ritual technique. They are the first manifestations of an extensive literature, nearly as old as they are, which together with them form the Four *Vedas.* Part of them, newly arranged, form the *Samaveda* ("knowledge in the form of melody"), a collection of liturgical songs. The *Yajurveda* ("knowledge in the form of sacrificial formulæ"), mainly in prose, completes the textual ritual of the great sacrifices, just as the *Soma* is the drink symbolic of immortality. The above-mentioned compilations comprise the fundamental group of the Triple *Veda.* The fourth, the *Atharvaveda* ("knowledge of the Atharvans"), which takes its name from that of a priestly family, is composed of hymns, just like the *Rigveda,* but they are generally associated with particular forms of ritual and magical conjurations.

A number of different categories of text may be added to these basic elements. There are the *Brahmanas,* which treat of liturgical speculations with regard to cosmological and physiological theories; the *Aranyakas* and the *Upanishads,* full of metaphysical speculations, works that have enjoyed popularity throughout the course of history; and finally the *Vedangas,* technical treatises of phonetics, ritual, grammar, interpretation of words, versification, and astronomy.

At the present stage of research no concrete vestiges have been found of the Vedic and Brahmanic civilizations which have handed down such a vast literature. The literature is difficult to date in the absolute sense, though it has been possible to compile a comparative chronology of the period at which the different works were written. It is believed that much of it was already in existence in a fully developed form in the sixth century B.C., at the time of the foundation of Buddhism, though generally speaking it is much earlier than that period. It is easier to localize geographically, on account of the rivers and regions mentioned. The people who were the authors of it appear to have lived mainly in the Indus Basin, and to have moved gradually eastward to occupy much of the Ganges Basin.

These people, who were divided into tribes, are the *Aryas* ("nobles"), in contrast with the *Dasas* ("slaves") or *Dasyus.* The *Aryas* were a pastoral people like the *Dasyus,* but the *Dasyus* had constructed fortified cities, which were attacked by the Arya Indra, the warrior god of the *Rigveda.* In the Indus valley there are extensive archæological remains of cities at Harappa, where traces of fortifications can be seen, and Mohan-jo-Daro, and they are also found as far south as Lothal, in Gujarat. It is possible that the walls attacked by Indra, always supposing that there was some human hero who was the prototype of this god, are those of the ancient inhabitants of the Indus valley. The Vedic *Aryas,* who appear to have been related to the ancient Iranians, if one is to judge by the linguistic affinities of Vedic Sanskrit and Old Persian, may well have been invaders of India who emigrated from Iran and attacked the peoples of the Indus valley, who already had a highly developed civilization. Whatever the truth may be, this civilization was one of the most remarkable in early antiquity. It was characterized by a high degree of urbanization and an advanced system of canalizations and drains. It possessed a writing, not yet deciphered, which may be seen on seals decorated with animal figures, some of them highly fantastic. Some of these seals, discovered in Mesopotamia in layers that have been dated, have enabled archæologists to estimate the duration of this civilization as approximately 2500-1500 B.C. The latter date coincides with the estimated age of the *Rigveda.*

Above: Painting of Krishna with embossed gilt ornaments (Tanjore school).
Below: Jain manuscript (sixteenth century)

Puri (Orissa): painting of Jagannath
(the black face on the right)
in the Temple of Jagannath

It is not only in matters of language that the Vedic civilization is linked with the ancient civilizations of Iran, for there is also the bond of ideas. From this we must infer the existence of a prehistoric Indo-Iranian family, from which the Vedic Indians and the ancient Iranians sprang. The "Indo-Iranians" themselves have affinities of language, ideas, and myths with the Greeks, Latins, Germans, Slavs, and Celts of Europe, as well as with the Armenians and Georgians and with peoples of Central Asia in the area near the western frontiers of China, the Kutcheans and the Agneans. The hypothetical ancestors of all these races are referred to as "Indo-Europeans".

The Vedic civilization was naturalistic and utilitarian,' though it did not exclude cosmological and religious speculation, as is shown in the hymns of the *Rigveda* and the *Atharvaveda*. But it is in the *Brahmana* that we find more significant ideas about the physical world, though they are still undetermined and take many forms. In the *Upanishads* we encounter the metaphysical conception of existence, man's *atman* (self), which is at the same time the Brahman, the essence of the universe ; essential knowledge reveals that they are but one.

One of the most significant conceptions of Vedic India is that of the *rta*, the concept of the true order of the world, a conception that may be considered as the forerunner of the *Dharma* of classical and even modern times.

The conception is even Indo-Iranian, for it is to be found in Iran under the name of *asha* in the language of the *Avesta*, the most important sacred book, and of *arta* in the language of the Achæmenids. One of the Achæmenid inscriptions even refers to an *arta brazmaniya* ("Brah-

manic order"). The idea of Brahman is allied to that of *Vak* ("the word"), which makes the sacred rites efficacious, and which regulates the movement of the world, conceived as a vast ritual development according to the *rta*. The *rta* is the law of nature in its normal course, as exemplified by the revolution of the planets and the rhythm of the seasons. There is a balance between the universe and the human and animal kingdom, which correspond with each other, element by element, and which mutually explain each other. Cosmophysiology and astronomy are the two fundamentals of Vedic science, based on the observation and understanding of real phenomena, though side by side with them flourishes a magic element operating mechanically and without rationalization. In astronomy a system of reference to the celestial movements was reached at an early period by means of twenty-seven or twenty-eight stars, the *nakshatra*, which mark out the ecliptic. This system allowed scientists to determine the various positions of the moon, which is most of the time visible between the *nakshatra*, and of the sun, which cannot be seen at the same time as the stars, but which is always opposite the full moon and the *nakshatra* crossing the meridian at midnight. The establishment of a calendar was essentially a matter of bringing religious rites into harmony with the laws of the universe, the general aim of such rites and something that could be used to advantage when the occasion arose. This astronomical system, with subsequent foreign additions, is the one that India has constantly used and which she transmitted to much of Eastern Asia. It was, moreover, in order to construct Vedic altars that India made her first steps in the

science of geometry. It is also in the Vedic texts that we find the first attempts to give a rational explanation of the major physiological phenomena, attempts that are the basis of the classical medical doctrines of the *Ayurveda*, still followed in traditionalist circles and among those to whom modern medicine is inaccessible because of financial considerations or distance from the main centres of modern medicine. Finally it is in the *Rigveda* that one finds the basis of the theory of the four natural social classes. The tradition is that the Brahmins, the Kshatriyas, the Vaisyas, and the Sudras issued from the head, the arms, the thighs, and the feet of Purusha, the great body of the universe conceived in the image of a man. This theory classes the different groups by their functions, but without making them distinct races, as they all come from one single being and constitute humanity as a whole divided according to activity in the community.

As the writing of the seals of the Indus region has not yet been deciphered, and as archæological excavations have produced very little evidence, and even that not of a precise anthropological nature, we do not yet know what type of men the Vedic Aryans encountered in India. Some scholars believe that they must have been Dravidians, and base their conclusions on the high degree of civilization that the Dravidians are known to have had at an early period, and the existence to-day of a Dravidian language (Brahhui) in Baluchistan, in an area remote from all other languages of the same family, which are found essentially in Southern India. If the Dravidians of the Indus had been forced southward by the Aryans, then the Brahui language could be considered as the residue of the Dravidian occupation of the North-west. But anthropologically speaking the Brahui are not Dravidians, and there is no trace of the Dravidian racial type anywhere in the Indus Basin. Nor was there any as far back as the first century B.C. for the Greek geographer Strabo stated in his writings that there were two types of men in India, the southerners, who were dark-skinned like the Ethiopians, but who were more like the white races as far as their features and hair were concerned, and the northerners, who were similar

*Konark (Orissa):
a temple to the sun built
in the form
of a processional chariot*

to the Egyptians. Moreover, the Munda have too rudimentary a way of life for it to be conceivable that the civilization of the Indus Basin belonged to them. The most probable supposition is that the Vedic Aryans found in the Indus Basin a race of people not so very different from themselves, and that they mingled with them, as subsequent invaders have done, thus producing the present-day racial types.

Whatever the explanation may be, the Vedic civilization encountered from the earliest times of its development a substratum of Indian civilization of a very advanced level, which was in contact with the Persian Gulf and Mesopotamia, as is proved by the discovery of Indian seals in the Tigris-Euphrates valley, and by archæological vestiges in the island of Bahrein, which bear witness to a wealth that can be explained only by considerable trading activity in this barren land on the borders of the Arabian desert. The Vedic civilization cannot therefore have failed from the very beginning to borrow elements from the civilizations around it. It underwent at the same time an internal evolution, for it shows considerable contrasts with the civilizations with which it has links, such as the Iranian, Greek, and Latin. Unfortunately we do not know

its history. It may have begun before it became established in India; many names of Vedic gods are mentioned in a treaty between the King of Mitanni and the King of the Hittites, in Asia Minor, in the fourteenth century B.C. But once it became established the Vedic civilization changed very little and was not subjected to any notable influences from outside, as it has come down to us intact, if incomplete, through its literary tradition preserved by the Brahmins.

This tradition, spread by the Brahmins, was not confined to its original geographical locality, but extended throughout India. It is honoured throughout the country in present times, as it was in the Vijayanagar Empire of the fourteenth century, and though it may be considered as quiescent it is always there as a source of inspiration or authority, though it has since been replaced by other traditions which have evolved. Its long, solemn, costly rituals could not be maintained indefinitely. The fact that it aimed at prosperity and wellbeing made it inadequate to satisfy the desire to go beyond humanity and nature, which from early times possessed the philosophers; this desire is not to be found in the most ancient traditions and, indeed, it came from different sources, but it finally found its

expression in the Upanishads. This is why the Vedic tradition was abandoned as far as his techniques were concerned, but preserved in its final form throughout the ages because of its thought, maintained, moreover, because of the prestige of its initial scientific studies of astronomy and medical theory.

Indian civilization in the sixth century B.C. was influenced by other movements in addition to Vedic Brahmanism. This is proved by the literature of the movements which succeeded it, and it shows the controversies in the midst of which they came into being.

BUDDHISM AND JAINISM

In addition to the Brahmins who followed the Veda, the hereditary guardians of knowledge, there were the Samanes who, through their own individual efforts, were in search not only of all kinds of practical knowledge, but more especially a state of existence in which they would not be at the mercy of outward circumstances, an existence that implied mastery of self. There were the Parivrajakas (" wanderers "), seeking truth outside the bonds of community life, living on the charity of pious people; the Pravrajins (" men who leave the world ") ; and also the Sannyasins (" renouncers "). But the main groups were those who were organized in communities, the Buddhists and the Jains. It is they who are the best known, for their communities, founded by highly eminent teachers with personal doctrines, have, by gathering together the details of the teaching of these masters, made a point of underlining their authenticity by reference to the circumstances in which they were formulated. They have thus preserved some historical links, a feature characteristic of neither Vedic orthodoxy nor Hinduism, whether Saivistic or Vaishnavistic; Hinduism is pre-eminent, but we see it only in its final form, through its literature or its secret art, as very little relating to its early stages has been preserved.

It was at the end of the sixth and the beginning of the fifth century B.C. in the heart of the kingdoms of the Ganges in North-east India, that the Buddha (" the awakened one ") and the Mahavira (" great hero ") or the Jina (" conqueror ") preached the doctrine of the misfortunes of human life and other conditions of existence through which the soul might have to pass in its transmigration.

Both doctrines founded techniques of the remoulding of the psychic existence, teaching that unconsidered actions leave their mark, and that disciplined activity liberates man, ridding him of those attachments that lead to suffering. Both repudiated or neglected theoretic speculation on the nature of things, in order to teach a practical discipline of thought and conduct. Their followers, and particularly the Buddhists, were to elaborate this teaching over the course of the years, with their many sects and schools of philosophy.

Buddhism and Jainism, more popular from their foundation than the learned Vedism, used in the early days the language of the people, the *prakrits* (" natural languages "), derived from Sanskrit in the same way as the Romance languages of Europe are derived from Latin. They maintained this policy until the early centuries

247

Base of the Temple of Tanjavur (eleventh century)

of the Christian era, when the *prakrits* had become so differentiated from each other that learned Sanskrit remained the only stable language in existence in all regions, and was therefore adopted as the common language of general relations.

Buddhism and Jainism cast aside the Vedic liturgies, which they considered as vain and worldly, but nevertheless did not repudiate all other forms of Vedic civilization. Both doctrines adopted Vedic science, though the Jains evolved their own theory of astronomy. Both accepted the Vedic ritual of the consideration of kings, even of kings converted to their faith, for, having retired from the world, they no longer had any laws with which to rule it. Even where their faith was dominant they handed over to the Brahmanic religion, as to a secular body, the government of the country and of a society from which their faith had compelled them to withdraw.

In this way we find at a very early period the Indian policy of mutual tolerance and even of division of social functions according to social communities; these customs were often violated locally and for limited periods, but the policy is nevertheless one which has persisted through the ages and one that explains the insistence on tolerance of the Republic of India to-day, and its attachment to a secular government respecting all different forms of belief.

Buddhism and Jainism nevertheless were harmful to Vedic ritual, and the fact that they spread throughout the country necessarily contributed towards weakening it. In the first place, the Vedic ritual included the shedding of blood in sacrifices, and this was condemned by Buddhists, Jains, and Hindus successively as contrary to their belief in the principle of non-violence. Then, while the kings often gave official privileges to various religious organizations in order to maintain them in peaceful coexistence, devout laymen gave exclusive support to the community of their choice, which was frequently a Buddhist or Jain monastery, to the exclusion of the Brahmanistic priestly groups.

The Brahmins nevertheless remained throughout history the main arbiters of social organization, because they themselves formed part of the general community and did not live outside it like the members of the Jain or Buddhist orders. The Brahmanic order, indeed, governs man at all the stages of his life, the *ashramas*, which are three in number: that of the *brahmacharin*, the student stage of the young man; that of the *grihastha*, his establishment, on marriage, in a family home; and that of the *vanaprastha*, the stage at which he can, alone or with his wife, retire to the forest, having paid his debts to society and to his ancestors by the procreation of a son, who will in his turn make his contribution to society and assure the sacrifices to the "Fathers". A fourth *ashrama*, not consecutive to the other

248

three, is that of the *sannyasin,* who can renounce the world and leave the community at any time in his life. He often did this, in accordance with a vow, in order to devote himself methodically to some form of of asceticism, *tapas* ("heating"), which assured an exceptional degree of self-mastery. The most typical form of this asceticism was to place oneself in the middle of four fires and to expose oneself to the full sun. It is now generally replaced by the psycho-physiological exercises of the Yoga, which are completely different, as they are not based on self-mortification, but are founded on the physiological theories of the *Ayurveda,* and on personal experiments under the guidance of a master *(guru).* Nevertheless certain *Sadhus* to-day still practise some of the ancient *tapas,* with their terrifying forms of penitence.

By means of ancient Buddhist and Jain texts we learn the names of the kingdoms and their rulers at the time of Buddha and Jina, and this knowledge is parallel with and completes the dynastic lists of the principal kingdom of the period, the Magadha, which are given in the Hindu *Puranas.* The *Puranas* also contain legendary and mythical stories and dynastic chronologies which are ill-preserved, but which can be linked to a certain extent with the general chronology when the dates of the sovereigns in question are known from some other source. This is true for Chandragupta, the founder of the Maurya dynasty of Magadha, of which he and his grandson Asoka were the most famous rulers. Chandragupta is referred to by Greeks and Romans as Sandrakottos or Sandracottus, at the time of Alexander the Great and immediately afterwards. This established date gives the relative dates of those who precede or follow him in the Indian dynastic lists. Such lists, going back for many generations, were already in existence at the time of Alexander, the end of the fourth century B.C. They reveal an India divided into a number of kingdoms or states, and the Buddhist texts inform us that these states often corresponded to republican confederations. But the different religions and the civilization in general were to be found throughout the country, with little distinction of political division.

Mount Abu (Gujarat): the ceiling of a Jain temple

249

LINKS WITH THE WEST THROUGH INVASIONS AND TRADE RELATIONS

Although contingents of Indian troops were recruited by the Persians of the Achæmenid Empire to fight in their armies, the India of antiquity enjoyed the reputation of never having of her own accord attacked a foreign country, and she still takes pride in having merited this praise. Indian expeditions into foreign countries have, indeed, been the exception, and though the country itself has always been liable to invasions, it has not been deeply disrupted by them.

The Persian Empire of the Achæmenids, founded by Cyrus in the sixth century B.C., soon gained a foothold in India, mainly under the leadership of Darius, from 518 B.C. onwards, and ruled the whole of the Indus Basin until Alexander the Great defeated the Persians in 330 B.C. Alexander's famous conquest of India was in reality only a passing occupation, from 327 to 325 B.C., of the former satrapies established by the Persians. The retreat and death of Alexander, and the subsequent elimination of the officers whom he had left in India, had the result of returning to Indian administration the provinces which had been taken from it for two centuries by the Persians. It was Chandragupta who reconquered them shortly before 313 B.C., taking possession of the kingdom of Magadha, formerly ruled by the Nanda dynasty, for which he substituted his own Maurya dynasty. The Kingdom of Magadha, the capital of which was Pataliputra, the modern Patna, was the seat of the unification of the whole of Northern India, and even, under Asoka (c. 264-227 B.C.), of the whole peninsula, with the exception of three Tamil kingdoms in the extreme South, Kerala-putra or Chera, the modern Kerala, the kingdom of the Pandyas of Madurai, and that of the

Cholas of the Coromandel Coast, the Sanskrit name of which, Cholamandala, means the threshing-floor of the Cholas.

The long Persian occupation of the Indus Basin on the one hand and the imperial expansion of the Gangetic kingdom of Magadha on the other greatly influenced the destiny of India. Apparently indifferent to the Persian occupation, Brahmanic civilization had flourished in the satrapies of the Indus as well as in the independent kingdoms of the East. Not only did the Persian Empire include Egyptian, Greek, Lydian, and Mesopotamian lands as well as Persian and Indian, but all these territories were administered by means of a group of officials who spoke an Aramaic Semitic language and whose education was based on Babylonian civilization. Communications were established in the field of learning between these officials and Indian scholars; Aramaic script was modified by Indian men of letters for the transcription of the current languages or *prakrits*. Thus, while spreading scientific theories to the Hellenistic world through the Persian Empire, India received new ideas from the Greek world as well as from the Babylonian and Persian, particularly in the realms of divination and astrology. When they came under the domination of the Kingdom of Magadha, the former satrapies of the Indus, Gandhara and Sindh and the areas of North-west India which to-day are Afghan, remained, after the fall of Persia, regions in contact with Greek, Babylonian, and Persian civilization. Alexander the Great had found in the satrapies Brahmins who were firmly established and eager to defend themselves against his invasion, and it was when he dominated these satrapies that Xerxes had wished to establish his *arta brazmaniya* in his own country. Later, in about 250 B.C., Asoka had inscriptions engraved in Greek and in an Aramaic tinged with Iranian vocabulary, advocating a code of conduct to the peoples of Arachosia, to-day the

Near Jingi (Madras):
rock sculpture representing the Jain Tirthakara

Temple at Khajuraho (tenth century) ▶

Afghan province of Kandahar. The people of this area were his subjects, but they counted no Brahmins among their number. And from the time of Asoka onwards important stone vestiges bear witness to Indian art, which at that time contained some elements of Persian inspiration.

Asoka himself was, indeed, the greatest ruler in the world of his period, and his reign marked a decisive upward trend in Indian civilization. He extended the empire inherited from his father and grandfather, and encountered the Brahmanic civilization which was already established in the South, particularly in Kalinga. The massacre of Brahmins and other people which this conquest entailed filled him with remorse. Soon after he was converted to Buddhism, and, adopting its laws against passion and violence, he devoted himself to the peaceful administration of his empire, and to propaganda among foreigners, particularly the Greeks, in favour of the establishment of *Dhamma* as it was called in his *prakrit*, or the Brahmanic *Dharma* as it is known in Sanskrit. As a Buddhist he particularly encouraged this faith, and it is he who, by means of missionaries, facilitated its introduction into Ceylon and spread it to other parts of India. But as a king he advocated to all his subjects, irrespective of their various religious beliefs, mutual respect, veneration for one's parents and for the aged, and abstention from harming or killing others, whether men or animals. The inscriptions that he had carved in an area extending from Afghanistan to Mysore, from Gujarat to Orissa, bear witness both to the extent and to the power of the constitution of a non-sectarian state, organized to promote general

Græco-Indian Buddha from Gandhara

peace and prosperity in an atmosphere of religious tolerance. Asoka's empire was a model which has been forgotten as an historical fact, in spite of the way in which the Buddhists for a long time sang its praises, though at the same time laying emphasis on the partiality shown to their community. This empire was equally important for spreading and offering a concrete example of the reign of *Dharma,* which Sanskrit literature, under whatever political régime it flourished, never ceased to extol and to comment upon; it is an ideal still present in the minds of Indians to-day, who have re-discovered the serene greatness of Asoka. Asoka's reign marks the beginning of the development of Indian civilization

Græco-Indian statuette from Gandhara

Scythians, who came from Bactria, but who were originally inhabitants of Central Asia. Under the Kushana dynasty, of which the most famous ruler was Kanishka, the Scythians had governed an empire that extended from Central Asia to the Mathura region of the Yamuna valley, and even as far as Banaras on the Ganges. All these Greeks, Iranians, and peoples from Central Asia settled in India for fairly extensive periods. The Indo-Greek kingdoms lasted from about 170 to 30 B.C. The Saka and Parthian dynasties, either as independent rulers or as vassals of the Indo-Scythians, were in India from about 90 B.C. until the fifth century of the Christian era, when the Indo-Scythians themselves, who had gradually become weaker, disappeared.

The various religions of these peoples were practised side by side with the Indian cults, in a general atmosphere of mutual tolerance. Movements of religious unification took place, especially among the conquerors from Central Asia, who were suddenly brought face to face with firmly established religious systems which had been elaborated over a long period. Buddhism, Jainism, and Vedic or Hindu Brahmanism were too fully established to undergo much influence from Greece or Iran or from Christianity. It is believed that St Thomas the Apostle had preached Christianity in the states of the Indo-Parthian sovereign Gondophares before going to settle in the Coromandel Coast area, where he finally underwent martyrdom. But some

in all its forms throughout the country and in the lands beyond the mountain barrier and across the seas. The main routes by which it spread to foreign countries were through the mountain passes in the North-west and across the Bay of Bengal. The North-western route has remained a route for caravans moving towards Iran and Central Asia, and, though it was the way by which foreigners invaded India, even these invasions meant trade relationships. From the ports were shipped the precious stones and other products of value that formed the basis of Indian trade with South-east Asia.

The presence of Iranians in North-west India and the Greeks who settled there gave rise to several invasions of the Indus Basin, from the second century B.C. onward, by Greeks and by Iranian groups, Sakas and Parthians, who were ousted from their areas of origin by the pressure of peoples who had themselves been driven westward from the borders of China and the Pamir plateau to Sogdiana and Bactria, provinces in the eastern part of Iran. These invasions accounted for the installation of a number of Indo-Greek and Indo-Parthian kindoms in North-western and Western India. In the early centuries of the Christian era the Indo-Parthians were subordinated to or replaced by the Indo-

Mamallapuram: Pallava monolithic temples and bull (seventh century)

Greeks were converted to Hinduism, notably Heliodora, who in about 100 B.C. had a votive pillar to Vishnu erected in India. Heliodora was a native of Takshasila (Taxila), a town in the North-west of the Panjab, an old-established point of contact with the Greeks, who, at the time of Alexander the Great, had referred to its king as Taxiles, and the Greeks who, in about A.D. 200, still considered it as partly Hellenistic and who wrote an account of the visit paid to it by Apollonius of Tyana, the Greek philosopher and miracle-worker of the first century of the Christian era. One of the more important Indo-Grecian kings, known as Milinda in Middle Indian and Menandros in Greek, who reigned over a large territory in the North-west in the second century B.C., showed a considerable interest in Buddhism, and for that reason was commemorated in the literature of the Buddhist community.

It was not only in the realm of religion that coexistence was to be found. The science, literature, and arts of the different peoples developed parallel with each other, as in the time of the Persians in lands in which Sanskrit or Prakrit Indian traditions were established. Trade was carried on with the Roman Empire. There were sea routes from Western or Southern India to Egypt ; while an overland route crossed Persia, followed the river Oxus to the Sea of Aral and the Caspian Sea, and finally reached the Black Sea by means of a series of trans-shipments. The latter was a route that had existed since Persian times. Another route which was partly maritime and partly overland followed the Persian Gulf, Mesopotamia, and Arabia to reach either Palmyra or Petra and Nabatæa. Many Greek gold coins of the last centuries before Christ, and Roman coins of the early centuries of our era, have been found in India, as well as examples of the local Indian, Indo-Greek, Indo-Parthian, and Indo-Scythian currencies. The excavations at Virapattinam, near Pondicherry, sometimes incorrectly referred to as Arikamedu, uncovered Roman pottery made in Italy in the first half of the first century of the Christian era. Geographical information collated by Strabo, Pliny, Ptolemy, and the anonymous author of a work on the lands bordering the Erythræan Sea (Indian Ocean) were spread throughout India up to the

Unfinished Pallava sculptures on a monolithic temple at Mamallapuram (seventh century)

*Mamallapuram: Vishnu, recumbent, worshipped by the Earth.
On the right, two Titans, who are vainly trying to attack him
(Pallava art of the seventh century)*

third century of our era. At that time, some five centuries after the reign of Asoka, the Iranians, whose power had increased since the foundation of the Sassanid dynasty, and who were the enemies of the Romans, restricted Indian relations with the Græco-Roman world, and strengthened the links with Iran itself. Shahpuhr I (A.D. 241-272), who vanquished the Roman Emperor Valerian in 259, established his suzerainty for a time over the Indus Basin, replacing the Indo-Parthians and the Indo-Scythians. It was during the reign of Shahpuhr that Mani, the founder of Manichæism, who spent some time in India, preached. The Sassanids encouraged the renewed activity of the old Iranian religion of the *Avesta,* which included the famous tradition of Zoroaster. Gundeshapuhr in Susiana, the capital of the Sassanids, became one of the principal centres for the exchange of scientific knowledge, in which India played her part.

The political development of Iranian influence in Western India was short-lived, but it had significant consequences. It stemmed the important current of relationships between India and the Græco-Roman world of the West, relationships that had been increasing since the first century of our era, and it took the place of those who had established the Indo-Greek dynasties in India in the time before Christ. The remarkable development of Græco-Buddhist art, Indian in inspiration and Græco-Roman in treatment, in Gandhara in North-western India, dates mainly to the time of this intense commercial activity, and it was terminated by the increasing political power of the Iranians, who were hostile to Rome. This period also marks the spread of Indian philosophical ideas in the Græco-Roman world and the influence of Greek science on India. India at this time borrowed much from the astronomy and astrology of Alexandria. It was then that the Indians added to their methods of cosmography and the establishment of a calendar according to

255

the system of the *nakshatra,* the zodiac system and the foretelling of destiny according to Greek astrological speculations. Indian books of the period refer to the Greeks as "Yavana," in Old Persian "Iauna" or Ionians. The centre of the new school of astronomy appears to have been Ujjayini, the city the meridian of which was chosen by the astronomers and astrologers and has been traditionally maintained as the one from which longitude is calculated.

Moreover, the tradition of peaceful coexistence, which had become established in Western and North-western India, of Indians, Greeks, and Iranians of all different origins, had, particularly under the Indo-Scythian Empire which linked India with Central Asia, allowed Buddhism to spread to Central Asia and then to China, where it is known to have been established as early as A.D. 65. This atmosphere of peaceful existence had been troubled on several occasions by Indian military reaction against the Saka invaders. An era still referred to in modern India was founded, according to classical tradition, in 58 B.C., by King Vikramaditya, after a victory over the Sakas. But another era even more widely used is the one referred to as the Saka era, which began in A.D. 78; and though its origins are obscure, it spread the name of the Sakas throughout India and even

as far as Indochina and Indonesia. Finally, the domination of the Sakas and other rulers from Iran or Central Asia was accepted by the people of the whole of Western India, provided that it practised the tolerance ordered by Asoka in bygone days and generally carried out by local rulers of foreign origin. But the enforcement of Iranian imperial rule from a seat of government outside Indian territory, and the anarchy resulting from this remote control appears to have provoked a reaction in India in favour of independence, similar to the one that followed the expedition of Alexander the Great. Just as the Maurya Empire of Chandragupta was formed around the nucleus of the eastern kingdom of Magadha, so the imperial dynasty of the Gupta was founded under another Chandragupta, who was also a prince of Magadha.

Chandragupta, the successor of a father and grandfather who were already Maharajas, though less famous, founded this dynasty in A.D. 320, styling himself Maharajadhiraja ("supreme king of the great kings"). His son Samudragupta (*c.* A.D. 335-375) was the great conqueror of the dynasty. He conquered some of the "great kings," and received the submission of many others, being content to receive tribute from them. He, indeed, allowed a number of dynasties of

Mamallapuram: Pallava temple
on the sea-shore dedicated to Siva
(eighth century)

Temple at Udaipur ▶

Mamallapuram:
an example of Pallava animal art
(eighth century)

Iranian and Central Asiatic origin to remain in power in the West and North-west, merely maintaining regular diplomatic relations with them. His son Chandragupta II (*c.* A.D. 375-414), known as Vikramaditya ("the sun of heroism"), extended the empire still farther, and probably established his authority as far as Bactria in the North-west and Bengal in the East. In the South his lands bordered on the Dravidian territories. His successors Kumaragupta I and Skandagupta fought against new invasions from the North-west by the Ephtalite Huns; they were first repelled in 455, but shortly afterwards they took possession of the North-western and Western territories, which became once more subordinate to a foreign power. This rule was distasteful to the Buddhists, but in 533 the Hun ruler Mihirakula was forced to yield to the Indian king Yasodharman, while shortly afterwards the Sassanids and the Turks destroyed the centre of the Hun Empire in Bactria.

The period of Hun intervention was also marked by the crumbling of the Gupta Empire. It had not been strongly centralized, and was a feudal state rather than a political unity, so it declined as the vassal kingdoms prospered, quite independently of the disorders caused by the Huns. Many of the kingdoms flourished after the collapse of the Gupta Empire, especially Kanyakubja and Bengal. A dynasty that had been in power under the Guptas at Sthanesvar, on the borders of the north-western countries that were

so subjected to invasions, made an alliance with Kanyakubja, a kingdom of the Ganges valley. The ruler of Eastern Malava and Sasanka, the powerful king of Bengal, were prevented by treachery, assassinations, and invasions from overpowering it. But Harsha, a young prince of Sthanesvar, with the aid of the ruler of Kamarupa, the modern Assam, who attacked Bengal from the east, repulsed the Bengali king and founded a powerful empire centred on Kanyakubja, though it was less extensive than the Gupta Empire. In 606, when he officially became Emperor, Harsha founded a new era. He died in 647.

Meanwhile Southern India had established its own kingdoms since the end of the Empire of Asoka, and these kingdoms, in Gujarat and along the eastern and southern fringes, bordered on the lands subject to invasion. The Andhrabhritya dynasty, also known as Satakani or Satavahana, which was established in the upper Godavari valley, was in contact with the Indo-Parthians and the Indo-Scythians, though the southern kingdoms were remote from this contact.

The Kanarese country was ruled by the Kadambas of Banavasi, and subsequently, from about A.D. 500 onwards, by the Chalukyas of Aiholi and Vatapi (the modern Badami).

In the Tamil country the rulers were the Pallavas, who came probably from Western India and established themselves at Kanchi to govern the whole of the Coromandel Coast area, which

Manuscript dating from the reign of Vigrahapala of Bengal
(eleventh century).
Above: scenes from the former life of Buddha. Below: Buddha

had previously been in the hands of the Cholas.

The most powerful Chalukya king was Pulakesin II, to whom the whole of the Andhra country between the Godavari and the Krishna submitted. In 611 he established at Vengi the Eastern Chalukya dynasty, which lasted until the twelfth century. He was attacked in about 620 by Harsha and won a victory over him; but in about 642 he was himself conquered by the Pallava king, Narasimhavarman I. Paranjodi, the victorious Pallava general, subsequently retired to his native village to devote himself to religion, and he became one of the saints still venerated by the Saiva sect. The Pallavas then became the principal rulers of the South until 740, when they were conquered by the Chalukyas of Vatapi, who were soon replaced by the Rashtrakuta dynasty. When the Pallavas were defeated their territory once more became a Chola kingdom, the capital of which was Uraiyur, near Tiruchirapalli; while the Pandyas once more ruled at Madurai and the Cheras in the Malabar Coast area, so that the distribution of Tamil power was similar to that which existed at the time of Asoka, and it was to remain that way until the Vijayanagar period.

Caves of Elephanta: Siva dancing

THE CULMINATION OF PRE-ISLAMIC INDIAN TRADITION

In Northern India, after Harsha and Sasanka, the political situation became increasingly complex by reason of the multiplication of regional dynasties, right up to the time when the Moslem invasions complicated it even more. The division of the country into a large number of kingdoms, though explained naturally by the diversity of the regions of which its vast territories are comprised, nevertheless facilitated invasions, which came from the part of the Indus Basin so often subjected to foreign colonization. But the political divisions did not impede the general development of all branches of Indian civilization in the country as a whole and outside its borders. These divisions have but little bearing on Indian society to-day, because the civilization that modern India has inherited did not undergo corresponding cultural divisions, and also because, especially in the North, these kingdoms have been forgotten.

Asoka and Kanishka are still remembered to a certain extent in Buddhist tradition, and Chandragupta Maurya among the Jains. Most of the other rulers are just names that figure in dry genealogical lists of the dynasties. Harsha is known in India because of a poem describing his life, written in classical Sanskrit by the eminent writer Bana. But the essential facts known about the Maurya, the Gupta, and the other dynasties are gleaned from inscriptions that have

Monolithic temple of Ellora

literature of the various *prakrits*, Jain, Buddhist, or secular in inspiration; the *pali*, which were written mainly in Ceylon, and transported with the Buddhist canon of the school of the Theravada to Indochina, principally from the thirteenth and fourteenth centuries onward, but which have disappeared from India itself; and finally the Tamil literature, second only to the Sanskrit in its volume and its scope, for it represents all branches of Indian learning.

Indian civilization owes its unity to the Sanskrit literature that it has inherited. This literature includes the Vedic or Brahmanic writings of the pre-Christian era, or, in terms of Indian chronological calculation, of the period before Vikramaditya and the Saka eras; but it has its roots in the period that preceded Buddhism and Jainism, which were founded five or six centuries before Christ.

been deciphered since the last century, and from foreign historical sources, such as the Greeks or the Chinese Buddhist pilgrims of the fourth and seventh centuries, like Fa-hian, Hiuan-tsang, who knew Harsha, or Yi-tsing. It is only in modern times that India has had access to the thoughts and examples of her ancient historical past. For a long time it was hidden from her. Only a more recent past, with the poems in honour of the Rajput heroes who fought against Islam, and the whole history of European intervention and domination, has made any direct contribution to the formation of her present outlook. It is her cultural tradition, not her politics and her arms, which has made India what she is to-day. Her outlook can be explained less by the vicissitudes to which she has been subjected than by the conceptions of the way of life and of the world which she has created for herself. To the foreigners whom she has influenced she has offered her ideas, not her history. And if foreigners have taught us something of her history, it is not what they have learnt from her, but what they have gleaned from chance observation.

The contribution that pre-Islamic India has made to the formation of present-day India is therefore the treasures of literature, oral traditions, and architecture which have been successfully and deliberately preserved.

Her literature, which was largely developed in the pre-Islamic period, consisted of the classical Sanskrit, current throughout the country; the

The Tamil poet Tiruvalluvar.
Modern painting from the Mémoires de l'Athénée Oriental

It also includes the classical literature which flourished from the beginning of the Christian era until the thirteenth century. The classical Sanskrit literature is based on a learned grammar which represents a continuation of the

Vedic science of speech, speech which created and ordered the universe, speech, the basic element of which is the cosmic sound, the rumble of the ocean which the voice of man reproduces by a lengthy prolongation of the syllabe *om*. But the grammar properly speaking has an essentially practical value, and sets out in precise fashion the rules of morphology and of the use of the different forms of speech. By means of the work of Panini it had already attained, several centuries before the birth of Christ, a degree of perfection which enabled Sanskrit to be taught methodically throughout the country and used, in a standard form, as a means of communication common to all the peoples of India and the foreigners with whom they were in relations. The use of Sanskrit as a current language appears to have developed particularly in Western India in the early centuries of our era at the time of the Indo-Parthian and Indo-Scythian rulers, as it represented a stable element in the linguistic confusion of their cosmopolitan court circles. The earliest important Sanskrit inscription known, which is already poetic in style, dates from the second century of

Interior view of the enclosure around the stupa at Sanchi (second century B.C.)

Buddhist stupa at Sanchi

the Christian era, is to be found in Gujarat, and was the work of the "Great Satrap" Rudradaman, whose name is Indian but whose title is Iranian.

In addition to the scholarly literature of the philosophic manuals, the great epics, the *Puranas*, and the vast literature dealing with the *Dharma,* there appeared in Sanskrit from this time onwards an extensive literature of a more secular nature, consisting of collections of tales like the *Pancatantra,* sententious maxims by authors such as Bhartrihari, plays, novels, such as *The Adventures of Ten Young Princes* by Dandin, and poems or poems in prose known as *kavya,* which recounted the exploits of the gods or of men, and which were invariably characterized by veiled allusions and play on words, using all the *alankara* ("ornaments") of a highly developed rhetoric, the taste for which has never disappeared. The masterpieces of these literary genres were produced at a very early period, at the time of the Guptas or even before. Indian animal stories were transmitted to Iran under the Sassanids, and from there, with additions, they found their way through Western Asia to mediæval Europe, and were known in the seventeenth century to La Fontaine, who acknowledged the Indian sage Pilpay as the source of some of his fables. Kalidasa, the most universal of the Indian poets, lived at the time of the Guptas. He has always been held as the supreme model, and is still considered as such among modern men of letters. Indeed, the whole of his work, even in translation, holds a

charm even for those foreigners who are most remote from Indian civilization. Part of it has been translated into Tibetan, and some of it was discovered in China, while European versions popularized India in the Romantic period. This is because it expresses the feelings of man's heart, offering descriptions of nature, rather than representing the thoughts of a particular Indian background. It is not a work of local significance, but one that embraces the whole of humanity. In addition to the poems, it includes a number of plays, the most famous of which tells the story of Shakuntala, who was wooed by a king who loved her sincerely, but who forgot her completely because of a curse placed upon her, even though she was innocent; but he finally recognized her again when the curse had been lifted. Poems written by Kalidasa include the *Meghaduta,* which tells of a message that an exiled lover sent to his beloved on a cloud that was moving towards his country; the *Ritusamhara,* a song describing the seasons; the *Raghuvamsa,* which is about Rama and his ancestors; and the *Kumarasambhava,* which tells of the birth of the god Kumara.

Up to the time at which it reached its greatest heights the whole of the secular Sanskrit literature was confined to Northern India. It was only later that it spread to Peninsular India and to foreign countries. In the early centuries of the Christian era secular writing in the north of the peninsula was in the local *prakrit,* and in the south in Tamil.

The Tamil was by far the most flourishing of

Bali (Indonesia):
the fountain of Guwagaja (restored)

these literatures, and it has remained more alive than others in India to-day; it soon eclipsed the *prakrit* literatures, and Sanskrit literature was developed side by side with it, sometimes acting as a source of inspiration and sometimes being itself enriched by the Tamil. An early detailed grammar, the *Tolkappiyam,* served to stabilize classical Tamil, thus making it a unified and living language and contributing to the value of its production. It has remained a living language not only for the people who speak it, but also for men of letters who have adopted Sanskrit concurrently with it, becoming *ubhayakavi* (bilingual poets). After the period known as the Sangam, to which belong the earliest surviving

Tamil poems, the literature developed parallel with Sanskrit, and to a certain extent adopted the same genres. Gnomic verse is well represented by Tiruvalluvar's masterpiece, the *Kural,* which is still extremely popular; it is a work in praise of family life, an account of its duties and the duties of kings to themselves and to society; it also tells of the joys and the impatience of love. Other famous Tamil works are the *kavya,* similar to those written in Sanskrit and of equally high literary value, and tales in elaborate verse forms, such as *Manimegalai,* and the *Silappadikaram.* But the most important side of this literature consists of the powerful religious and devotional element, the hymns in honour of

Tenth-century temple of Siva
at Bantay Srei, Cambodia (restored)

Temple of Siva Mahadeva
at Prambanan, Java (restored) ▶

the Nayanar and the Alvar, the saints of the Saiva and Vaishnava sects. These hymns tell of the miracles of the manifestation of God, Siva or Vishnu, the Supreme Being, who exists in everything and under countless forms, grandiose or moving, even amusing, within the comprehension of man. They were written between the fifth and tenth centuries, particularly under the Pallavas and the Cholas; while their authors were not unacquainted with the religious ideas of the North, and even the vocabulary used, they wrote in their own individual style, and with unsurpassed vigour. To this devout and eager background belong the classical *Vedanta* of Sankara, Ramanuja, and their successors, characterized by the integration of the greatly exalted feeling of the unity of the Supreme Being with the universe and with man himself into the interpretation of the *Upanishads* and the Sanskrit philosophical treatises that had been imported from the North.

Contemporary with the development of secular literature describing the beauties and the fervour of the world, and the renaissance of the ancient naturalistic Brahmanism through Hinduism with its adoration of the Infinite manifested in the world, masterpieces of art and architecture were produced, thanks to the progress of science and new techniques. The ancient monuments of Northern India have disappeared with the exception of the huge Buddhist *stupas,* such as those at Sanchi and Bharhut, dating to the second century B.C., they are *tumuli* covering relics of Buddha or of his disciples, who preached the necessity to free oneself from the ties of the world; but they have nevertheless been decorated in a spirit of devotion and surrounded by enclosures characterized by elaborate ornamentation, the poetic fantasy of the scenes, and sculptures depicting the beauty of nature with highly realistic reproductions of animals. Materials recu-

Sanchi: defiant peacocks

perated from ruined temples were used to construct mosques and Moslem tombs. It is only in areas that did not experience conquest and Moslem influence that the great temples of the times of the Chandella dynasty, which were mainly constructed during the tenth and early eleventh centuries, have survived. There are important temples of this period still standing at Khajuraho.

It is therefore in the South that the great sanctuaries of Indian art, Hindu or Jain temples, and Buddhist or Jain monasteries, with their chapterhouses and monastic cells, have been preserved. Many of these monuments replaced timber buildings, and reproduce in stone the general form and features of the earlier edifices. They were often natural or artificial caves, arranged and carved in the rock, whether it was granite or one of the softer rocks. There are numerous Buddhist, Jain, and Hindu sanctuaries in the western part of the peninsula and the Deccan plateau area; these include the sanctuaries of Siva on the island of Elephanta, near Bombay; the Buddhist sanctuaries of Kanheri near Bombay and Ajanta near Aurangabad, the latter famous for its paintings; and the numerous Saivistic, Vaishnavistic, and Jain sanctuaries in places such as the Badami of the Chalukyas. In addition to all these cave constructions there are complete sanctuaries carved in masses of natural rock which have been hollowed out and ornamented with columns, statues, and decorative motifs. The most famous of the monolithic temples are the Pallava temples at Mamallapuram and the temple of Ellora, which represents the Kailasa, the sacred mountain of Siva. Few of these temples are now used for worship, and the local inhabitants scarcely know their names and the purpose for which they were built, and are completely ignorant of their history, which has nevertheless been preserved in the inscriptions on the buildings themselves and in documents. These local people have their own legends about the temples, which frequently represent the conjectures of their comparatively recent ancestors, who had forgotten their original significance. They do not, however, belong to a different religion from that practised to-day, but remain as witnesses to its extension and its former strength, which is unshaken even though they have been abandoned. The temples where the greatest numbers of worshippers gather to-day are the Chola temples such as those of Tanjavur and Gangaikondacholapuram, built in the eleventh century, and more particularly those of the Vijayanagar period. They were decorated with statues of the divinities and legendary scenes taken from the Saivistic and Vaishnavistic documents known as *Tantra*, *Agama*, and *Samhita*, which describe the rites to be carried out, the decorum to be observed, and the Yoga techniques to be practised by the worshippers, in addition to offering doctrinal teaching. The most important of these texts, to which must be added a whole host of special treatises and manuals, were, like the *Puranas*, mainly written when the period of religious fervour and general prosperity of the whole country was at its height, before the advent of the Moslem invaders and the European merchants.

This same period, which began in the early centuries of the Christian era, was also marked by the extension of Indian influence in Tibet from the seventh century onward, and eastward to Indonesia and Indochina at an even earlier date. Excavations in Indochina, such as those at Oc-èo in South Vietnam, have uncovered both Indian and Roman influences dating back to the first centuries of the Christian era. Throughout South-east Asia are to be found monuments that are Indian in inspiration though original in conception, and which include the whole architectural ensemble of Cham, Indonesian, and Khmer art, the last-named being one of the most impressive in the world. The island of Bali, which lies east of Java, has even preserved Sanskrit texts and forms of worship inspired by the India of antiquity, even though the Indonesians have for centuries been adherents of Islam; and the Balinese and Javanese have given a new beauty to the art borrowed from India through their own sparkling genius.

To this great period of creation or renewal of Brahmanic antiquity belong the basic elements of which Indian civilization consisted in the period prior to the establishment of Islam and the Western powers. This period, with its creative force and its expansion, explains the breadth and the continued existence of a proud Indian civilization, devoted to calm tolerance, to an ideal of law and order, and to the modern conception of peace, and it shows also how India is a nation able to live in unity with invading civilizations which she accepted and absorbed in her own territories, without yielding up her country to them.

SELECT BIBLIOGRAPHY

L. Renou and J. Filliozat: *L'Inde classique, manuel des études indiennes* (2 vols., Paris, 1947-53; 3rd vol. in preparation).

Madeleine Biardeau: *Inde* (Paris, 1958).

Cambridge History of India (Cambridge, 1922-37).

The Oxford History of India (Oxford, 3rd ed., 1958).

K. A. Nilakanta Sastri: *History of India* (3 vols., Madras, 1950-52).

Alfred Foucher: *La vie du Bouddha*, d'après les textes et les monuments de l'Inde (Paris, 1949).
Les vies antérieures du Bouddha (Paris, 1955).
L'Art gréco-bouddhique du Gandhâra (Paris, 1905-51).

Louis Renou: *Sanskrit et culture*. L'apport de l'Inde à la civilisation humaine.
La civilisation indienne, d'après les textes sanskrits.
Anthologie sanskrite (Paris, 1947).

UNESCO collection of representative works, Indian series, 1956, etc.

The Upanishads.

Publications of the Institut de civilisation indienne, Paris.

Publications of the Institut français d'Indologie, Pondicherry.

NOTE ON THE SPELLING OF INDIAN NAMES

The question of the spelling of Indian names is a complicated one. As we are still in a period of transition, it has been considered advisable as a general rule to adopt the spelling with which the English-speaking public is familiar, though in certain cases the latest transliteration is also given.

ILLUSTRATIONS

Figures in bold type refer to the pages of this book

Frontispiece. Elephant. Detail of a Bundi painting (1750). Prince of Wales Museum, Bombay.

THE INDIAN NATION

1. — The Country

15. Capital decorated with lions (Sanchi). (Photo Y. Bongert). — **16.** The Vale of Kashmir with the mountains beyond. (Photo Brian Brake-Magnum). — **17.** Lake in Kashmir. (Photo Weiss-Viollet). — **18.** The Dhauli valley in the Garhval massif of the Himalayas. In the foreground a deodar, or Himalayan cedar. (Photo J. J. Languepin — French Expedition to the Himalayas (F.E.H.)). — **19.** Aerial view of the outskirts of Patna (Bihar). (Photo Jean Filliozat). — **19.** Terraced slopes in the Garhval. (Photo J. J. Languepin — F.E.H.). — **20.** On the banks of the Brahmaputra. (Photo Paul Popper-Atlas). — **21.** The Brahmaputra valley. (Photo Atlas-Doumic). — **22.** Landscape in the hinterland of Bombay, with the Western Ghats in the background. (Photo Hurliman — P. Popper). — **23.** Fishing installations alongside a river. (Photo Bouron). — **24.** Parliament House, New Delhi. (Photo Indian National Tourist Office). — **25.** Village council in Northern India. (Photo Indian Embassy, Paris). — **26.** Vinoba Bhave marching in quest of gifts of land. (Photo Atlas-Doumic). — **27.** Trivandrum. (Photo Bouron).

2. — The People

28. Men towing boats on the banks of the Jhelam (Kashmir). (Photo Weiss-Viollet). — **29.** Girl selling cigarettes and betel gum. (Photo Atlas-Dubois). — **30.** Man smoking a *nargileh*. (Photo J. J. Languepin — F.E.H.). — **31.** Mountain dwellers from Lata (Garhval). (Photo J. J. Languepin — F.E.H.). — **32.** Basket-seller from Rajasthan. (Photo Paul Popper-Atlas). — **33.** River craft in Kerala. (Photo Gaussen). — **35.** Tea-picking in the Mannar area (Southern India). (Photo André Petit). — **36.** A Tamil girl returning from the well. (Photo Ecole française d'Extrême-Orient). — **37.** A typical Moslem. (Photo Y. Bongert). — **38.** A Bengali mendicant pilgrim carrying the *ektar* with which he accompanies singing. The *ektar* bears an inscription in Bengali. (Photo J. J. Languepin — F.E.H.). — **38.** The poet Rabindranath Tagore, surrounded by a group of his students, girls from the University of Santiniketan. (Photo Almasy). — **39.** Transplanting rice. In the background raising water from a well with oxen. Coromandel Coast. (Photo Y. Bongert). — **41.** Tamil girls. (Photo Pierre Filliozat). — **41.** A typical Sikh. (Photo Almasy). — **42.** Fish-seller. (Photo Bhanzali — Holmes-Lebel).

3. — Language

44. One of the inscriptions of King Asoka (third century B.C.). (Photo Weiss-Viollet). — **45.** A treatise of modern anatomy in Sanskrit. — **46.** Adults learning Urdu and Hindi in a village school in Uttar Pradesh. (Photo Press Information Bureau, New Delhi). — **47.** Different scripts: 1. Kanarese (Kannara), 2. Hindi (from the *Ramayana* of Tulsidas), 3. Tamil (from a history of Indian art), 4. Bengali (from original version of *The Home and The World*, by Rabindranath Tagore). — **48.** Nagari musical notation. — **49.** A bookstall at the entrance to a temple in Kanchipuram. (Photo André Petit). — **50.** An autographed poem by Rabindranath Tagore published by Kshitis Roy, Santiniketan).

4. — Social Background and Town Life

51. Bombay: Marine Drive. (Photo Paul Popper-Atlas). — **52.** Bombay: public washing establishment. (Photo Gaussen). — **52.** Bombay: juxtaposition of Anglo-Indian and modern buildings. (Photo Jean Filliozat). — **53.** Street in the centre of Srinagar (Kashmir). (Photo Brian Brake-Magnum). — **54.** Street barber in Poona (Maharashtra). (Photo Atlas-Dubois). — **55.** Modern houses in Bombay close to slums. (Photo Keystone). — **56.** Mathura (Uttar Pradesh): vegetable-seller sitting near a pillar-box. (Photo Jean Filliozat). — **56.** Photographer in the market at Delhi. (Photo Weiss-Viollet). — **57.** Delhi: drug-seller and snake-charmer. (Photo Weiss-Viollet). — **58.** The Red Fort, Delhi: view on to the gardens. (Photo Jean Filliozat). — **59.** New Delhi: India Gate, a memorial to the Indian soldiers killed in World War I. (Photo Hérault). — **59.** Amber (Rajasthan): the Temple of Jagacchiromani. (Photo Paul Popper-Atlas). — **60.** New Delhi: the Central Secretariat. (Photo Indian National Tourist Office). — **61.** Delhi: the Red Fort. (Photo Almasy). — **62.** Udaipur: the lake and the palaces. (Photo Paul Popper-Atlas). — **63.** Anglo-Indian architecture: a Jain temple in Calcutta. (Photo Brian Brake-Magnum). — **64.** Pondicherry: The French Institute. (Photo Jean Filliozat). — **65.** Banaras: one of the ghats leading down to the Ganges. (Photo Almasy). — **66.** Street in the centre of Calcutta. (Photo Indian National Tourist Office). — **67.** Street scene in Old Delhi. (Photo Cartier-Bresson-Magnum). — **68.** Madras: street sanctuary. (Photo André Petit). — **69.** View of Pondicherry from the old pier. (Photo Pierre Filliozat). — **71.** Calcutta: the waiting-room of a station. (Photo Almasy). — **72.** Shops in Pondicherry. (Photo Hérault). — **73.** One of the humbler shopping streets in Calcutta, with advertisements for films, medicines, and hair-oil. (Photo Almasy). — **74.** Banaras: northern bathing-place. (Photo J. Auboyer). — **75.** Delhi: villagers at the Red Fort. (Photo Pierre Amado). — **77.** Canal in Kerala. (Photo Bouron). — **79.** Calcutta: street scene with rickshaw. (Photo Almasy). — **80.** Yoked oxen in the Coromandel Coast area. (Photo Filliozat). — **81.** Women at a well. (Photo Pierre Amado). — **83.** Chandigarh: women students from the Panjab. (Photo Chinwalla-Holmes-Lebel). — **84.** Banaras: one of the ghats. (Photo J. Auboyer). — **85.** Chandigarh: University students. (Photo Chinwalla - Holmes-Lebel). — **86.** Banaras: cremation site. (Photo Almasy).

5. — Working Conditions

87. Flower market in Southern India. (Photo Hérault). — **88.** Buffaloes grazing on an irrigated plain (Coromandel Coast). (Photo Hérault). — **89.** Ghogargaon: country scene. (Photo Bouron). — **90.** A *picottah* (machine for raising water from a well for irrigation). (Photo Jean Filliozat). — **91.** Market scene in Pondicherry. (Photo P. Filliozat). — **93.** Furnace for extracting lime from sea-shells. (Photo Bouron). — **93.** Srirangam: millstone for crushing stone or shells to obtain lime. Note the symbol of Vishnu on the temple wall behind. (Photo Y. Bongert). — **94.** Banyan-tree on the banks of the Hooghly, between Chandernagore and Calcutta. (Photo G. Martel). — **95.** Rice-harvesting, Kanchipuram (Southern India). (Photo André Petit). — **96.** Village temple at Viliyanur (Southern India). (Photo Hérault). — **97.** Woman pounding condiments on a grindstone. (Photo Bouron). — **98.** Winnowing. (Photo Paul Popper-Atlas). — **99.** River craft at Quilon (Kerala). (Missi-Photo). — **100.** Women pounding rice in a mortar. (Photo Jean Filliozat). — **101.** Fisherman on a raft made of tree-trunks lashed together. (Photo Atlas-Dubois). — **102.** In the Tata steel-works. (Missi-Photo). — **103.** Tobacco factory (Andhra Pradesh). (Photo Indian Embassy, Paris). — **103.** The Howrah Bridge, Calcutta. (Photo Gaussen). — **104.** Third-class compartment in a train. (Photo Atlas – Dubois). — **105.** Ferry on the road from Khajuraho to Jhansi. (Photo Y. Bongert). — **105.** Transporting grain-jars. (Photo Ecole française d'Extrême-Orient). — **106.** Dam across a river. (Photo Indian National Tourist Office). — **107.** Construction of the dam for the Nugu reservoir (Mysore). (Photo Indian Embassy, Paris). — **108.** Carpenters. (Photo Holmes – Lebel). — **109.** Woman weaving woollen cloth at Mana. (Photo J. J. Languepin – F.E.H.). — **110.** Man selling baskets. (Photo Ecole française d'Extrême-Orient). — **110.** Implements for fanning the fire. (Photo J. Auboyer). — **111.** Village houses with mud walls (Javadi Mountains). (Photo Gaussen). — **111.** Women at the well (Javadi Mountains). (Photo Gaussen). — **113.** Potter at his wheel. (Photo Jean Filliozat). — **113.** Woman spinning (Southern India). (Photo André Petit). — **114.** Painting on matting (Calcutta). (Photo Brian Brake – Magnum). — **115.** Woman at a loom (Calcutta). (Photo Brian Brake – Magnum). — **116.** Village school at Ghogargaon (Aurangabad region). (Photo Bouron). — **117.** Madras, University buildings. (Photo Hérault). — **117.** Jamnagar : the new college of electricity and naval technology (1955). (Photo Indian Embassy, Paris). — **118.** Embroidery work (Kashmir). (Photo Weiss – Viollet). — **118.** Machine tools in an instruction shop at Ambarnath (near Bombay). (Photo Indian Embassy, Paris).

6. — Aspects of Cultural Life

119. Man in meditation near a sacrificial fire. (Photo Doumic). — **120.** Mamallapuram : Somaskanda cave. Vishnu recumbent (seventh century). Siva, Uma, and Skanda are inside the central shrine on the right. (Photo Y. Coffin). — **120.** Mamallapuram : Somaskanda cave. The goddess Durga fighting a buffalo-headed demon, Mahisha (seventh century). (Photo Y. Coffin). — **121.** An ascetic saint, Karaikkalammaiyar, sitting at the feet of Siva dancing, and listening to the final echo of the cymbals. (Photo Institut français d'Indologie). — **122.** Temple of Madurai (sixteenth century). The pool of the Golden Lotus and two towers *(gopuram)*. (Photo Institut français d'Indologie). — **123.** Pattadakal : Lambani women dancing. (Photo Institut français d'Indologie — Pattabiramin). — **123.** Lambani woman (Mysore). (Photo Institut français d'Indologie – Pattabiramin). — **125.** Mamallapuram : group of monolithic sanctuaries sculpted in the rock (seventh-eighth centuries). (Photo Y. Coffin). — **125.** Unfinished sanctuary of Durga, carved in a rock, north of Mamallapuram (eighth century). (Photo Jean Filliozat). — **126.** Terra-cotta statues of warriors of the god Aiyanar on the road between Villapuram and Selam. — **127.** Banaras : a temple visited by monkeys. (Photo Almasy). — **128.** Temple musicians at Bahur. — **129.** Procession bearing the statue of the goddess Draupadi (heroine of the *Mahabharata*). — **130.** Modern statue of the god Aiyanar, guardian of the fields. (Photo Gaussen). — **131.** Har ki padi (Hara's staircase), a place of pilgrimage at Haridvar. (Photo Paul Popper – Atlas). — **132.** Entrance to the temple of Jagannath at Puri (Orissa). (Photo Jean Filliozat). — **133.** Offerings presented to Krishna. (Photo Atlas – Doumic). — **135.** Chariot decorated for a religious procession. — **136.** Modern statuette of Ganesa. (Photo Lavaud – Horizons de France). — **136.** Modern steatite statuette of Subrahmanya. (Photo Lavaud – Horizons de France). — **137.** Jain monks at Delhi. (Photo Weiss – Viollet). — **138.** Bronze statuette of Virabhadra. (Photo Lavaud – Horizons de France). — **139.** A pilgrim camp. (Photo Atlas – Dubois). — **140.** Delhi : Moslems at prayer. (Photo Indian Embassy, Paris). — **141.** Mosque at Delhi at the time of a religious festival. (Photo Indian Embassy, Paris). — **142.** Saiva monk receiving massage. Deccan, eighteenth century. (Musée Guimet, Paris). — **143.** Catholic church in Kerala. (Photo Chinwalla – Holmes-Lebel). — **144.** Kraunca, white bird of the marshes. Mogul miniature, eighteenth century (Musée Guimet). — **145.** Sri Saccidananda Sivabhinava Nrsimha Bharati, philosopher of the school of Sankara, *jagadguru* 1879-1912. — **146.** Yoga postures *(Sivayogamandir)*. (Photos Jean Filliozat). — **147.** Attitude of meditation. (Photo M. Mahesh Ghatradyal). — **148.** Hermit living in a cave. (Photo Atlas – Doumic). — **149.** Painting on fabric. — **150.** Sitar player. Mogul miniature, eighteenth century (Musée Guimet). — **151.** Painting by Jaimini Roy. (Bossenec Collection). — **152.** Bharatanatya dance pose : shooting with bow and arrow. (Photo Louis Frédéric – Rapho). — **153.** Manipuri dance pose. (Photo Louis Frédéric – Rapho). — **154.** Bharatanatya dance pose : Krishna playing the flute. (Photo Louis Frédéric – Rapho). — **155.** Popular songs and dances at Delhi on Republic Day. (Photo J. Filliozat). — **157.** Making-up an elephant for a torchlight procession. (Photo Indian Embassy, Paris). — **158.** Actors of the Kathakali. (Photo Louis Frédéric – Rapho). — **158.** Kathakali dance gestures *(mudra)*. (From Le Journal Asiatique). — **159.** Scene from the Indian film of *Aladdin and his Wonderful Lamp*. (Films Régence – Algérie). — **160.** Advertisement of the Tamil film *Parttipan Kanavu (The King's Dream)*. (Photo Jean Filliozat).

THE PAST AND ITS TRADITIONS

1. — India Under British Rule

163. The temple of Minakshi-Sundaresvara at Madurai (seventeenth century). Gate tower *(gopura)*. (Photo Institut français d'Indologie). — **165.** Jewellery of an Indian dancer. (Photo Horizons de France). — **168.** Indian Cynocephali shown among those who were to receive the Mission of the Apostles. Vézelay, interior portal (twelfth century). (Photo Archives Photographiques). — **169.** A Skiapod. Sens Cathedral (twelfth century). (Photo Archives Photographiques). — **170.** Harvesting pepper in the Malabar Coast area. From the *Book of Marco Polo* (Ms fr. 2810 XIVᵉ siècle, Bibliothèque Nationale (B.N.), Paris). — **171.** The goddess Kali, copied by a European from a popular Indian picture. (Thomas Maurice : *Indian Antiquities*, London, 1794). — **171.** How the King of Malabar wears his jewels. From the *Book of Marco Polo* (Ms fr. 2810 XIVᵉ siècle, B.N., Paris). — **172.** Portrait of an English gentleman in India. The Earl of Denbigh, attributed to Van Dyck (1599-1641). (National Gallery, London). — **173.** The Mosque of Asaf-ud-daula, Lucknow (end of the eighteenth century). (Photo Jean Filliozat). — **174.** Goa. From Souchu de Rennefort : *Mémoire pour servir à l'histoire des Indes Orientales*, 1702. (B.N., Paris). — **175.** Moslem tomb at Lucknow (end of the eighteenth century). (Photo Jean Filliozat). — **176.** Collège La Martinière, Lucknow. This was a palace bequeathed as a school by Claude Martin (1735-1800) of Lyons, a general in the service of the Nawab of Audh. Martin's tomb is in the crypt of the palace. (Photo Jean Filliozat). — **177.** Travellers' resting-place and pavilion on the road from Delhi to Agra (Indo-Moslem style). (Photo Gaussen). — **178.** Presumed portrait of Anandaranga Pillai, an agent of the Compagnie Française des Indes at Pondicherry. About 1740. (Photo Horizons de France). **179.** Gold medal of the Compagnie Française des Indes, 1750, from the trading-post of Masulipatam (Andhra) (B.N., Paris). — **180.** The foundation of the Compagnie des Indes Orientales by Louis XIV in 1664. From Souchu de Rennefort : *Histoire des Indes Orientales*, 1668 (B.N., Paris). — **180.** Gold pagoda (coin) known as "the three svamin", Vishnu and his two wives. Currency of Yanaon, minted at Pondicherry (eighteenth century), (B.N., Paris). — **181.** Pathan (Afghan) chieftains from Peshavar (Cabinet des Estampes, B.N., Paris). (Photo Horizons de France). — **182.** A Hindu temple as seen by a European artist. De la Flotte : *Essais* *historiques sur l'Inde*, Paris, 1769. — **183.** A young horseman, Mogul painting of the beginning of the eighteenth century. (Musée Guimet). (Photo Horizons de France). — **185.** An employee of the East India Company in Bengal (Cabinet des Estampes, B.N., Paris). (Photo Horizons de France). — **187.** Banaras, by W. Daniell (nineteenth century). — **188.** Shuja-ud-daula, Nawab of Audh (Gentil). — **189.** Indian painting of the nineteenth century from Orissa. In the centre, British officers and sepoys (Mss. indiens 1401, B.N., Paris). — **190.** Dancer and musicians playing the *tabla* and cymbals. Woodcut by Rani Chanda, Santiniketan, 1938. — **191.** Siege artillery of the Anglo-Indian army in the nineteenth century. (Capt. G. F. Atkinson: *A History of the Indian Campaign)*. (Photo Associated Press, London). — **193.** An elephant of the temple of Vishnu Varadaraja at Kanchipuram. (Photo Viollet). — **195.** The Hindu University at Banaras. (Photo A. M. Loth). — **196.** Rabindranath Tagore. (Bossennec Collection). — **197.** An Indian carnival. Krishna is using a syringe to squirt women with coloured water (eighteenth-century painting). (Musée Guimet). (Photo Horizons de France). — **199.** The Mahatma Gandhi. (Photo Indian Embassy, Paris). — **200.** Jawaharlal Nehru, Prime Minister of the Republic of India. (Photo Indian Embassy, Paris). — **201.** Dr Rajendra Prasad, first President of the Republic of India (Photo Indian Embassy, Paris).

2. — Hindu and Moslem India Before British Rule

202. Avudaiyarkovil (Tanjavur district): King Arimardana-pandya (Photo Institut français d'Indologie). — **203.** Madurai: the marriage of Minakshi and Sundaresvara, with Vishnu playing the part of the bride's father (seventeenth century). (Photo Institut français d'Indologie). — **204.** Stucco decoration on a temple in Tiruchirapalli (eighteenth century). (Photo J. Auboyer). — **205.** Tiruvadavur (Madurai district): bronze statue of Manikkavasagar, a saint of the Saiva sect. (Photo Institut français d'Indologie). — **206.** Pallavanesvaram (Tanjavur district): bronze statue of the goddess Uma and her child Skanda. (Photo Institut français d'Indologie). — **207.** Twentieth-century imitation of a temple pillar of the Vijayanagar style. (Photo Y. Coffin). — **208.** Pursuit (twentieth-century imitation of Vijayanagar style). (Photo Y. Coffin). — **208.** A prince worshipping (twentieth-century imitation of Vijayanagar style). (Photo Y. Coffin). — **209.** Vyaghrapada, the "tiger-footed", one of the mythical sages of Chidambaram (twentieth-century imitation of Vijayanagar style). (Photo Y. Coffin). — **210.** Vishnu in his incarnation as the child Krishna (twentieth-century imitation of Vijayanagar style). (Photo Y. Coffin). — **210.** A dancer: sculpture in the temple of Chidambaram. (Photo Institut français d'Indologie). — **211.** The pool and one of the towers at the entrance to the temple of Chidambaram. (Photo Jean Filliozat). — **213.** Chidambaram: Nagas (mythical creatures, half human, half serpent). (Photo Y. Coffin). — **213.** A dancer: sculpture in the temple of Chidambaram. (Photo Institut français d'Indologie). — **214.** Chidambaram: the sage Agastya. (Photo Y. Coffin). — **215.** Chidambaram: a dancer. (Photo Institut français d'Indologie). — **216.** The Fort of Jingi near Tiruvannamalai. (Photo Y. Coffin). — **218.** The siege of a fortress. Mogul painting of the seventeenth century (Musée Guimet). — **219.** A princess receiving a painter, who is presenting her with her portrait, and a musician. Mogul painting of the eighteenth century (Musée Guimet). — **219.** A girl reading and smoking a hookah. Mogul painting of the eighteenth century (Musée Guimet). — **220.** A combat on fantastic elephants. Mogul painting of the eighteenth century (Musée Guimet). — **221.** Akbar. From Manucci: *Histoire du Mogol* (B.N., Paris). — **222.** A girl and an antelope. Mogul painting of the eighteenth century (Musée Guimet). — **222.** A bird-catcher. Provincial school of the eighteenth century (Musée Guimet). — **223.** Hindu woman worshipping before a sanctuary of the Linga of Siva. Provincial Mogul school (Murshidabad?) of the second

half of the eighteenth century (Musée Guimet). **224.** Akbar at a combat between two black antelopes. Mogul painting of the eighteenth century, copy of a work of the school of Akbar (Musée Guimet). — **225.** Jahangir with a portrait of Akbar (seventeenth century). (Photo Archives Photographiques). — **226.** Jahangir visiting a hermit. Indo-Persian painting of the seventeenth century. (Photo Archives Photographiques). — **227.** Agra: The Red Fort. — **228.** Decorative detail from the tomb of the Itmad ud-daula. — **229.** Agra: The Taj Mahal. — **230.** Shah Jahan in ceremonial procession. Mogul painting of the eighteenth century, presumably a copy of a seventeenth-century work (Musée Guimet). — **231.** Shah Jahan as an old man. Mogul painting of the seventeenth century (?) (Musée Guimet). — **233.** Agra: the marble tomb of the Itmad ud-daula, the father of Nur Jahan (seventeenth century). — **234.** New Delhi: astronomical instruments in stone at one of Jaysingh's observatories (eighteenth century). (Photo Viollet). — **235.** Kutb Minar, near New Delhi. (Photo H. Gaussen).

3. — Ancient Indian Civilization

237. Bhuvanesvar: Temple of Lingaraja. (Photo Y. Bongert). — **238.** Bhuvanesvar: decorated pillar (Photo Y. Bongert). **239.** Khajuraho: Temple of Vamana, south side. (Photo Bouron). — **241.** Painting of Krishna with embossed gilt ornaments. (Photo Pierre Filliozat). **241.** Jain manuscript, sixteenth century (Sanskrit 1453, B.N.). **243.** Puri (Orissa): painting of Jagannath (the black face on the right) in the Temple of Jagannath (Mss indiens 1041, B.N.). — **244.** Khajuraho: One of Siva's games: disguised as a young ascetic, he disturbs the women in a hermitage by his beauty (tenth century). (Photo Y. Bongert). — **244.** Khajuraho: Jain temple. Jina in meditation (eleventh century). (Photo Bouron). — **245.** Temple of Muktesvar (Orissa). (Photo Jean Filliozat). — **246.** Konark (Orissa): a temple to the sun built in the form of a processional chariot. (Photo Viollet). — **247.** Statue of Jina (Musée Guimet). — **248.** Base of the Temple of Tanjavur (eleventh century). (Photo Ecole française d'Extrême-Orient). — **249.** Mont Abu (Gujarat): the ceiling of a Jain temple. (Photo Indian National Tourist Office). — **250.** Near Jingi (Madras): rock sculpture representing the Jain Tirthakara. (Photo Y. Coffin). — **251.** Temple at Khajuraho (tenth century). (Photo Bouron). — **252.** Graeco-Indian head of Bodhisattva from Gandhara (Lahore Museum) (Musée Guimet, Gandhara Exhibition, 1959). — **252.** Graeco-Indian Buddha from Gandhara (Lahore Museum). (Musée Guimet, Gandhara Exhibition, 1959). — **253.** Græco-Indian statuette from Gandhara (Lahore Museum). (Musée Guimet, Gandhara Exhibition, 1959). — **253.** Mamallapuram: Pallava monolithic temples and bull (seventh century). (Photo Y. Coffin). — **254.** Unfinished Pallava sculptures on a monolithic temple at Mamallapuram (seventh century). (Photo Y. Bongert). — **255.** Mamallapuram: Vishnu, recumbent, worshipped by the Earth. On the right, two Titans, who are vainly trying to attack him (Pallava art of the seventh century). (Photo Goloubev – Musée Guimet). — **256.** Mamallapuram: Pallava temple on the sea-shore dedicated to Siva (eighth century). (Photo Y. Coffin). — **257.** Temple at Udaipur. (Photo Morrisson – Holmes-Lebel). — **258.** Mamallapuram: an example of Pallava animal art (eighth century). (Photo Y. Coffin). — **259.** Manuscript dating from the reign of Vigrahapala of Bengal (eleventh century). Above: scenes from the former life of Buddha. Below: Buddha. (Sylvain Lévi Collection). — **261.** Caves of Elephanta: Siva dancing. (Photo H. de Coral – Musée Guimet). — **261.** Monolithic temple of Ellora. (Photo India Office). — **262.** Artificial grotto at Ellora. (Photo Viollet). — **262.** The Tamil poet Tiruvalluvar. Modern painting from the *Mémoires de l'Athénée Oriental*. — **263.** Paintings in the caves of Ajanta. (Photo Goloubev – Musée Guimet). — **263.** Interior view of the enclosure around the stupa at Sanchi (second century B.C.). (Photo Y. Bongert). — **264.** Detail of a doorway of the enclosure to the stupa at Sanchi (second century B.C.) (Photo Y. Bongert). — **265.** Buddhist stupa at

Sanchi. (Photo Y. Bongert). — **266.** Bali (Indonesia): the fountain of Guwagaja (restored). (Photo Jean Filliozat). — **266.** Tenth-century temple of Siva at Bantay Srei, Cambodia (restored). (Photo Ecole française d'Extrême-Orient). — **267.** Temple of Siva Mahadeva at Prambanan, Java (restored). — **268.** Angkor Vat (Cambodia): women of Vishnu's entourage. (Photo G. Martel). — **268.** Sanchi: defiant peacocks. (Photo Goloubev – Musée Guimet).

Layout: Guy Chabrol

MAPS (Cartographer P. Simonet)

20. India: Average annual rainfall and direction of monsoons.
43. Simplified linguistic map.
160-161. India: Physical. India: Economic. India: Political. India in the Eighteenth and Nineteenth Centuries. The India of Vijayanagar, the Brahminsa and the Moguls. John Fryer's Map of India.
169. Trade Routes to India in the early centuries of the Christian era.

The binding is illustrated with a calligraph of the syllable *Om,* symbol of the Absolute.

INDEX